hamlyn

History of
Ships

Bernard Ireland

Editor: Tarda Davison-Aitkins
Executive Art Editor: Mark Winwood
Design: Les Needham
Picture Research: Jo Carlill
Production: Clare Smedley/Julian Deeming

First published in Great Britain in 1999
by Hamlyn, an imprint of
Octopus Publishing Group Limited
2–4 Heron Quays, London E14 4JP

Copyright © 1999 Octopus Publishing
Group Limited

Reprinted 2000

ISBN 0 600 59590 0

A catalogue record for this book is available
from the British Library

Produced by Toppan
Printed in China

CONTENTS

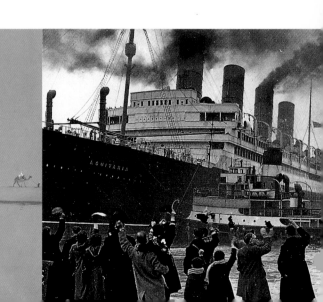

INTRODUCTION

A GENERATION PAST, the term 'Romance of the Sea' was common, and there is, indeed, something undefinably attractive about the ways of ships, distant ports and strange cargoes.

The Author considers himself fortunate to have grown up in a world where ships seemed more accessible than they are today. Youngsters could freely wander on quays now barred by virtue of mechanised hazards or the operator's fear of litigation should they 'fall in'. Long hours could be idled watching sweet-smelling Baltic timber being bundled and discharged, or huge stacks of crated Breton cauliflowers being cleared from coasters with strange names.

To a boy, as to his counterpart on the Hook or the Hooghly, the London River was a magic place. Yet battered by war, overlaid with centuries of grime, atmospheric with damp, clammy fog stemming from a million coal fires, it was a living thing. Crowds, crossing London Bridge on their way to humdrum tasks in dark offices, would pause briefly to watch activity in the Upper Pool, with the produce of the Canaries, of Poland and Denmark going ashore or overside into barges. Or a 'flatiron' collier, funnel and masts lowered, threading the arches with Geordie coal for the city's power stations.

Around high water, locks would open and the river would be instantly athrob with traffic bound for and from the big enclosed dock groups – West India, Millwall, the Surrey Commercials and the Royals. Sombre black-and-stone freighters of the P&O, spotless Ellerman 'Citys', Blue Star and Strick with their striking funnel livery. Pale blue and white funnels of the Argentinians, the black cross of the Hansa, the aluminium-coloured cargo gear of the Americans.

Like urchins dodging this stately parade were the small fry. Inevitably a 'Bird' of General Steam, inward-bound from Harlingen or Hamburg; a clutch of tall-stacked British steam coasters, loaded to the hatch beams with Tyne coal for a score of riverside wharves; a grey Dutch schuyt, the characteristic 'ker-tonk' of her machinery reverberating from the warehouse walls that hemmed the river.

Nothing stands still. The world of shipping, like all else, has changed dramatically and is still changing. Investment is seen as bringing limited and uncertain return. Major maritime powers have either 'flagged-out' extensively or have left it to others, preferring to sell their expertise in management or regulation. Great companies, once bitter trading rivals, have been obliged to merge or cooperate yet, even with their enormous combined assets, still contrive to lack the confidence that once was taken as read. A P&O ship of the 1950s or 1960s could be named simply *Cannanore* or *Socotra*, and her Red Ensign and London registry said the rest. Her modern counterpart is a container ship of six or seven times her deadweight capacity yet needs to be named something as corporately dreadful as *P&O Nedlloyd Damietta* and to be registered in *Hamburg*. *Tempora mutantur* ... Times have, indeed, changed.

This, then, is a book about ships. Clippers and colliers, corvettes and cruisers. It is also about people, those who created and those who strove. My thanks, as ever, are due to my wife, who translated endless longhand to the wonders of the disk, and to those who tracked down an impossibly long illustration list.

Bernard Ireland,
Fareham, 1998

7

Inset: A graceful ship of Queen Hatshepsut, c. 1500 BC. The complex rigging supports the weak spar and shapes the sail. Note the hogging truss.

Main picture: An Egyptian low-relief depicting a typical river craft. Its form directly influences that of the sea-going ship above.

Ancient Civilisations to Medieval Europe

BEGINNINGS

THE COMMONLY-STYLED 'Cradle of Civilisation', the Near and Middle East, has provided a rich assortment of pictures and artifacts which, related to the age of the find, have enabled us to get a fair idea of how man progressed from rivers and lakes to crossing the open sea.

Probably the earliest-known representation of a boat is a clay model of a dug-out canoe, dating from about 5000 BC in pre-dynastic Egypt. A dizzying 1500 years separates this simple model from vases decorated with illustrations which indicate the development of river craft long enough to accommodate 25 paddlers per side. Artistic conventions of the time are sometimes ambiguous but what is clear is that by this time such a craft had a continuous sheerline to increase freeboard at either and, perhaps surprisingly, had multiple steering oars.

Egypt, then as now, produced little useful timber, and boats were constructed of short and irregular pieces of wood, keyed together to create a spoon-shaped hull which, lacking framing, was braced by transverse beams set at intervals below what, today, would be termed a gunwale.

Later depictions, spaced irregularly with respect to time across the nation's long history, provide snapshots of evolution in boat building technique. Crews are shown facing backward rather than forward, indicating a shift to rowing, a more efficient method of progression than paddling. As the frameless construction conferred little longitudinal stiffness, the craft were fitted with a 'hogging truss', a stout continuous rope secured near the bow and stern and led over high vertical crutches. Tautened by means of a simple 'Spanish windless', it pulled the hull elements tightly together, preventing the extremities from drooping, or 'hogging'.

Rowing and ramming

Well before 3000 BC, the mast and squaresail had made their appearance. The mast, of course, required precious continuous lengths of timber and, like the yards at the upper and lower edges of the sail (the one supporting it, the other keeping it spread in the region's characteristically light breeze) it was often 'fished' together from two or more pieces. Used only in favourable conditions, it could be lowered onto a substantial crutch, the movement being assisted by large stones lashed to its heel to act as a counterweight. Perhaps because the operation was frequent, permanent shrouds could

Left: This Assyrian example shows the essentials for galley warfare – oars to power the ram into the enemy's hull, soldiers to board for hand-to-hand combat.

not be provided, so the mast was built as a bipod to give it transverse stiffness, the standing rigging comprising only fore- and backstays. This development was inefficient, requiring twice as much long timber and adding topweight.

Such craft were able to make not only coastwise voyages up to the Levant but also sea crossings to Minoan Crete. Trade, including timber, was a two-way matter, and cross-influence becomes evident between Aegean and Egyptian ideas.

Tomb-paintings, low reliefs and pottery shards, which often give the researcher puzzling perspectives, were joined about 2000 BC by increasingly-detailed models, buried in tombs to assist the incumbent on his journey to the world beyond.

Egyptian boat builders, even when trade gave them access to improved timber, appear to have been a conservative bunch. When, for instance, the Queen Hatshepsut undertook her expedition to the yet-unidentified Land of Punt, it was in 80–90 ft (24–27 m) versions of essentially riverine craft.

By about 1200 BC, Egypt was in decline and, under the redoubtable Ramses III, was fighting for its continued existence against threats from the north. These included the Phoenicians, possibly the sea-going element of the war-loving Assyrian Empire. Their ships, in the few known representations, show much in common with those of the Greeks, and were built for seagoing. Having access

to suitable timber, boat builders of the Aegean and the Levant developed framing early on, their craft being planked over a keel and ribs.

The keel was a vitally important element, giving a craft the longitudinal strength necessary to withstand the enormous stresses imposed by the open sea. It enabled the craft also to be deepened in section, permitting a desirable increase in freeboard and also, in time, a second bank of oars, the inclusion of which required the hull to be sponsored along each side. As the rig was still an unsophisticated squaresail, progress on most points, or in light winds, depended greatly upon the oarsmen. An extra bank meant extra speed or range. It meant also the power to drive deep the ram which, in all portrayals, is shown as a forward extension of the keel, there being no stempost.

Here, then, are the features of the first warships. In action, the oarsmen just rowed, leaving the fighting to soldiers sited on the long centreline walkway that ran nearly the length of the ship. Ranging alongside an opponent in order to board was virtually impossible due to the oars. Boarding end-on, following a successful ramming, would have exposed would-be boarders to being cut down one at a time. Tactics were thus probably built around the skill of the bowman, picking off an enemy crew until ramming or boarding became feasible.

FIRST DEVELOPMENTS – GREECE AND ROME

Right: While little contemporary impression has survived, this model of a Greek trireme of 480 BC is probably accurate in its depiction of oar layout.

Below: Coins and seals provide much information of ships at specific dates. This coin of Sextus Pompeius shows a Roman galley of about 44 BC under sail and oar.

THE AEGEAN IS NOT A LARGE SEA, it being about 200 miles (320 km) from Athens to the Turkish Dardanelles and perhaps twice that from Thessalonika in the north, to Crete. Because of the comparatively short distances involved and the uncertain nature of local winds, Greek warships were heavily biassed towards rowing, with sail assistance when available. Like the Phoenicians, the Greeks were building biremes, or double-banked galleys, by 700 BC. Records show that these could easily cover 150 miles (240 km) in a day, and maintain nearly nine knots over short distances. A key to such performance lay in the oarsmen being freemen rather than impressed, allowing them to take their part in associated expeditions.

Although hull planking of some 3 in (76 mm) thickness is quoted by some authorities, it is on record that crews were able to carry their craft ashore when necessary, which suggests that construction was somewhat lighter. Within the dimensional limitations imposed by then-current techniques, designers sought to maximise the number of oarsmen.

Built for speed, early biremes were probably about 80 ft (24.5 m) in length by no more than 10 ft (3.5 m) beam. Beyond the gunwale ran a continuous light structure, or outrigger, that supported the rowlocks for the outer bank of oars. Twenty-five rowers per side sat alternately on upper and lower thwarts. The difference in level was, perhaps, only some 18 in (460 mm), but this was sufficient to separate the two banks.

Again, the ram was a prominent feature of the hull, and was now carved into fantastic and fearsome shapes. Due to the lightness of the hull's construction, it was stiffened by heavy external belts of doubled timber ('wales'). These were brought together at the forward end both to reinforce the stempost and the ram against the shock of collision. A centreline fighting deck is obvious in representations, with the addition of a light, portable brow for use in boarding. References are made to the so-called 'Greek Fire', a naphtha-based compound, slung in pots from flexible poles, which burned fiercely on contact with water.

In common with every warship since, biremes steadily increased in size and complexity and, perhaps by 500 BC, could accommodate 59 oars per side. Having grown to an estimated 120 ft (36.5 m), however, their extra size was not matched by their extra power, and they were inevitably slower. The answer was the trireme which, for only a slight increase in dimensions, could accommodate three rows of oarsmen in staggered lines. On a length of about 150 ft (45.5 m), careful design allowed 85 oars per side, the oars in each bank differing in length. A still-extant slipway near Athens confirms the general sizes.

Later references to 'quadriremes' and 'quinqueremes' have caused much argument among scholars as to their layout. If, however, the term 'reme' is assumed to apply to the oarsmen, rather than their oars, it is easy to visualise the longer oars being served by two men, the shorter by one.

Roman tactics

Being a military state, Rome had much to learn in its wars against the sea-skilled Carthaginians. Copying design from both their opponents and the Greeks, they built quickly but with heavier scantlings. With superior fighting men, the Romans devised tactics to enhance boarding an enemy. As the galleys were being built, fighting men and rowing crews were trained in especially-created establishments ashore. Because boarding was as much in evidence as ramming, Roman galleys (known as 'liburnians') were equipped with heavy hinged boarding bridges. Fitted with a spike on their undersides, these bridges were effectively pinned to an opponent's deck. For over a century, between 264 and 146 BC, the Romans contested mastery at sea before finally beating the Carthaginians.

During the first century BC the Romans campaigned northward, their war galleys supporting advances ashore. Julius Caesar described how his ships, ill-suited to north European conditions, battled with those of the Veneti off what is now the coast of Brittany. The local ships depended upon sail rather than oars, were strongly built and, with their high free-board, were difficult to board. The Romans used an effective tactic of heaving grappling hooks on ropes to snare and damage their rigging in order to immobilise them. Differences between ships of northern and southern Europe would long be marked.

Trade, of course, flourished in parallel with war, with both Greece and Rome operating similar full-bodied merchantmen. The former appear to have been the more lightly constructed, sometimes portrayed as proceeding with oar assistance. Roman ships were stoutly-built with a single mast, probably about 90 ft (27.5 m) in length and capable of stowing up to 250 tons of cargo. Besides a poopdeck, or aftercastle, they had also acquired a bowsprit, steeved-up at a sharp angle and supporting a small square sail, spread on a light yard. Ships such as these were not very manoeuvrable and this sail, known as an 'artemon', could be backed by hand to assist in going about. There is also evidence of triangular topsails, set above the main yard and, possibly, laced to the main lifts.

Left: The aggressive aspect of a warship of Imperial Rome is here well portrayed. A reefed squaresail aids manoeuvrability but there is no bowsprit or artemon.

WARRIORS AND EXPLORERS
THE NORSEMEN

Below: Burial mounds at Oseberg and Gokstad in Norway give us insight into the development of the Norse longship. The relatively shallow sections of this Oseberg ship, dating from c. 850 AD, suggest the ships were designed for inshore use

Right: 'Dawn raiders'. A depiction of a Norse Longship as seen in *The Story of the British Nation*.

During the centuries that followed the birth of Christ, while Polynesians colonised the western Pacific, the Arabs and Indians moved with the seasonal monsoons and the Chinese navigated their great rivers, the great empires of the Fertile Crescent and the Mediterranean rim were in sharp decline. In the north, however, the Baltic provided another natural arena for trade and conquest. To its west lay a seemingly limitless ocean, whose horizons beckoned irresistibly.

Scattered widely over the coasts of what is now Scandinavia, the Norsemen left durable records scratched into their rock. Depictions of local craft abound, their evolution again shaped by local environment and local materials. Greatly stylised, their doodlings show a range of objects which, together, run a gamut from the sledge of the northern winter to oar- and sail-propelled boats. What they represent are lightly-framed craft, clad in animal hides, a style of construction that still lives in such as the curragh of the Aran Islands and the umiaks and kayaks of the Inuit peoples. Between uses, such craft are run ashore (and may even be inverted for shelter) and naturally require sledge-type bottom runners

to avoid damage. Virtually keels, these runners add longitudinal strength and, extended forward and aft, provide a convenient and distinctive feature for lifting. These extensions were long assumed to be for use as rams but this was not the case in northern craft.

Wood construction – Hjortspring to dragon boats

As wood-working skills developed, larger craft evolved, their shape influenced by what had gone before. The so-called Hjortspring boat dates from the third century BC yet, while being 45 × 6 ft (13.7 × 1.8 m) in size, remains very much a wooden version of a hide boat.

Early northern wood construction was based not on a keel proper but on a solid section of timber, cut and formed, possibly using fire and steam, and grooved to accept carefully-shaped planks. These, the garboard strakes, were bound solidly to it using pliable withies. Early examples, well preserved by the peat bogs in which they were found, comprise three planks, or strakes, per side, carefully formed to create a classic boat shape. An interesting feature of northern practice was the overlapping of successive strakes in what is termed

'clinker-build', as opposed to Mediterranean craft, which adopted edge-to-edge planking in so-called 'carvel-build'.

The Nydam boat of the second century AD shows the introduction of selected fastenings in iron, the development of characteristically-similar stem and sternposts, and just one steering oar. This latter was lashed to the 'steer board', later star-board, quarter. Compared with Mediterranean practice, scantlings are much lighter.

Besides the Nydam boat, which was a 75 ft (23 m) inshore craft, designed to be propelled by 14 oars per side, there were the full-bodied, cargo-carrying 'Knorrs', equipped with a mast and a single squaresail, but fitted for rowing if sufficient crew was carried. It was, however, excavations in burial mounds at Oseberg and Gokstad in Norway that were to give full insight into the later development of that most fabled of craft, the Norse longship.

Dating from about 850 AD, the Oseberg ship is about 70 x 17 ft (21 x 5 m) in size, whose nearly flat rise of floor results almost in V-sections. The 12 strakes per side are fastened with a mixture of lacing, iron fastenings and wooden pegs. There is a genuine keel, but transverse ribs and frames were added after the planking. Designed to sail, she also has 15 circular oar ports per side, each with its own cover.

The relatively shallow sections of this ship suggest that it was designed for inshore use but the example from Gokstad was longer and deeper. From gunwale to keel her section follows a graceful complex curve, encompassing 16 planks per side. While she also pulled 16 oars per side, Norse sagas speak of craft with 34, indicating possible dimensions of 140 x 28 ft (43 x 8.5 m).

Although the sailing qualities of such craft were early disputed, full-scale replicas have sailed the Atlantic inside four weeks and have demonstrated an ability to beat to windward. That this style of craft became general throughout Europe is evidenced by the Bayeux Tapestry, which depicts remarkably similar examples of the eleventh century AD.

The Norse drakkars, or 'dragon boats', exhibit an exquisite feel for balance and line, set off by low-relief carving of the endposts with delicate and intricate design. The Norsemen themselves, however, were savage, regularly pillaging the east coast of an eighth-century Britain painfully emerging from the Dark Ages, and thrusting southward to ravage even Spain.

Steering boldly westward, they moved successively from the Shetlands and Faroes to Iceland and Greenland. Thence they explored southward to the more temperate climes of fabled Vinland (probably Newfoundland and Nova Scotia) and, possibly, New England. And this before the Normans had crossed the English Channel.

Right: The Norse long-ship from Gokstad (c. ninth century) was longer and deeper than the Oseberg ship. Full-scale replicas have sailed the Atlantic inside four weeks, demonstrating their ability to beat to windward and prove their sailing qualities.

NORTHERN DEVELOPMENTS

Above: Bayeux tapestry depictions of William of Normandy's invasion fleet show that his ships were closely related to Viking craft.

Right: The Seal of Dunwich. It is one of the few excavated remains which have helped us to identify Norman craft.

THE ALMOST PURE NORSE DESIGN of the craft in which William of Normandy invaded Britain in the eleventh century provided the basis for slow evolution over the twelfth and thirteenth centuries. Artistic depictions are, however, limited to little more than sketches in the odd manuscript, and our knowledge derives from coins, seals, carvings and a very few excavated remains.

With the gradual establishment of the rule of law, trade began to flourish in staple commodities — salt and dried fish, grain, coal, timber and building stone. As many northern ports grew wealthy they adopted civic seals to mark their legal incorporation. While designers of these regularly included the craft that were the source of their prosperity, they also modified their proportions to fit the circular space available. There are, however, a number of useful examples and, as they are accurately dated, lines of development may be traced.

Depictions of Roman ships often indicated a small, castle-like feature toward the after end. Although arched below and with crenellated bulwarks above, it was probably of wooden construction although painted to resemble stone. Small for fighting purposes, its primary function was probably to give commanders a better view forward. Thirteenth century seals show this structure reinstated, forward as well as aft, and detailed according to contemporary architectural style rather than as a permanent part of the ship's structure. Besides their use in navigation, they are depicted as platforms both for fighting and for ceremonial purposes.

Oars, or even provision for rowing, were no longer portrayed by this time. Masts were permanent features, with shrouds as well as fore and backstays. While only one, primitive squaresail is still evident, it has been improved. Up to three lines of reefing points show that its area could be reduced in over-strong winds. Conversely, horizontal lines across the lower part of the sail probably indicate that strips of canvas ('bonnets') may be laced on to increase its area.

A bowsprit is almost universal, its outer end supporting blocks which enable the sails to be set broader when beating in contrary winds. The spar might also have been used to assist in handling of grapnels and anchors. It is sometimes shown tipped with a leafy branch, possibly to indicate a ship's trading status.

Hansa Ports and the Cinque Ports

Hulls were clinker-built with some of the heavy transverse beams extending through the sides for extra strength. Stem and stern remained virtually identical, often capped with carved ornamental extensions, until early in the thirteenth century, when the unwieldy and vulnerable steering oar began to be superseded by the rudder.

To hang the rudder, the sternpost had to be made straight, inclined at a steep angle to meet the keel. This brought the hull planking further aft, often terminating in a small triangular deadwood. Such modification of line would have improved sailing qualities by increasing longitudinal stability and reducing the tendency to make leeway.

Despite steady improvement in society, lawlessness was still rife and, for mutual protection and prosperity, thirteenth century ports often grouped together. Notable among these associations were the Hanseatic League and the English Cinque Ports, which granted certain trading privileges in return for obligations. Hansa ports spread from the German North Sea and Baltic coasts to Scandinavia and the English east coast, creating a near-monopoly for about two centuries. Grouped along the Dover Strait, the Cinque Ports prospered over much the same period, enjoying the favour of the Crown in return for making available a significant squadron in

time of war. At this time, there were neither dedicated warships nor a regular navy.

The hegemony of the League resulted in something of a trademark ship. Referred to universally as a 'cog' there is, tantalizingly, no known definitive representation of one. Again, however, the seals of newly-appointed member ports give a fairly accurate indication of their characteristics. A straight stern post, with hung rudder, is matched, unlike in English vessels, by a straight stem, set at a slightly more gentle angle. The stem continued upward to replace the separate bowsprit. By filling out the forward lines the ship's weatherliness would be further improved.

The 'fore-castle' appears to have diminished in size and function, perched almost as an afterthought atop the stemhead. At the after end, however, the structure was extended, sometimes incorporating a raised poopdeck, which suggested accommodation below. While it still does not give the impression of being an organic part of the hull, its size and proportion were by now more in harmony.

Few statistics may be gleaned, but a mid-fourteenth century cog appears to have been about 100 ft overall by 24 ft (30.5 x 7 m), dimensions which suggest a displacement of about 400 tons and a cargo capacity of perhaps half that.

Below: A more common type of northern warship of the fifteenth century, with a lateen mizzen. The rudder, quarterdeck, fore- and after-castles are evident.

Warships to the Time of the Spanish Armada

A replica of a Spanish nao, with which Columbus would have been familiar. The rig combines the driving power of a squaresail on the mainmast with the aid to manoeuvring of a lateen mizzen. Note the heavy wales on the hull.

FROM THE SEVENTH CENTURY AD, Arab influence spread westward from the Indian Ocean. Fine seamen, their craft – generalised as 'dhows' – were characterised by fore and aft rig, whose triangular sails were termed 'lateen'. Compared with the European square rig, it had a vastly superior performance to windward. The first indication of the dhow in the Mediterranean is its portrayal in a late nineth century Greek manuscript.

Hard data on developments in the area is sparse but, by the mid-twelfth century, biremes are shown with a lateen mainsail, their rams raised to waterline level and the hull strengthened accordingly.

By the time of the Third Crusade in the 1190s, twin-masted, lateen-rigged ships were common in the region, their mainmast stepped nearly amidships, the foremast well forward and given a pronounced forward rake to assist in reversing the sail when going about. An account of the crusade speaks, tantilisingly, of a battle between Christian ships and an unusually large Saracen three-master, of which nothing else is known.

In the north, two-masted square-riggers were introduced in the early fifteenth century but, with

EAST MEETS WEST

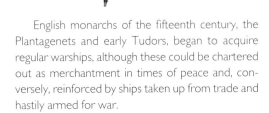

the foremast stepped, again well forward, the rig was unbalanced. An after, or mizzen, mast was therefore adopted, in addition bearing a lateen sail which greatly assisted manoeuvrability. The increasing size of such ships, known generally as 'carracks', was reflected in their also acquiring a main topsail, spread on a separate main topmast. Contemporary depictions indicate the mainmast with rope bindings ('wooldings') at regular intervals, showing that to tolerate the increased stresses the mast was now of larger section, requiring several timbers. To further improve manoeuvrability, an artemon-type square sail (the 'spritsail') was re-adopted. Another example of southern influence was the gradual abandonment of clinker construction in favour of the stronger carvel build.

Trading contacts spread influences in the opposite direction also. By the late fourteenth century the rudder had arrived in the Mediterranean, together with the combination rig of square and lateen sails. Adopted by the city state of Venice, the carrack sprouted a diminutive second mizzen (the 'bonaventure mizzen'), stepped right aft.

Up to 125 ft (38 m) overall length by about 34 ft (10.5 m) in beam, the carrack dominated the fifteenth century scene. Fully capable of extended voyages it, in several variations, conveyed many of the early discoverers. As Spain and Portugal, in particular, quickly appreciated the potential wealth in lands yet unknown, a spate of expeditions was despatched. In the 1490s alone, Columbus explored the Caribbean to the Venezuelan coast, da Gama skirted South Africa to reach India, while Vespucci, Cabral and others began to chart the South American coast. In the north the Cabot brothers were looking at Canada, long before settled temporarily by the Norsemen but, in the south, the Iberian powers claimed the New World as their own, dividing it according to the terms of the 1494 Treaty of Tordesillas, a piece of diplomatic arrogance guaranteed to generate war through its rejection by others.

A growing influence at sea was the gun. Venetian galleys of about 1380 are usually credited with being the first ships to mount guns of significant size. These were 'bombards', with barrels made up of several cast segments and firing stone balls of up to 50 lb (22.7 kg). The coming of artillery exposed the major weakness of the galley which, flanked by its oars, could effectively mount only end-on-fire, there being space forward for two 10-pounders (4.5 kg) in addition. Smaller 'anti-personnel' swivel guns could be mounted along the fore and aft walkway.

English monarchs of the fifteenth century, the Plantagenets and early Tudors, began to acquire regular warships, although these could be chartered out as merchantmen in times of peace and, conversely, reinforced by ships taken up from trade and hastily armed for war.

English 'galleons'

Like their Spanish counterparts, the English ships took the generic name of 'galleon', although this was never accurately defined as a type. Both were directly descended from the four-masted carrack but the English ships, depending on gunnery rather than boarding, were lower and more manoeuvrable, with far lower fore and aft castles, and setting topgallant sails above the topsails on fore and mainmasts. Both could be pierced with square gunports along various levels, their heavy broadside fire governing their tactics as much as the galleys' centreline armament.

This obvious deficiency in the galley led to the development of the galeass which combined the manoeuvrability of a single protected bank of rowers on either side with a three-masted lateen rig. Between the rowers rose a superimposed gundeck, complemented in firepower by further cannon mounted in fore and aft castles. The high-mounted ram was retained. Although ill-suited to northern conditions, this clumsy hybrid also appeared in the sixteenth century Royal Navy's order of battle.

Left: Battle of Lepanto, 7 October 1571. A depiction of the victory of a combined Spanish, Papal and Venetian fleet led by Don Juan of Austria over the Turkish fleet near Navpalitos in the Corinthian Gulf.

Above: This model of a Flemish carrack of c. 1470 shows well the deck layout. Probably from the first representation of a gun-armed ship, the model emphasises the importance of fighting tops.

EARLY GUNNERY AT SEA

Right: A cast iron demi-culverin of the Armada period mounted on a carriage for military use. Small-wheeled carriages for shipboard employment had only recently been introduced.

Below: The seal of Southampton shows a late Tudor warship with two gun decks and complicated fore- and after castles. On her main course appear the arms of Hampshire.

AS MENTIONED EARLIER, cannon probably first went to sea in Venetian galleys. With its painfully low rate of fire and its wild inaccuracy, however, it impressed more by its discharge than by the damage it inflicted. The major weapon was still the well-tried, massed longbows of embarked soldiery, and the taking of an enemy was dependent upon boarding and hand-to-hand combat.

Development of cannon capable of causing structural damage was limited both by cost and technique. Early cannon were reckoned to weigh 80 times the weight of their shot and, while brasses and bronzes could be cast accurately and melted in the quantities required, they were four times the cost of iron. The latter's higher melting point made founding difficult. The necessary techniques were eventually mastered in Germany and the Low Countries, being brought to England by Flemish master-founders hired by Henry VIII in the 1540s.

Early fifteenth century warships were still carrying four or so cannon with barrels comprising

either a series of cast bobbin pieces, or built up from wrought iron strips. Secured to solid timber beds these could be only crudely trained, but not elevated.

Complementing these were topside-mounted swivel guns. Known generally as 'serpentines', or serpent pieces, these could be surprisingly large, capable of firing a 9 lb (4 kg) iron ball, some 4 in (100 mm) in diameter. As gunpowder improved in quality and reliability, so guns needed to become progressively heavier to withstand the explosive stresses of firing.

By the time that Henry VIII was expanding the royal fleet, heavy cannon were moving rapidly to cast muzzle-loaders, mounted on wheeled carriages. Logistics were complicated by there being about 20 recognised types. These ranged from the close-ranged (1,600 yard/1460 m) cannon royal, with a calibre of 8½ in (216 mm) and firing a ship-smashing 66 lb (30 kg) shot, through the useful, long-ranged culverins and basilisks, firing 15–18 lb

(7–8 kg) shot some 2,500 yards (2,300 m), to a range of small 'murderers', or swivel guns, such as the falconet or robinet.

On a overall length of 120 ft (36.5 m), a large warship might have a beam of 32 ft (10 m). Long-barrelled weapons such as culverins were 12 to 14 ft (3.7 to 4.3 m) in length and, to run them fully inboard for re-loading via their muzzles, meant that their positions on opposite sides of the gundeck needed to be staggered. Guns might be run inboard by their own recoil forces, or by block and tackle. There is adequate evidence that they were often loaded from outboard, under conditions of great danger and difficulty.

The cumulative weight of, say, a score of large cannon dictated their being sited on a lower gun deck, firing through square gun ports with hinged covers. This feature marked the end of the practice of arming merchantmen for use in war. The 'race-built' English galleon also possessed considerable sheer towards the ends, necessitating a 'fall' of a half-level at the after end of the gundeck, visible externally as a break in the line of the gunports. The fall allowed the after castle to be reduced in height.

Above: Artillery was still rarely able to sink a ship, so the soldier, with his heavy and cumbersome weapons, still had an important role in naval combat.

1,000 tonners and 100 gunners

In 1502, Vasco da Gama's numerically-inferior squadron of broadside-armed ships inflicted great execution on an Arab fleet off Malibar. Guns of the time were, however, rarely able to destroy larger vessels outright. Besides this, there was great credit to be gained through the capture of an opponent, while her prize value and contents enriched many a family. There was, therefore, every incentive in dis-abling an enemy by the destruction of her more vulnerable rigging, clearing her gundecks by a raking broadside and, while picking off key personnel by sharpshooters sited in the fighting tops, closing quickly, grappling and boarding.

Henry's fighting instructions, and the tactics adopted during battles with the French in 1545-6, embodied such procedures but, where the size of enemy ships and the number of embarked per-sonnel were too great, as during the later Armada actions, boarding was not advisable and few ships were lost other than by mishap or through stress of weather.

By the obscure method of measurement of the time, the largest warships were of some 1,000 tons 'burthen'. In 1610, before his nation became embroiled in trade wars with the Dutch, James I launched a 1,200-ton 'super-ship' in the *Prince Royal*, which carried 55 guns on three levels. In 1637, this ship was eclipsed by the magnificent *Sovereign of the Seas*, built for Charles I. This was the first 100-gunner, carrying her armament on three continuous gundecks. With overall dimensions of 234 × 48 ft (71.3 × 14.6 m) her lines and proportions were less extreme than those of her predecessors, there being, for instance, no need for falls in the gundecks. She was the first to set royals above the fore and main topgallants, a topgallant on the mizzen and a sprit topsail on a diminutive mast stepped at the bowsprit end. As a further aid to manoeuvrability, this latter sail was the precursor of fore staysails.

This romanticised portrayal of a Spanish galleon by Nicholas Hilliard emphasises the great height of the poop structure. Note the bonnets, increasing the area of the mainsail.

UNFORTUNATELY, THERE IS NOT SPACE to follow the politics and machinations that preceded the decision by Philip I of Spain to invade England. Despatch of an army, conveyed in one of the most powerful naval armadas yet seen would, it was hoped, convert England to Catholicism and quell the growing rebellion in the Spanish Netherlands, where there was already an army under the Duke of Parma.

Although Philip had had to water down the over-grandiose proposals of his appointed planner, the Marquis of Santa Cruz, preparations were still lengthy and impossible to conceal from the English themselves. In 1587, Francis Drake descended on the Iberian coast, destroying or taking 37 incomplete ships in Lisbon and Cadiz. This inevitably delayed the enterprise, which then suffered further through the sudden death of Santa Cruz, early the following year. Brooking no more delay, Philip appointed in his place the totally unsuitable Duke of Medina Sidonia.

During the night of 11 July 1588, the Duke left Corunna with 130 sailing ships. These included 65 galleons, 8 galleys and galeasses and over 15,000 troops. Many of the ships were Portuguese and Neopolitan. His instructions were to keep to the, deeper, English side of the English Channel, ignoring the English fleet, if it appeared in force. He was to gain an area east of the Dover Strait, whence he could both control the Thames Estuary and cover the passage of Parma from the Netherlands. Parma himself was to be reinforced by Medina Sidonia's troops.

Key BATTLE

1 THE SPANISH ARMADA

Based mainly on Plymouth, the English fleet was commanded by Lord Howard of Effingham, whose vice and rear-admirals were Drake and Hawkins respectively. It had fewer 'great ships' than the Spaniards, but its more numerous smaller units were far more heavily armed. Although the Spanish galleons were not significantly larger than the English, they were far loftier, to suit tactics based on boarding. Their adversaries, however, were handier and faster and, known to be far superior in gunnery, and had no intention of being closed beyond cannon shot.

Scattered by adverse weather, Medina Sidonia's force dallied off the Lizard (Cornwall, South West England) to regroup, incidentally missing the chance of catching Effingham embayed in Plymouth Sound. Proceeding slowly up-channel the following day, 21 July, in a vast crescent formation, the Spanish found their port wing harassed by Drake, Hawkins and Frobisher, who captured two great ships.

Following a pause to re-ammunition on the 22nd, the English enjoyed a 'wonderful sharp conflict' the following day. Shifting winds allowed the Spaniards to split the attacking force, which had to fight hard to protect its auxiliaries, eventually forcing the English to close up for mutual support.

South of the Isle of Wight on the 24th, the English, now organised into four divisions, managed to isolate Recalde, one of the Spanish commanders. He was rescued by the manoeuvrable galeasses but his ship was so injured that it was sailed to the French coast and beached.

Effingham, in insufficient strength to seek an all-out battle with an enemy that he described as 'wonderfully great and strong', had adopted a policy of 'pluck(ing) their feathers little by little'. Always able to run in for replenishment or repair, his opponent gradually accrued losses and damage, together with doubts regarding the eventual outcome.

On 27 July, Medina Sidonia anchored off Calais, Effingham laying 'within culverin shot'. As the Spanish commander waited to contact and confer with Parma, the English were joined by a large contingent of minor warships from the Thames. Eight fireships were prepared and, during the night of 28 July, these were sailed into the Spanish anchorage. In the ensuing disorder the largest Neopolitan galeass lost her rudder, went ashore and was taken by the English.

On the following day the Spanish were still anchored, but scattered between Calais and Gravelines awaiting Parma's arrival, complicated by the presence, offshore, of a Dutch squadron. Anticipating Parma, Drake led the first headlong attack on the enemy. After nine hours of battle, mostly conducted 'within arquebus shot', two large Spaniards were grounded on the hostile Netherlands coast, where they were taken by grateful Zeelanders. About 40 ships had been driven into the North Sea and many of those remaining were greatly battered by the English fire, the rate of which was reckoned by the Spanish as being three times their own. By their own reckoning, the latter had suffered 600 dead and 800 injured.

Medina Sidonia's resolve broke. He ordered the enterprise to be abandoned and his armada to use the southerly wind to get home northabout around the British Isles. In unfamiliar stormy seas and on unknown coasts the enemy left his bones, only half the force ever returning.

The expedition failed largely because the Spanish had not established sea control before attempting a major landing. From the tactical standpoint, superior manoeuvre and gunnery had defied superior force long enough to break its morale.

Above: **Henry VIII's flamboyant *Henry Grâce à Dieu* of 1545 featured topgallants above her topsails, as well as mounting a diminutive bonaventure mizzen.**

Below: **John Pine's rendering of the Armada sailing up-channel shows well the crescent formation that made it difficult to attack. Oars are still retained on some Spanish ships.**

Development of the Battle Fleet

THAT THE WARSHIP HAD PRESERVED England from the Spaniards was acknowledged by both Sovereign and Nation. While this guaranteed a navy's future, it begged the questions of its strength and how it was to be financed and administered.

Queen Elizabeth had almost doubled the size of the navy, bequeathing in 1603 a 42-strong service to her successor, James I. Only two ships were greater than 1,000 tons burthen, and a dozen were small fry.

Presiding over a relatively quiet spell in history, James viewed the fleet as a symbol of the Crown's dignity and authority, typified by his building of the great *Prince Royal* in 1610. Its administration how-ever, was a mess of graft and sinecure. At the King's death in 1625, between 50 and 60 ships appeared on the order of battle but a detailed survey established that only 39 were fit to be commissioned.

A listing of the fleet broke it down into 'Ships royal, Great ships, Middling ships, Small ships and Pinnaces'. In general, a ship's tonnage, the number of her guns and the size of her crew were related functions. By the middle of the seventeenth century, at a time when a 1,000-tonner had a crew establishment of 500 men, there emerged six categories, or 'rates', of ship, based on crew numbers. This, however, soon gave way to a new system, based on guns carried. A First Rate thus carried over 60 guns,

COMING OF AGE – THE WARSHIP IN THE SEVENTEENTH CENTURY

a Second about 50 to 60, and a Third about 40 to 50. 'About' because the system did not take account of the great variety of guns in service so that in, for instance, the 1652 fleet list, we can find 50-gun Second and Third Rates, and 40-gun Third and Fourth Rates. The categorisation was, from personal points of view, very significant as most named posts aboard were paid according to a ship's rate.

In 1677, a First Rate was standardised as a 100-gun ship of 1,550 tons, a Second as a 90-gunner of 1,307 tons, and a Third as a 70-gunner of 1,013 tons. Their size appears larger than before only because the builder's measurement, previously based on length of keel, was now changed to be calculated on the length of the gundeck. Rating systems, however, never ceased to be revised.

Guns were still a confusing mix of the modern and the medieval. The hundred guns of a First Rate comprised 26 lower deck 'cannon' (probably 42-pounders), 28 middle deck culverins (18-pounders) and 44 sakers (6-pounders) distributed around the upper deck, forecastle and quarterdeck. There was also a pair of 3-pounders.

Although they were later to be referred to more simply by weight of shot, guns still showed confusing variations. As battle tactics were usually to close to within half pistol-shot before exchanging full broadsides, long range gunnery was an irrelevance and the guns themselves could be made shorter and lighter, their muzzle velocity much maintained by improved powder.

Charles I, unhappy with the state of the fleet, which incidentally, became the 'Royal Navy' only after the Restoration in 1660, levied a hugely unpopular tax, known as 'Ship Money', on the nation. It certainly expanded the force, but to his detriment because, despite the defection of a large part of the service to the Royalist cause, the remainder were well able to deter the French from direct support to his restoration to the throne.

The quasi-war with the French justified a further fleet expansion to nearly 160 ships. Most of the new vessels were of the Fourth to Sixth Rate and, of these, the Fourth, typically of 32 or 34 guns, was significant in developing into the Frigate, one of the fleet's most versatile categories.

The Dutch in the course of liberating themselves from Spanish domination, had delivered a crushing naval defeat in the Downs in 1639. Spanish naval decline followed, allowing the astute Netherlanders to take over much of their trade. Their sudden rise in fortunes were noted by Cromwell in England who, intent on a share of the action, inflamed Dutch sensitivities through passing restrictive navigation acts and acting at sea with general high-handedness. As a result, between 1652 and 1673 three totally maritime wars were fought.

The Line of Battle

Designed for shallow and constricted waters, Dutch ships were smaller, beamier and less deep than their English counterparts. Their tactics were still based on boarding. Relying on artillery, the English fleet was divided into three squadrons (Red, White and Blue), which would engage in separate melees with smaller ships supporting their flagship.

To command his new fleet, Cromwell appointed several generals from the army. Known as 'generals-at-sea', they proved very able and it was probably Monck who regularised the formal Line of Battle. Very much suiting broadside-armed ships, the Line had already been used spontaneously in actions, even by the Dutch, but the Fighting Instructions now strung First to Third Rates into a single line ahead. Each ship covered the vulnerable ends of adjacent ships and the formation was nearly impossible to outflank. Individual captains left the Line only for the direst reason. The formation persisted until the twentieth century and resulted in many stalemated actions. It encouraged unquestioning obedience in subordinates, with the consequent loss of initiative.

Above: The royal warship *Vasa*, built in 1628, as seen from the richly decorated stern.

Below: A fine longitudinal cross-section of a First Rate of the late seventeenth century. Note the great depth of hull and the close spacing of the frames.

Opposite: The 100-gun First Rate, *Sovereign of the Seas*, built in 1637, was the prestige flagship of the King and noted for her extravagent ornamentation.

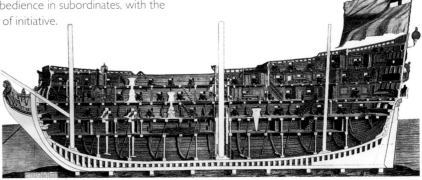

THE WOODEN WARSHIP – FROM THE RESTORATION TO THE REGENCY

THE SEAMEN WHO MANNED the warships of Charles II would have been quite at home on those of Nelson or Collingwood for, in terms of construction, rig and armament, developments were slow for 150 years.

English ships could out-manoeuvre those of the Armada, but this edge in performance, with respect to both French and Spanish ships, was slowly eroded. Each had their strengths and limitations in specific conditions but it became almost the norm for the English to lift the lines of prizes and to build copies. In quality of construction, however, English ships were superior.

With the passage of time, characteristics became less extreme. The pronounced sheerlines of the late seventeenth century, for the purpose of producing a high and imposing afterstructure, were progressively flattened. The rake of the stem, earlier intended to produce a fine forward entry, was steepened to increase fullness and the buoyancy necessary to support the weight of forecastle and armament, and to reduce the tendency to plunge in a headsea. The marked tumblehome of the sides, designed to make boarding more difficult

and to site the higher guns further inboard (in the belief that this improved stability), largely disappeared by the end of the eighteenth century. This was true also of extravagant decoration, with ships becoming more austere.

The slow trend was to increasing size and to heavier, but fewer, guns. First and Second Rates, together with three-decked Third Rates, formed the Line of Battle, lesser ships often being termed 'cruisers'. By the end of the century, strong French influence had resulted in the adoption of the 110-gun First Rate and the famous '74', a large two-decked Third Rate. In the former, 42-pounders were mounted on the lower gundeck and, in order to give the necessary freeboard to work them, ship dimensions increased to the maximum that could be built using traditional methods. Only with the introduction of Seppings' diagonal framing, early in the nineteenth century, were hulls stiff enough to permit further enlargement.

In practice, the 42-pounder proved unwieldy and, by the end of the eighteenth century, had been replaced by the 32-pounder, with its higher rate of fire. Newly introduced was the carronade. Better metallurgical understanding enabled this short-barrelled, large-bore gun to be cast very lightly. With ship-smashing balls of up to 68 lb (31 kg) weight, it proved very popular for close-range combat.

Some captains, enthusiastic at their effect, mounted carronades almost exclusively, paying the price when coming up against opponents who were happy to lay off and play 'long bowls' with conventional long-barrelled 18- and 24-pounders.

Wooden warships – the final phase

Certain classes proved more useful than others. First Rates of 100 and 110 guns, now exceeding 2,300 tons, increased at the expense of the 9-gun Second Rate, which ceased to be built. Crank, three-decked Third Rates made way for longer, two-deck versions. Third Rates of 64 guns also stopped being built in favour of the ubiquitous '74' which, by the close of the century, formed virtually half the fleet. Frigates of 32 to 38 guns appeared in large numbers while French influence again led to the introduction of the 1,500-ton 'heavy' frigate with 24-pounders in place of 18s.

Below: Often known as the 'smasher', the Carronade was designed to fire a large projectile over a short distance. Lighter than conventional cannon, it also required fewer crew.

These ships were also built by the Americans, and proved redoubtable opponents in the War of 1812.

Improvements in rigs were complemented by the successful development of copper sheathing of the submerged hull to reduce fouling by marine growth. During the first half of the eighteenth century, the sprit-topsail, a weak affair and difficult to handle, gradually disappeared, and the bowsprit extended by the jib boom, beneath which were spread two square sails. Staysails, triangular and quadrilateral canvas spread on the stays between the masts, developed also to triangular headsails, easy to work and a powerful aid to manoeuvrability.

After about 1710, the lateen mizzen slowly lost the triangle of canvas ahead of its mast, followed by that section of its long yard. The remaining length of yard became a gaff which, complemented by a boom, spread a quadrilateral sail termed the 'driver', or 'spanker'.

During the first three decades of the nineteenth century, the wooden warship had entered its final phase. By stages, the forecastle and quarterdeck were linked, finally roofing-in the waist and forming a continuous upper deck. Forward, the leaky and vulnerable bulkhead abaft the beakhead gave way to a more powerful, rounded structure, better able to resist raking fire while offering several positions for chase-firing weapons.

Right aft, the towering tiers of stern and quarter galleries were modified to new round, then eliptical, form. The earlier structure was both heavy and weak, imposing great strains on the counter that supported it, while offering little scope for axially-firing gun positions.

Above: A painting by Samuel Scott depicting Lord Anson's victory off Cape Finisterre in July 1805. The two fleets met again later that same year off Cape Trafalgar.

BUILDING A 'WOODEN WALL'

FOR PREFERENCE, ENGLISH SHIPS were built of indiginious oak which, when well seasoned, was highly durable. An extremely tough wood, oak grows naturally into the convoluted shapes required by the shipwright. Unfortunately, a mature tree requires over a century of growth, and periodic peaks of shipbuilding were not, in general, accompanied by planned re-afforestation, so shortages sometimes became critical, necessitating imports of timber from as far afield as India, where some ships were also built.

In times of protracted peace, it was the practice in Royal dockyards to leave incomplete hulls standing for years at various stages in order to complete shrinkage and settling. Private contractors could not afford this luxury and, in any case, were appointed to build generally in times of tension or emergency, when ships were required quickly.

Contractors usually built close enough to a dockyard to allow the Admiralty overseer to ensure the quality of the work, but it was usual for the fit-ting-out of the bare hull to be undertaken in the dockyard. Dockyard-built three-deckers might be constructed in drydock, but the contractor had surprisingly few resources. He required a foreshore suitable to support a building slip, perhaps two score skilled men and a continuous supply of timber, either carted in or brought by coaster. About 85 per cent of the weight of a '74', or some 1,500 tons, was wood, and 90 per cent of this was oak, measured and purchased in 'loads' of about 1½ tons.

Paradoxically, the first wood actually laid was elm, strong and straight enough for keels. A line of blocks was set up to support the hull's considerable weight, and on this was laid the 'false keel', which protected the keel proper from minor damages caused by touching bottom. Both false keel and the keel proper, which was laid on top, were constructed from four or more lengths of elm, linked by strong oblique joints called 'scarphs'.

There being no cranes, a line of stout vertical posts was erected along either side of the slip to

Right: A launch at Deptford c. 1757. At this time, the River Thames was a busy shipbuilding centre, with further yards at Chatham, Sheerness, Woolwich and Blackwall.

assist in the raising and support of large elements. While some shipwrights worked on the hull, others worked in the mould loft, using Admiralty drawings to produce full-sized templates ('moulds'), employed by others to hew timbers to approximate shape ('converting'). Rough and converted timber lay in large stacks, seasoning further until required.

Constructing wooden ships

The straight sternpost, bolted to and strengthened by an inner sternpost, was then erected, followed by the stempost. This, being of pronounced curvature, was scarphed from several pieces and, again, backed by an inner timber.

The keel was then crossed by up to 50 'floor timbers'. These were shaped like inverted coat hangers, almost flat amidships but rising to a steep vee section towards the ends, where they were jointed not the keel but to triangular deadwoods. Atop the floor timbers, and locking the whole assembly together, was laid the 'kelson', which followed a long, continuous curve, rising steeply towards each end.

The floor timbers formed the bottom section of the ship's transverse frames. These, owing to the complex curvature of the ship's cross-section, were also fabricated from several sections ('futtocks'). There were two sets of these, their joints staggered and bolted together. Gunport positions were staggered so that every second transverse frame was continuous to the upper deck. Between them, alternate frames abutted the lower sills of the gunports. Following this, timbers were trimmed to their final shape and longitudinal ribbands fitted to ensure fairness of line. This was particularly important at the ends where, in plan, the hull curved in sharply to meet the line of the keel. Frames in these areas ('cant' frames) closed up until they were a continuous wall of timber.

Forward, the line of the stem was built out into a gracefully-curved 'knee', which supported a substantial figurehead and the beakhead. The stern was the weakest point of the construction. Short vertical timbers rose from the deadwood supporting horizontal transoms and thence, the counter.

From this grew the structure that comprised the galleries of the after accommodation. Heavy wales were then fitted along the outside of the frames, and planked between. Inside, the frames were fitted

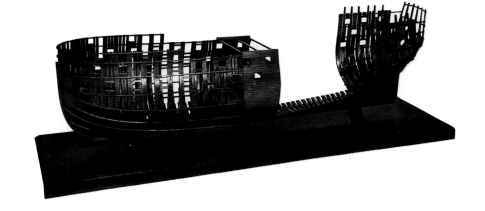

with the knee pieces that supported and braced the transverse beams. These, complemented by lighter members in way of heavy loads, such as cannon, supported the deck planking. Diagonal bracing was originally added in the 'hold', or lower spaces, but proved too space-consuming, being superseded by vertical pillars. With virtually no diagonal members, hulls were limited in size until Seppings' reforms of the early nineteenth century.

For launching, the ship had cradles built around her, forward and aft, and groups of props installed at the same points. Removal of the keel blocks then transferred the hull's weight to the cradles. Knocking away the props allowed the whole to slide, stern first, down the slip and into the water.

Top: Ready for launch, a 64-gun two-decker is shown supported only by the launching cradles and props.

Above: This model of a 74 of about 1815 shows several stages in her construction. Note how the bluff bow causes the cant frames to be close-spaced.

Turner portrayed Trafalgar through the eyes of an artist rather than draughtsman. The battle has become a triumphant spectacle, the ships arranged and scaled to suit the composition rather than tactical realities.

BY THE END OF THE EIGHTEENTH century, the concept of the Line of Battle had been *de rigueur* for over 100 years. Enshrined in Fighting Instructions, it resulted in many stereotyped and stalemated actions. If it were ignored, the heresy required to be offset by considerable success.

In 1782, Admiral Rodney met de Grasse off the Saintes in the West Indies. In very light conditions the British line of 36 ships was heading roughly northward, the 31-strong French line on a reciprocal course. Having the advantage of the breeze, Rodney allowed half his line to pass beyond his opponent's rear before he suddenly tacked, cutting de Grasse's force in two. His second-in-command, Hood, quickly grasped the situation and repeated the manoeuvre, thus isolating a second group. Before the remainder of the French line could beat back to assist their colleagues, the British van had doubled back. The two isolated groups were in real trouble and were fortunate to lose only five ships, including their flagship. Only the 63-year old Rodney's reluctance to pursue his beaten, retreating enemy spoiled the day.

Nelson was 16 years younger, bold and equally unorthodox. He belived in victory by annihilation. In 1805, Napoleon was poised on two occasions to invade Britain and, for this operation, required his battle fleet to establish temporary sea control in the English Channel. The fleet, allied to that of the Spanish was, however, scattered in ports from Toulon to the Texel and watched or blockaded by the British. Its Admiral, the Comte de Villeneuve, greatly pressured by his Emperor, spent months slowly

Key
BATTLE
2 TRAFALGAR

assembling his squadrons, being pursued by the British from the Mediterranean to the West Indies and back in the process. Making for Ferrol, he was intercepted off Cape Finisterre in July 1805 by Sir Robert Calder. Although two Spanish ships were captured, Calder earned himself a court martial for failing to press Villeneuve with sufficient vigour. The upshot was that the combined fleet was concentrated on Cadiz.

Napoleon, who had been obliged to abandon his plans for invasion due to Villeneuve's difficulties, ordered his recall, but the Admiral, getting wind of the development, pre-emped it by sailing his fleet on 19 October 1805. In this he was assisted by Nelson who, having arrived to reinforce Collingwood's blockading force, withdrew well out to sea leaving only frigates to keep watch.

The British captains had known their commander's intentions for ten days or more. Assuming that he would have 40 sail against 46 (actually 31 against 38) Nelson would head for the enemy in two columns. The first, led by his flagship, *Victory*, would break their line ahead of its centre, ie adjacent to Villeneuve's flagship. In parallel, Collingwood's *Royal Sovereign* would head the second column, aiming to burst through at about 'the twelfth ship from the rear'. The rear end of Nelson's force would prevent the enemy van from doubling back.

A considered version of the plan which Rodney had improvised some 23 years earlier, Nelson's carried more risk in that it had already been tried successfully before and would be known to the enemy. In addition, his long, end-on approach, particularly in light winds would place his leading ships under heavy fire for a considerable period without their being able to respond effectively.

Villeneuve's orders to his fleet, which included 15 Spanish ships, showed that he fully anticipated Nelson's intent, yet had no real counterplan.

On 21 October 1805, some 20 miles west off Cape Trafalgar, the two fleets met in calm conditions, but with a heavy swell presaging a blow. Villeneuve was steering northward in a ragged, almost double column, with French and Spanish vessels mixed. As planned, Nelson's and Collingwood's line ran in with a following wind. Limited to only about three knots, however, the lead ships were punished for nearly 40 minutes without being able to return fire.

The *Victory*, closely followed by several others, barged through a small gap in the enemy line, immediately astern of the French flagship, *Bucentaure*, which was raked by each in turn. Treated similarly by the French *Neptune*, *Victory* fell off and grappled with the *Redoubtable*. As the ships exchanged broadsides, muzzle to muzzle, sharpshooters and grenade throwers swept upper decks with death. After about 20 minutes, Nelson was mortally wounded and taken below. As the *Redoubtable* made preparations to board, she was taken from the other side by the British *Temeraire*, which saved the situation.

Both centre and rear, where Collingwood had repeated the process, degenerated into melees but, as required, the enemy van was kept from the fray by backmarkers from Nelson's group. Its efforts were, in any case, irresolute and, by 16.30 hr, after some four hours of action, surviving ships to lee were breaking off and making for Cadiz.

Within an hour, it was all over. Seventeen of Villeneuve's ships were in British hands, another had blown up. With many of Collingwood's own ships severely mauled, prizes took low priority in the fate that followed and only five survived being wrecked, foundering or being re-taken. Five ships that had run into Cadiz were promptly blockaded there, while four surviviors from the French van ran into a British squadron under Sir Richard Strachan off Finisterre on 2 November, and all were captured.

Trafalgar came close to Nelson's creed of annihilation. With no British ship lost, French and Spanish seapower had been greatly blunted.

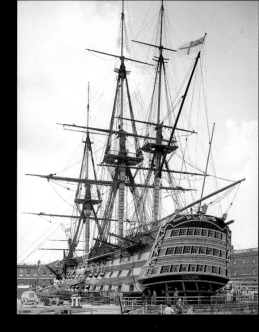

Above: Still a commissioned ship, over 230 years after her completion, the *Victory* permanently occupies a Portsmouth drydock. Docked in 1927, she was almost destroyed by bombing in 1941.

Below: During the gale following Trafalgar, the *Victory* is towed into Gibraltar. She is under jury rig, having been heavily damaged in the final stages of the approach, before breaking the enemy line.

Merchant Sail Until the Coming of Steam

YESTERDAY'S WORKING SAILING SHIPS had a lofty appearance that disguises to modern eyes just how small they were. The sixteenth century carrack, which had provided the baseline for European merchantman and galleon alike, began to evolve in other directions. In the Netherlands, which were becoming fierce trading competitors with the British, it developed into the three-masted 'flute', usually characterised by apple-cheeked after sections, crowned by a narrow and high quarterdeck. Variants, favoured by British owners, who called them 'fly-boats', had severer, rounded sterns which lacked the ornamentation usually favoured by the Dutch. The latter, at the height of the 'trade wars', were reputed to own 10,000 ships, the largest, loading a bare 1,000 tons, trading with India. With piracy and privateering still rife, these were built with a single gundeck, making them virtually indistinguishable from contemporary warships.

Later, common derivatives were the 'cat' and the 'hagboat', the British, with generally deeper water, preferring the 'pink'. Ships at this time were named for their hull form rather than their rig, which could vary considerably.

By the later eighteenth century the 'bark' was common among the larger cargo carriers, with exceptional examples being of 1,250 tons burthen, for which they would measure about 150 ft (46 m)

THE SAILING MERCHANTMAN

in hull length and under 40 ft (12 m) beam. Ships of only a few hundred tons were engaged in the 'triangular' slave trade, the supply of British military forces in North America and in whaling in high latitudes. Design compatability between cargo capacity, passenger accommodation and the provision of a gundeck was beginning to be difficult, resulting in an irregular upper deck profile.

A renowned example of the bark was the Whitby collier, built with minor differences throughout the north east of England. Starting as a three-master, not necessarily 'barque'-rigged, this developed in time to a two-master, commonly termed a 'Geordie brig'. Powerfully built for the coal trade, such ships were often taken up for naval service, one such being the *Endeavour* which, despite being of only 368 tons, roamed the world under Cook's captaincy.

Besides coal, timber was as important a freight as it is now. Lengths of wood and masting material being incompatible with the small hatches of the time, it was common to cut large, rectangular ports in the bows and stern of ships involved in the trade.

Until the mid-nineteenth century, trade to the east of the Cape of Good Hope was monopolised by the powerful East India companies whose ships had advanced from the equivalent of a 32-gun, single-deck frigate to a 64-gun two-decker. Looking like warships, armed and run like warships, they often needed to fight and were, on occasion, taken up for naval service.

Sail gives way to steam

The Americans were also becoming proficient builders in their own right as industries and skills became established. In particular they developed the schooner which, like so many other types, had originated in the Netherlands. With anything from two to seven masts its rig combined the advantages of squaresail and fore-and-aft, and a considerable sail area manageable by a small crew.

The mid-nineteenth century erosion of the monopolies enjoyed by the great chartered companies provided great incentive for the development of 'private' ships to exploit the trades. It was a boom period for British shipbuilding which, in general terms, now constructed iron ships in the north, and wooden in the south. Iron ships, requiring less bulk of material in their construction, could stow up to 15 per cent more cargo than a wooden vessel of

similar dimensions. Transitional composite construction thus became common, with wood planking on iron frames.

Ships began to be built to suit their trade, from big bluff cargo carriers to smaller, fine-lined examples, built for speed, with every variation in between.

Speed was becoming important for survival and the steamship was now making a growing impact. Slowly, the sailing ship was relegated to hauling only non-urgent bulk cargoes and it entered its final phase with the big steel barques, commonly stowing two to three thousand tons, their huge sail area broken down into individual canvas that could be handled by a crew of minimum size.

Even hauling the likes of nitrates from Chile or grain from Australia, their economics became hopeless. While they consumed no fuel, they took twice as long, or more, on a voyage. A steamer, arriving 'light' for such a freight, would simply pump out her ballast water and accept a grain cargo via the suction hoses of an elevator, her large hatches facilitating trimming. The crew of a sailer would first need to dig out a thousand tons or more of solid, shingle ballast, then assist in bagging-up the grain, which would be carted aboard and stowed by hand. While their way of life is now seen as romantic, most sailing men were happy 'to leave the sea and go into steam'.

Above: Cotman's watercolour of a dismasted brig emphasises the stark reality of major damage at sea. The sheer economy of the work makes it one of the artist's masterpieces.

Opposite: A fine impression of a West Indiaman in a fresh breeze off Deal. Perhaps about to come-to, she has only her fore topsail fully drawing. Note the deliberate resemblance to a regular frigate.

PRIVATEERS AND PIRATES

Right: Edward
Teach ('Blackbeard')
cultivated a ferocious
aspect, reputedly even
attaching smoking slow
matches to his beard.

Right: Edward
Teach ('Blackbeard')
cultivated a ferocious
aspect, reputedly even
attaching smoking slow
matches to his beard.

Below: The redoubtable
Henry Morgan
successfully followed
a buccaneering career
that just straddled
the boundary of
respectability.

Sᵗ HEN: MORGAN
Part. 2. Chap. 4.

KNOW YE THAT WE have granted and given licence to – and – and their companions to annoy our enemies by sea or by land ... so that they share with us the half of all their gain ... ' With this form of the so-called Letter of Marque Britain's King Henry III created, in 1243, the first known privateers.

As the monarch's coffers were invariably depleted, it was usual to minimise the number of 'King's Ships' (which were, in any case, available for hire for trading purposes in time of peace) and to grant privileges to certain corporate bodies in return for an obligation to provide an agreed number of ships and men for the King's use in time of war. Any shortfall would then be made good by licensing adventurers to conduct hostilities in the above fifty-fifty partnership with the Crown.

In early days, there was a distinction between a 'letter of marque ship' and a privateer. The former was specifically licensed to extract from ships of a foreign flag goods to a value (agreed with the Admiralty Court) equal to that of a previous loss caused by that flag. This changed gradually to mean an armed merchantman, engaged on normal business but licensed to attack targets of opportunity. A privateer was fitted out exclusively to 'annoy the enemy' as a temporary man-of-war. In time, distinctions blurred and all were termed 'privateers'.

Piracy – the 'golden age'

Over six centuries privateering proved a popular pastime, attended by great risk but, always, the prospect of great gain. Britain, which defined it, always had most to lose from it, her sprawling, worldwide trade ever vulnerable. In contrast, some British privateers, such as William Dampier and Woodes Rodgers, had very successful careers.

Through centuries of hostilities with the French the Royal Navy could contain its counterpart but could do little against the many privateers. These had fast ships and attracted the best seamen, who were exempted from impressment. Their crews were large, both to fight the ship and to provide personnel to sail prizes to a safe port. British shipping was at risk principally in its home waters and in the distant areas to which it traded. During their War of Independence and the War of 1812, the Americans proved equally adept at causing injury to commerce.

It was thus Britain that engineered the prohibition of privateering. The war with Russia, the

so-called Crimean War, terminated with the 1856 Treaty of Paris, which carried a rider, or Declaration, abolishing privateering (although it flourished during the early stages of the later American Civil War) and defining the relationship between flags, goods and contraband.

Privateers were often castigated as behaving like common pirates, whose occupation was as old as seafaring itself. At a time when all merchantmen were armed many Masters were not averse to offering 'protection' to a weaker vessel on pain of her being sacked. Although piracy was, and remains, a curse not related to geography, its heyday is commonly associated with the Caribbean and the coast of Central America, the so-called Spanish Main. Its origins here were with French hunter-settlers, driven out of Hispaniola (now Haiti) by the Spanish about 1630. Settling in the Tortugas, their staple diet was dried, smoked meat, whose Carib name of boucan gave rise to their nickname of 'buccaneers'. Endlessly moved on by the encroaching Spanish, their hunting grounds lost, these resourceful people turned to fitting out ships to prey on Spanish trade. This, more warlike existance was marked by a change in French terminology to 'flibustier' corrupted in English to filibuster, or freebooter.

The lifestyle began to attract others from France, starting with Pierre le Grand but, despite

Above: With his mercenary attitudes and total hatred for the enemy, Sir Francis Drake was at one with Queen Elizabeth I. With such patronage his buccaneering was granted respectability.

Left: As remains the case today, large seagoing ships proceeding close to land were often subjected to surprise boarding by armed gangs in fast small craft.

the romantic aura that it has since acquired, the life of the average pirate was brutal and short, terminated by disease, excess, treachery or at the end of a yardarm.

The ranks of piracy were soon swelled with the likes of Bartolomao Portugues and Francis l'Olonois, reducing Spanish seaborne trade to the point where the only way to make a living was to sack townships. Into this zone of irregular and undeclared war were attracted others, notably the Welshman Henry Morgan, who rose to command an ad hoc Anglo-French force of a dozen sail and 700 fighting men. In time, he laid waste Port-au-Prince, Maracaibo, Porto Bello and Panama. Following personal complaint from the King of Spain, Charles II conferred respectability on Morgan with a knighthood and deputy governership of Jamaica. Old habits died hard, however, and the old rogue again fell from grace.

France and England combined in the 1698 Peace of Rijswijk to end freebooting by an amnesty, but few of these brigands could settle down and piracy entered a new 'golden age' of frightfulness, typified by the likes of Edward Teach ('Blackbeard'), Captain Kidd, and Mary Reed and Anne Bonny.

SAILING RIGS

BY THE END OF THE AGE OF SAIL, there had developed a wide range of different rigs, mostly refined to be effective yet economic with respect to manpower. Only in the nineteenth century had it become customary to classify sailing vessels by their rig, rather than by hull type or trade. Then, for reasons of fashion or economy, a quite minor change in rig might be sufficient to alter a vessel's category, or to give her an individual quirk that would earn the description of 'jackass rig'.

It will, by now, be apparent that there were two major classes of sail, i.e. the squaresail and those set fore-and-aft. The former, and the more ancient, was most efficient at driving before the wind. It was set from a transverse spar, or 'yard', which was raised and lowered by 'lifts', and trimmed, for other than a following wind, by 'braces'. Square rig, correctly, is set on masts with 'tops', signifying that they comprise two or more sections, e.g. lower mast, topmast and topgallant mast. Setting, shortening or taking in canvas required the yard to be manned by line of seamen, often in hazardous conditions of numbing cold and wind, combined with powerful accelerations and general fatigue.

For the most part, squaresails were named for their masts and the position occupied, e.g. mainsail, maintopsail and maintopgallant. The largest, lower sail was, however, usually referred to as a 'course' while, for ease of handling, the topsails might be divided. The above example would, therefore,

more likely read: main course, lower and upper maintopsails and maintopgallant. Length of yard and area of canvas diminished rapidly with height in order to reduce the strain on the rigging and top-weight, and to lower the centre of pressure of the wind and, thus, capsizing moment. Some 'crack' ships, such as clippers, could set further small areas of fair weather canvas above the topgallants. The first of these was the 'topgallant royal', later contracted to 'royal'. Very rarely, a tiny scrap of canvas was set even above this; known as a 'skysail', sailors often termed it a 'kite'.

Multi-masted ships

In dependable weather, such as seasonal tradewinds, sail area could also be increased laterally by 'studding-sails' (pronounced 'stunsails'). Studdingsail booms were rigged to extend the length of the topgallant and topsail yards, the studdingsail itself having the depth of upper and lower topsails combined but rigged outboard of them.

As we have seen, the earliest fore-and-aft sail adopted in northern waters was the lateen mizzen, which developed into the spanker, set on gaff and boom abaft the aftermost mast. The next advance was to set fore-and-aft canvas on the heavy stays that supported the masts. These, logically enough, were termed 'staysails'.

Forward, the difficult arrangements for setting squaresails above and below the bowsprit were replaced by triangular staysails, set before the foremast and known collectively as 'headsails'. The largest and innermost, set on the forestay, was termed the forestaysail. Up to six headsails were carried on extreme rigs but the number was usually four – forestaysail, inner and outer jibs and flying jibs. To set them the bowsprit, like the masts, comprised two or three sections, i.e. the bowsprit proper, a jib boom and a flying jib boom. Of considerable length, these were braced upward to the foretopmast and foretopgallant mast tops, and downward by the 'martingale' to the stem directly or led via a short, downward-pointing strut known popularly as the 'dolphin striker'.

Staysails set between the masts were originally of irregular quadrilateral shape but became almost universally triangular. They, too, took their names from the stays upon which they were set, e.g. main and mizzen topmast staysails. Hanked in general to standing rigging, fore-and-aft canvas could be

Below: A water colour featuring barges under sail on the River Thames.

Right: This three-master is 'ship-rigged', her mizzen built in three sections and crossed for square rig. Note that she is carrying studding sails on the foremast.

Below right: The brig-rig of the *Cupido* is the two-masted equivalent of ship-rig. The vessel in the background is setting topgallants and studding sails to run before the wind.

handled by a few hands, working the peak halyards. Vessels with predominantly fore-and-aft rigs could thus be worked by smaller crews, accounting for the popularity of the schooner in American waters and the brigantine in British. The latter developed from the brig, a two-master square-rigged on both, but modified to take three headsails, four squaresails on the foremast, a mizzen spanker and three staysails between the masts.

Among larger cargo carriers, the standard 'ship' rig saw squaresails on each of, usually, three or four masts. This developed into the 'barque' with the adoption of fore-and-aft rig on the aftermost mast. Thence, by retaining square rig on only the foremast and converting the remainder to fore-and-aft, it became a 'barquentine'.

One problem with multi-masted squareriggers was that several of their sails could be ineffective by virtue of being blanketed by those adjacent. Popular also was the sprit rig, originating in the Netherlands but familiar in British waters on numerous Thames barges. Easily handled, the rig was spread on just a mast and a standing diagonal sprit.

LOCAL CRAFT

SAILING RIGS IN THE WEST were always in a process of development yet in the nineteenth century, having reached an apparent peak of complexity and sophistication, were displaced by another Western development, the steam engine. This sense of continuous evolution was not apparent in the East, where local requirements, in general, produced local solutions.

In China, particularly, it was believed that there remained nothing to be learned. That which was ancient was revered and anything new was viewed with suspicion. Junks, as familiar today, were described recognisably by the thirteenth and fourteenth centuries traveller Marco Polo and then, at infrequent intervals, by the few educated Westerners to travel the area. Having evolved the craft to a perfectly acceptable standard, the logical Chinese saw no merit in further change. That this was not entirely complacency may be seen by considering some of its features. We have seen elsewhere in the book how, in the West, the rudder displaced the steering oar during the thirteenth century. It may have been delayed because of the universally-used curved sternpost, which was not compatible with hinging. Although of seemingly infinite variation in design, on the other hand, the majority of junks featured a long, overhanging counter, beneath which protruded the rudder post. Unsupported at its heel, this would have required to tolerate considerable torsional forces at its upper end but for the fact that the Chinese balanced the rudder blade. With about one-third of its area forward of the rudder post and two-thirds abaft, it used a principle appropriate to Western designs of today, yet was in service routinely with the Chinese a millennium before the West even adopted the rudder.

Marco Polo mentions the use of watertight bulkheads. These may have been a prudent feature facilitated by the junk's generally uncomplicated trapezoidal cross-section, or simply to fulfil the practical need of a floodable live fish compartment or the carriage of oil in bulk.

Right: Although seen here on a Maltese craft, the cutter rig was common internationally. All sails are fore and aft, and there are two foresails, one set on the forestay.

Left: Junks sail in Hong Kong Harbour near the American Pier on the Kowloon Peninsula.

Leeboards, greatly characteristic of Western shallow-water craft and lowered to assist sailing to windward, were in use by the Chinese centuries before they spread westward. To enable them to be speedily struck, junk masts are not stayed by standing rigging but rely on tabernacles for their support. As with rudders, a sail's area is balanced about its mast. Sail design is ingenious, their many subtle variations betraying their origins to the experienced eye. Common to all is a complex arrangement of horizontal bamboo battens, which shape the sail and allow it to be collapsed rapidly in an emergency, after the fashion of a Venetian blind. The battening permits economy in both size and weight of sailcloth employed, while providing a convenient means of going aloft.

Seagoing junks have sails that tend to a peak, but riverine craft have narrower, higher sails, squared-off at the top. In this they share a feature common to many craft, worldwide, which need to ghost along waterways over which faint breezes may be blocked by embanking or by vegetation. In Britain, for instance, high-peaked sails were typical of such as the Norfolk wherry (evolved for shallow fenland waterways but which may also have fathered the American Gundelo sailing barge) and the 'keels' of the Humber and the north-eastern rivers, employed in the latter area to shift coal from up-river staithes to colliers waiting downstream. In enclosed dock systems, Thames bargemen would set their small triangular topsail to assist in shifting berth, while the fickle breezes of the Douro River have shaped the high rig of the ancient Portuguese craft designed to move vast barrels of wine.

The birth of multi-hull craft

The high peak is a natural feature of the lateen rig and is seen to advantage in the Egyptian gaiassa, whose Nile habitat has its tiny breezes baffled by high embankment and extensive groves of palms. Running before the wind the gaiassa will 'goosewing' her two sails, setting them on opposite sides.

The gaiassa's lateen rig was probably borrowed from that of the Arab dhow, the latter being a generic term used to describe a wide variety of (usually) single-masted craft of up to about 200 tons capacity and common from the Persian Gulf to Zanzibar. Rakish craft, often beautifully built in teak they, like so many, now more frequently exist in a cut-down form and propelled by the ubiquitous diesel engine.

Limited by local resources, Eastern boatbuilders could often construct only narrow-gutted craft, which they learned to stabilise with outriggers. Potentially very fast, these appealed to the West as recreational craft, the hull-plus-outrigger combination developing into two equal-sized 'demi-hulls' to form a catamaran. As usual, it is the West that has taken the concept further, refining the basic catamaran into such as the SWATH and, through multi-hull craft in general to the current research into trimaran warships.

Below: The rakishly-attractive appearance of this two-masted Arab dhow is evident, as is the complication of manhandling the feet of the long yards around the masts when going about.

WHALING IN THE DAYS OF SAIL

Above: **This John Ward painting depicts whalers in a deceptively peaceful environment. Reliance upon small boats for whale catching produced magnificent seamen but many casualties.**

MAN'S PURSUIT OF THE WHALE extends back to pre-history and is not confined to any particular part of the world. With the creatures' migratory habits bringing them close inshore, many coastal communities became dependent upon an annual bounty hunted from open boats. A century before the Normans invaded Britain the Basques were active, gaining skills that saw them working the Newfoundland Grand Banks by the close of the sixteenth century.

Known long before to the Norsemen, the large Arctic archipelago of Spitsbergen was 're-discovered' by Willem Barendsz in 1596. His accounts of numerous pods of whales close inshore was quickly followed up by the Basques, whose expertise was, by now, widely acknowledged.

Spitsbergen lay within the purlieu of the English-based Muscovy Company, given a royal charter in 1555 to discover and to exploit a north-east passage route to Cathay and, incidentally, to foster trade with the Russians. In 1610 the company hired Basque skills to fit out an experimental whaling expedition. Backed by the company's monopolisitic powers the enterprise expanded into an industry that was described as 'prospering strangely'. Whatever that actually meant, its lead was soon usurped by outsiders, including British but, predominantly, Dutch. Within a decade, the latter had effectively taken over but the acquired skills of the British were to surface elsewhere.

Baleen whales (such as the blue and fin whales) abounded in season off the coasts of Newfoundland, New England and Greenland, while sperm whales followed the eastern seaboard. The British colonies in America were already prospering with an alliance of developing skills and seemingly unlimited resources. At the time that the colonies revolted for independence, for instance, one-third of British-registered tonnage was American-built.

Cook's hugely-informative Pacific voyages attracted both settlers and whalers. Even the famous First Fleet, once it had deposited its transportees at Botany Bay in 1788, went about its whaling business in regional waters. British and Yankee whalers working the Pacific were soon numbered in hundreds, the trade faltering only in the mid-nineteenth century, when the development of onshore oil deposits greatly reduced demand for whale oils.

The extreme difficulty of hunting whale in the days of sail ensured that over-fishing occurred only in specific areas, and it was only in the twentieth century that science and power combined to drive most types of whale to the verge of extinction. A total of 860,000 creatures taken in the 1960s and 1970s alone contrasts starkly with just 15 or so taken by a Yankee sailing whaler on a successful voyage.

Whales – catching and processing

New Bedford whalers were stoutly built but with a surprising turn of speed. Wood-built and ship-rigged they were typically some 130 ft in length with a tonnage of perhaps 400. Slung along either side were double-ended whale boats, each of which had its own crew, mate and harpooner. On sighting a whale the ship launched the craft as a flotilla, guided by signals from lookouts perched high in the whaler's rigging. Once achieving an attacking position to the lee of his quarry a harpooner would aim an iron into its head. It would immediately take off at high speed, towing the boat on a long line which would be led around the boat's bitts, or 'loggerheads'. The huge beast would need to be 'played' to exhaust it and there was continuous risk of capsize or being dragged under if it 'sounded', or dived deeply. As other

boats and the ship closed to assist, the struggle ran its course. A well-aimed iron would see the whale unable to dive as its vent clogged with blood, and it would be quickly dispatched on the surface.

Hove-to, the ship would secure the floating carcass by chains to its starboard side. Staging was then lowered from the ship's side for the process of 'cutting-in'. From the staging, which extended above the carcass, it was first necessary to have a man, secured on a short line, to stand on the slippery, rolling surface and make the initial cuts and footholds.

The head, one-third of its bulk, would be removed first. 'Heaving-in falls' would then be rigged via blocks slung between the ship's masts and attached to winches. As men with flensing irons and spades separated the overlaying blubber it would be thus peeled off as a 'blanket piece' and swung inboard. Here, it would be quickly cut into mangeable chunks and reduced to oil in the 'try pots', the permanent fires under which often gave the ship the appearance of being herself ablaze. Cooled, the oil was run into casks. Lacking refrigeration the ships could make little use of the meat but the head, particularly of the sperm whale, yielded large quantities of high grade and valuable oil. Straps and tackles removed the teeth, sold as ivory. After an investigation into the intestines for lumps of ambergris, prized by the perfume industry, the remains were set adrift to be picked clean by marine scavengers before settling to the bottom.

Above and below: In his leisure time the whaling sailor indulged in various handicrafts. Besides carving wood, decorating sea chests and creating delicate fancy ropework, he turned his hand to 'scrimshaw', the incising of pictorial scenes onto the teeth of sperm whales.

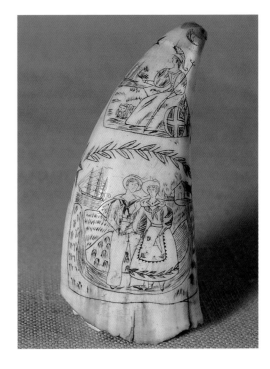

THE CLIPPERS

Right: An unusually workmanlike impression of one of the most famous clippers, the *Cutty Sark*, running before the wind with studding sails set.

Below: The *Ethiopean*, close-reaching and setting full plain sail. She is ship-rigged, with four headsails and staysails between the masts. The mainmast is crowned with a minute skysail.

WHILE THERE EXISTS NO PRECISE definition of the term 'clipper', it is accepted to apply to a ship built for speed rather than for economic cargo carrying. Its origins are thought to lay with the fast New England-built brigs and schooners that profited greatly as privateers and blockade runners during the war of 1812. Known collectively as 'Baltimore clippers', examples even found their way into the Royal Navy. With peace they lost their lucrative trade and many engaged in running slaves directly from Africa.

During the 1840s, yards such as Donald McKay's at Boston and William Webb's at New York were successfully applying square rig to fast hulls of 750 tons and more. These vessels were well-timed to take advantage of the 1847 'Gold Rush' to California. As this involved American ports at either end, only American ships could participate. Huge profits could be made by ships capable of making the long haul around the Horn in good time. Once arrived on the west coast, however, crews often deserted to join the throng of hopeful prospectors, and owners were obliged to keep them through the payment of premium wages. In addition, the passage back was virtually freightless, and a dead loss.

In 1849, however, Great Britain repealed her restrictive Navigation Acts, and American clipper owners found it profitable to proceed from the west coast, across the Pacific to China, to load a cargo of tea for the British market. Faster than existing British ships engaged in the trade, the Americans soon made deep inroads, prompting a British response, notably from Richard Green of Blackwall, famous for his 'frigates'.

Rivalry, races and records

To maintain high speed, a clipper required huge spreads of canvas and large crews. Most thus favoured 'shiprig', three masters which, unlike barques, carried both square rig and spanker on the mizzen. To studdingsails and huge staysails were often added strange scraps of sail with odd names such as 'moonrakers', which gave the illusion of more speed. The real key was a skilful captain, hard-driving mates and a crew endlessly trimming sail and setting up standing rigging. Driven too hard, many just disappeared, their fine lines offering insufficient buoyancy to lift to the odd rogue sea.

British owners, unable to find in home yards the quality and delivery that they required, also went to McKay, who thus built classic ships such as the *Lightning* and *Champion of the Seas*, *Red Jacket* and *Shalimar*. Vessels were also increasing rapidly in size, with Webb building the *Challenge* and *Ocean Monarch* of over 2,000 tons. The latter, still only about 242 ft (74 m) between perpendiculars, could accommodate no less than 880 passengers. Most travelled 'steerage' in conditions that, today, would be considered primitive.

Although clippers could make 16 knots in good conditions their average speed over a long haul could be surpassed by the meanest steamship. For instance, the record 71-day passage of the *Cutty Sark* from Australia to England, represents an average of 8 knots only. It was fortuitous, therefore, that the 'golden age' of the clipper coincided with the period of the Crimean War, when most available steamers went on lucrative government time-charter.

The next challenge, however, was the construction of a railroad across the Panama Isthmus (the canal was still a half-century in the future)

with steamship connection to either end. This put many fine sailers out of business, offset somewhat by the discovery of gold in Australia. Early steamships were having trouble coping economically with such a long haul and fast sailing ships scooped the mail contract (rather optimistically quoting a 65-day delivery) to complement a cargo of hopeful diggers outward and a full load of wool with which to return.

Clippers built for the China tea trade were finer and faster than the Australian wool carriers. The first tea of the season commanded a high premium on the London market and brought great credit to the company and skipper that had shipped it.

Intense rivalry resulted in fiercely-contested races, none more so than that of 1866 when five crack ships, *Ariel, Fiery Cross, Serica, Taeping* and *Taitsing,* left Foochow at the end of May, all within a space of 36 hours. For much of the 16,000-mile passage the ships were actually in sight of each

other but *Ariel* built up a short lead on the run north from the Cape of Good Hope, sighting the Bishop Rock light on 5 September. The *Taeping* had also crept up while, as the two raced neck and neck up the English Channel, the *Serica* ran, unsuspected, up the French side. Taking tows from the Downs, all three docked in London at the same time on 6 September, the other pair just two days behind.

'China Birds' fared poorly on the Australian run. Iron construction enabled the existing fuller-bodied design to be stretched, increasing capacity to some 3,000-tons and improving sailing characteristics by the addition of a fourth mast, termed the 'jigger'. When, in 1869, the Suez Canal opened, it struck the greatest single blow at the continuing viability of sail in the face of the march of steam.

Above: The *Montezuma,* one of the crack American Black Ball Line clippers, 'makes her number', displaying her signal letters as a request for her sighting and position to be reported.

SUEZ AND PANAMA

WHEN, IN 1859, Ferdinand de Lesseps' French-led consortium commenced digging a canal across the isthmus of Suez, it promoted vehement opposition from the British, whose powerful shipping lobby feared that much of its tonnage (designed for the traditional Cape route) would be made obsolescent. Shipping using the Cape route also tended to use British ports for the transshipment of cargo parcels destined for continental Europe, which trade was also threatened.

Ten years later, when the project was completed, attitudes had changed, with operators looking at means of capitalising on the new facility. Although business built slowly as services were adjusted, the canal's long-term potential was obvious and, in 1875, the British prime minister, Disraeli, took advantage of the improvident Khedive Ismail in purchasing the latter's 44 per cent shareholding for just £4 million sterling. Rarely was public money better invested.

Schemes had existed since antiquity to create a waterway linking the 80-odd miles separating Port Said on the Mediterranean from Suez on the Red Sea, the most recent one prepared for Napoleon. De Lesseps' masterpiece was 92 miles in length, including 20 miles which used the existing Bitter Lakes and Lake Timsah. South of the lakes there is a weak tidal effect.

On opening, the stated depth was 26 ft (7.9 m) permitting passage by ships with draughts not exceeding 24 ft (7.5 m). As navigable width was only 72 ft (21.9 m) passing places (or 'gares') were provided about every six miles. Early passages took up to 55 hours, but further dredging, easing of the sharper bends and the introduction of shipboard searchlights to permit night navigation reduced transits to under 24 hours by the turn of the century.

Below: The enormous size of the Gatun Lock on the newly-opened Panama Canal dwarfs a private steam yacht and freighter. Note the 'mule' locomotives at right.

The Atlantic and Pacific Oceans links

The opening of the canal made a considerable impact on shipping. Steamship services to the Far East via the Cape had hitherto been uneconomic due to the lack of suitable coaling stations and the consequent huge quantities that were required to be carried in bunkers. Suez shortened the routes to India and the Far East by 3,000 to 4,500 miles, offering coaling points in addition. Sailing ships were unable to navigate the Red Sea for much of the year and, no longer able to compete profitably with steamships around the Cape, went into significant decline.

Having crossed the isthmus of Panama, Balboa sighted the Pacific in 1513, an event initiating schemes to link the Atlantic and Pacific oceans. Sea to sea it was barely 50 miles, but the terrain was hilly, the tropical climate enervating, and the region rife with malaria and yellow fever.

There were two favoured routes: through Nicaragua and that roughly following the old Spanish trade route which ran from Old Panama to the Chagres River and thence to Portobello. This track had been so well trodden during the 1849 Californian Gold Rush that a railway had been opened in 1855.

Keen to capitalise on his success at Suez a by now-elderly de Lesseps began work on a waterway but was defeated by corruption, mismanagement and a mortality rate of one worker in six. A further French undertaking fared no better. However, consequent to their successful 1896 war with Spain, the United States had acquired territories in both the Pacific and the Caribbean, and were keen to create a waterway. Taking advantage of Panama's 1903 secession from Colombia, the Americans acquired a 99-year lease on a six-mile-wide Canal Zone, purchasing building rights from the French.

More logically, the Americans first tackled the root causes of the region's diseases following which, in 1907, the Corps of Army Engineers went to work. In August 1914 the first ship transit was made, an event overshadowed by events in Europe. Unlike the sea level Suez Canal, that at Panama utilises major flights of locks, such as those at Pedro Miguel and Miraflores, to cross the watershed of the Gatun Lake, some 85 ft (25.9 m) above datum. This lake, together with the dammed Chagres River, provides the water to replace that lost each time a lock is lowered. Generously-dimensioned when completed, the 1,000 x 110 ft (304.8 x 33.5 m) locks quickly proved to be limiting to the design of large ships, due to beam restrictions. At construction,

minimum bottom width was only 300 ft (91.4 m), a dimension imposed by the difficult Culebra Cut, where major landslips plagued the waterway for years following its inception.

By being able to switch naval units rapidly from the east to the west coast, the United States required fewer ships. The canal also decreased the distance from Europe to the Pacific coasts of North and South America by anything between 1,500 and 6,000 miles and stimulated the region's accelerated development.

Through basing canal dues on parameters such as dimensions, cargo and passengers carried, both Suez and Panama have exerted a powerful influence on ship design as operators tailored their newbuildings to wring the maximum advantage from each clause.

Above: Unlike the Panama Canal, whose opening was overshadowed by war, Suez was inaugurated with great ceremony. Although of much the same length as Panama, Suez is unencumbered by locks.

EARLY MARINE STEAM ENGINES

ALTHOUGH THE BASIC TURBINE principle was known to the ancients, it was the reciprocating engine that long dominated the application of steam power to marine propulsion.

Early steam enthusiasts, notably William Symington, were much engaged by the 'atmospheric' engine, the invention of which is credited to Newcomen as early as 1710. It worked by lifting a piston in a vertical cylinder under the action of steam pressure and some form of counterweight then, with the piston at the top of its travel, suddenly cooling the expanded steam below it with a cold water jet. With the steam turned near-instantaneously to water, the pressure in the cylinder was lowered. Normal atmospheric pressure, acting on the top of the piston, then forced it down for the cycle to be repeated. Although practicable, the action was slow and inefficient.

An alternative, with a single cylinder arrangement was to add a flywheel, whose inertia could return the piston to the bottom of its travel. Better, a second cylinder and piston could be added, with an action exactly opposed to that of the first, producing a balanced and continuously re-set system. Whatever arrangement was adopted, the expanded steam and water resulting from each cycle needed to be returned to a condenser, for the quantity of fresh water that could be carried was small and boilers could not accept saltwater.

Development of steam propulsion

Although many experimental prototypes had appeared over the years, the *Charlotte Dundas*, of 1802, is credited with being the first to demonstrate useful work by towing barges on the Forth & Clyde Canal. Her layout was remarkable in foreshadowing the sternwheeler, her single large paddle wheel being sited on the centreline and working in a notch in the stern. A engine, built by Symington, was sited on the deck and the single cylinder was of 22 inches (559 mm) diameter, permitting a 48-inch (1,219 mm) stroke. Being of atmospheric design, it was not particularly efficient, but drove the paddle shaft by crank and connecting rod, with the cylinder's crosshead structure being powerful enough to asborb and transmit the thrust generated.

In 1812, the smaller *Comet* began a regular passenger service between Glasgow and Greenock. She was only 40 ft (12.2 m) in length and her engine, built by John Robertson, had a cylinder of 12½ inches (318 mm) diameter, its piston having a 16-inch (406 mm) stroke. The piston was reset by a heavy flywheel.

Boilers in these early craft generated pressures of five pounds per square inch (5 psi) or less. They were shaped rather like a round pot, set in a brickwork structure to form the flue and, occasionally, the funnel itself. From about 1820, the structure took the form of an iron box whose internal water containment was bounded by large-surfaced, flat-faced flues. Flat surfaces have poor resistance to pressure and a further complication was caused when the boiler was allowed to cool because, as its steam condensed, a partial internal vacuum was created, putting the structure in danger of implosion by atmospheric pressure. Boilers were thus heavily braced internally and fitted with both 'internal' and 'external' safety valves.

The 1820s saw the first practical railway locomotive, whose boiler was arranged with the hot combustion gases passing through a bank of tubes set in the water case. This arrangement provided a much greater heating area and, being more efficient, was slowly accepted into marine practice. Steam pressures were still commonly less than 5 psi.

Below: Symington's *Charlotte Dundas*, reputedly the first practical steam boat, worked the Forth & Clyde canal. Note the huge centreline casing for the single paddle wheel and the tall stack necessary for natural draught.

WILLS'S CIGARETTES.

THE "CHARLOTTE DUNDAS".

Left: A side lever engine of 1836. Its 'architectural' design has great functional beauty, the individual members following exactly the direction of imposed forces.

A feature of early steamers was the high funnel. This was not a fashion but a necessity to induce sufficient draught for the rapid and complete combustion of coal. A later refinement was to build a steam-driven fan into the uptake to further improve airflow.

An important development in machinery was Boulton & Watt's side-lever engine. This could be given a lower profile by linking the crosshead, driven by the piston rod, to one end of a centrally-pivoted, low-set horizontal beam. The other end of this oscillating beam drove the crank that actuated the paddle-wheel shaft. Through the use of two cylinders, a smooth, balanced action could be obtained and, by setting the cranks mutually at right angles, the engine could be started or reversed irrespective of where its pistons had come to rest.

While of low profile, the side-lever engine was quite space-consuming and the next logical development was to build its various components into an assembly fitted below the paddle shaft. This, in addition, saved weight and shortened the drive path, the machinery now being termed 'direct-acting'.

By the time that Victoria ascended the throne in 1837, ships the size of a frigate could be propelled by auxiliary steam machinery at a speed of 10 knots, and the long transition from sail to steam had begun.

Left: Compound machinery, with its multiple cylinders, always impressed with its size. Usually termed a *cathedral engine* this example was built by Elder in about 1890 for the liner *Orient*.

45

Pax Britannica and the Era of the Transitional Fleet

Most ship-to-ship encounters of the war went to the Americans. An exception was the taking of the *Chesapeake* by HMS *Shannon* whose captain, Philip Broke, was a noted gunnery enthusiast.

THE WAR OF 1812

IN THE YEAR OF 1812, just a third of a century after the United States had gained their independence from Great Britain, attitudes on both sides were still raw and easily inflamed by a small incident. Decades of fighting the French had seen the Royal Navy expand to about 600 seagoing fighting ships, the manning needs of which, coupled with the hastily disciplined existence, required continuous impressment to maintain. With the arrogance bred from decades of accustomed superiority at sea, British warships routinely stopped American merchantmen to remove British deserters or nationals, 'new colonials' and, all too often, American citizens, for service in the Royal Navy. Matters were facilitated by United States-flagged neutral bottoms shifting much of the cargo which, but for the activities of French privateers, would have been shipped in British vessels. An added source of resentment was the huge profits being made by American traders on these high-risk ventures.

War nearly erupted in 1807 when the British ship *Leopard* stopped the American warship *Chesapeake* after a brief fight in order to impress four personnel. This was a national affront, and only the conciliatory powers of President Jefferson prevented overt hostilities breaking out. Provocations continued, however, and when James Madison took office in 1809, attitudes hardened. Despite British concessions, war commenced on 28 June 1812. Its maritime aspects were important and, unusually, were divided between the open sea and the Great Lakes.

America's Fledgling Navy

The infant US Navy comprised mainly seven frigates and nine assorted corvettes, sloops and brigs. British naval presence on the station was of much the same strength but could always be reinforced, whereas the Americans could not.

Six of the Americans were so-called 'heavy frigates', nominally carrying 42 to 44 guns but actually armed with 52 to 54. Larger than British frigates, usually 36s or 38s, they were good sailers, well manned and well handled.

With ships spread thinly, the war at sea was notable for a series of duels between frigates, at which the British usually came off worst. The first occurred in August 1812 when the over-confident British *Guerriere* (herself captured from the French in 1806) sought a battle with the *Constitution*

Left: Built in 1806, the *Shannon* was not scrapped until 1859, and into the era of photography. This picture gives an excellent idea of the upper deck of a 38-gun frigate, the still-primitive cannon and the uniforms of the period.

whose 24 pounders proved decisive over her challenger's 18s. Indeed, the 18-pounder shot, for the most part, bounced off the American's hull, earning her the soubriquet of 'Old Ironsides'. The *Guerriere*, reduced to a defenceless hulk by her fore- and mainmasts going by the board, was burned and sunk, the myth of British naval invincibility being badly dented.

In October 1812 matters progressed with the British *Macedonia* 38 being captured by the *United States* 44, and in December, with the 38-gunned *Java*'s sinking by the *Constitution*. Front line replacements were sent by Great Britain as part of the institution of a blockade of the Eastern Seaboard. In June 1813 the equally-matched 38s, *Shannon* and *Chesapeake* met by appointment outside Boston. Following a bloody duel, and despite the American commander, Lawrence's dying exhortation, 'Don't give up the ship', the *Chesapeake* was taken.

The privateering *Essex* 32, preying on a British whaling fleet off the Chilean coast, was hunted down by the British *Phoebe* 36 and *Cherub* 18. Armed mainly with short-range, ship-smashing 32-pounder carronades, the American was shot to pieces by the British long 18s.

In the summer of 1814, their blockade complete, the British captured the *President* which was trying to break out of New York, then landed a

4,000-strong military detachment, which advanced on Washington, burning its public buildings.

The Great Lakes marked, for the most part, the border between the United States and British Canada. Communications were virtually non-existant and control of the lakes was essential to the objectives of both sides. Each had maintained pre-war squadrons of minor warships but operations were now delayed until ad hoc yards could construct larger units capable of forcing a decision. In September 1813 the carronades of Oliver Hazard Perry's ships proved superior, in light weather conditions, to the long guns of the British whose commander, Barclay, surrendered his whole squadron.

In Montreal, in 1814, a veteran British army was poised to advance down the Hudson valley to take New York but a bloody British naval defeat on Lake Champlain prevented their proceeding along its shores. The abandoning of this campaign led to the Duke of Wellington advising the cabinet that nothing was to be gained in America and the war was concluded by the Treaty of Ghent in December 1814.

Never having given 'Mr Madison's War' the attention it deserved, the British emerged empty-handed. The Americans gained a strong sense of unity and their fledgling navy the heroes it needed. Ships today still commemorate the names of the likes of Decatur, Macdonough, Perry and Bainbridge.

PRIVATEERS AND WARS AGAINST COMMERCE

ANY NATION WHOSE ECONOMY is dependent upon seaborne trade is vulnerable to war waged specifically against that trade. Since the thirteenth century such warfare has been recognised as legitimate but, dignified by the title of Guerre de Course, it must be conducted according to international law. From earliest times, rather than commit scarce resources to regular warships, states found it expedient to licence individuals with suitable vessels. This licence, the Letter of Marque, elevated the holder from being classed a common pirate and obliged him, in theory at least, to bring in his prizes for condemnation at an Admiralty Court for subsequent division of their value between the state and the privateer. As, in later days, the latter took the lion's share it was a profitable, if risky, occupation that attracted many of the best men, although encouraging them to ignore the stricter requirements of the law.

The 1856 Declaration of Paris outlawed the practice by its signatories but, as these did not include the United States, their shipping suffered badly from it early in the civil war. To anticipate somewhat, privateering might have passed into history, but for the curious paragraph of the 1907 Hague Convention which approved the use in war of armed merchant cruisers in a raiding context. Hostilities quickly demonstrated their inadequacies, with submarines assuming the role. These proved totally unable to operate within the prescribed 'prize rules', which were abandoned for unrestricted warfare and the consequent appalling loss of life and ships

John Paul Jones – hero and villian

Over the years, many trading nations have suffered from privateering, often in periods short of war. British shipping attracted the attention of many, perhaps the most celebrated of whom being the adopted American John Paul Jones. A Scot by birth, he commanded a merchantman in the West Indies trade from his early twenties but, having killed in self-defence, sought refuge in Virginia. When the colonies went to war with Britain to gain independence Jones was commissioned into the Continental Navy. In 1777 he was given the 18-gun sloop *Ranger* and ordered to operate against trade and to cause disruption in British waters. His openly hostile crew, who mistrusted him as a foreigner, were further antagonised when Jones took several ships in the Irish Sea but sank them, having too few hands to sail them to a port where they could have been declared prizes.

Entering the port of Whitehaven, which he knew, Jones had intended to fire the colliers there but failed owing to the sheer ineptitude of his crew. A party was then landed to kidnap the Earl of Selkirk but, he being absent, it took his family silver instead (it was later returned). Off Carrickfergus Jones duelled with and took the 20-gun British sloop *Drake*, successfully bringing her to Brest.

France was assisting the American cause and gave Jones a decrepit East Indiaman for his next command. Named *Bonhomme Richard*, she was given a scratch armament of 40 guns and an equally scratch crew. In company with the American *Alliance* 36, the French *Pallas* 32 and two smaller French sail, the now Commodore Jones, sailed in August 1779 to circumnavigate the British Isles. His squadron failed in an attempt to take the port of Leith but had already disposed of 17 British merchantmen when it encountered a 44-strong convoy near Flamborough Head. Jones' hopes of

Below: This 1781 engraving of John Paul Jones shows him as naval hero. Although a bonny fighter, he was an indifferent leader, mistrusted by his own crews and French allies alike.

adding to his prizes were dashed when the convoy's two escorts interposed themselves, allowing their charges to reach safety. The cost of this attention to duty was the British 20-gun sloop *Countess of Scarborough* being captured by the *Pallas*.

Her compatriot, the 44-gun *Serapis* should, in the light airs prevailing, have laid off to take advantage of her superior firepower. Foolishly, she grappled the American, whose large crew then had the advantage. Blasted with point-blank gunfire during the bloody, two-hour hand-to-hand struggle, the aged *Bonhomme Richard* was obviously foundering. Summoned by the British captain to capitulate, Jones made his now-celebrated retort: 'I have not yet begun to fight'.

Persistence paid off for, unnerved by a powder fire aboard his ship, it was the British skipper who struck his flag. It was a disappointing outcome for the British although the escort had achieved its primary purpose in safeguarding the convoy. His own ship sinking, Jones took over the *Serapis*, sailing the squadron into the Texel for repair, thence to France.

Jones could not settle with peace and briefly joined the Russian navy. Ever difficult, he fell out with his new patrons and returned to France where he died in relative poverty in 1792 at the age of just 45 years. In 1905 he was honoured by his adopted nation when his remains were re-interred at the American Naval Academy at Annapolis.

Below: In a bloody moonlight duel off Flamborough Head, Jones captured the British frigate *Serapis* but had his own Bonhomme *Richard* sunk under him. Over 400 men in all were killed or injured, but *Serapis*' convoy escaped unharmed.

IMPROVEMENTS TO THE NINETEENTH CENTURY WOODEN FIGHTING SHIP

BY THE END OF THE NAPOLEONIC War, the Royal Navy had expanded to a record total of over 800,000 tons displacement, this at a time when its largest battle unit, the 120-gun three-decker, was of only 2,600 tons or so. Although one major ship in ten was a prize, there was an acute shortage of good timber. Repairs to battle damage, general maintenance and the generally profligate attitude of the Royal Dockyards meant that timber needed increasingly to be imported from sources as widespread as Canada, Burma, Germany and the Cape.

The average lifespan of a sailing warship was only some 25 years. 'Working' in a seaway, the elements of a wooden hull move relative to each other. This effect was especially pronounced towards the ends of the full amidships sections, where the bow and stern tended to sag, having insufficient buoyancy to support their weight. As

Right: Launched as the *Royal Frederick*, the *Queen* was so renamed in 1839 as a complement to the new monarch. A three-decked First Rate mounting 116 guns she was cut down and converted to steam propulsion 20 years later.

this was appreciated by the master shipwrights, they tended to fill out the lines somewhat, adding upthrust but to the detriment of sailing qualities.

The lack of diagonal framing in such construction presents something of a mystery. An examination of any timber-framed medieval building will show that its constructors well understood the need of working diagonals into each rectangular bay in order to confer rigidity. Somehow, this principle was not translated to shipbuilding where hulls comprised largely a series of transverse frames and beams whose stability with respect to each other depended greatly on longitudinal planking and wales. From about 1772 the French, the Spanish and the Russians attempted to introduce major diagonal members but failed, not least because of the typical hull's complex curvature.

Strengthening and copper bottoms

Credit for resolving earlier attempts into a satisfactory system went to Robert Seppings who, from 1806, gradually introduced a new arrangement, based on trussed frames in the sections below the turn of the bilge, diagonal riders in the deck above and diagonal bracing between gunports. Jointly, these measures increased a hull's longitudinal stiffness, enabling it to be made longer and to tolerate the increasing weight of armaments. The demand for particularly difficult timber sections was reduced through simplification of construction, for instance the excessive tumblehome that caused much complex curvature. Knee sections, used by the score to connect transverse beams to frames, had become scarce in their natural grown state and proved to be perfectly satisfactory when made of iron. This material quickly became usual for many standard components and, as early as 1827, the first iron mast went to sea in a Fifth Rate.

Broadside ships were always vulnerable to raking fire. The huge expanse of glazed stern galleries, and the flimsy bulkhead that backed the beakhead, provided no protection from axial fire, which could clear a gun deck. Again it is curious that the extremities of the gundecks were not closed-off with substantial transverse bulkheads to mitigate these effects, and it was only after the wars that the round bow and round (later elliptical) stern were introduced. In the latter case it reduced the massive overhung load imposed by the stern galleries, while allowing arming at all levels. Although the improve-

ments detracted from the sailing warship's classic beauty, they permitted guns to be sited to fire axially and on the quarters. In this they were something of a counter to armed steam ships, whose freedom of manoeuvre better enabled them to adopt a raking position in a fight.

There had grown a widely-held belief in the Service that foreign warships, particularly French, were superior sailers. As with most broad assumptions, it contained only an element of truth but brought about 'experimental sailing', somewhat unscientific contests to compare varying hull forms and sail plans in ships of similar rating. Unsurprisingly, it was found that the majority of designs exhibited both good and bad points.

During the 1760s, ships employed in tropical waters began to have their bottoms coppered to deter the marine growth that rapidly affected their performance. The measure was successful but was found to result in the rapid deterioration of adjacent iron fastenings. Urgent experiment by no less than Sir Humphrey Davy of the Royal Society correctly identified galvanic action as the cause. Its partial cure was effected by a more careful selection of neighbouring metals and the installation of passive sacrificial anodes.

At much the same time it was discovered that proper attention to the ventilation of a ship not only improved the health and well-being of the crew but also reduced the incidence of rot in timbers and assisted in the preservation of stores. Subsequent designs thus aimed to encourage natural air flow although most old seamen preferred a foul smell, for stagnant bilges denoted a tight ship!

Above: Notable in this cross-section of the 92-gun *Rodney* of 1833 is the pronounced tumble-home and double curvature of the hull, the diagonal framing and the immense size of the coiled anchor cables.

Below: The elliptical stern of the 90-gun *Albion* of 1842. It will be apparent that the considerable weight of the stern galleries is not weakly overhung but solidly supported by curved timbers faired into the after run.

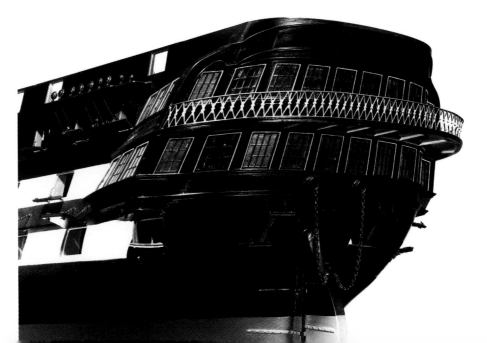

STEAM ENGINES AND WOODEN WARSHIPS

THE BRITISH ADMIRALTY HAS OFTEN BEEN accused of reluctance to adopt the new technologies of the nineteenth century. In truth, none who had responsibility for the immense instrument of power that was the Royal Navy could allow innovations to go unremarked, or yet pioneer advances that would themselves render the Fleet obsolescent. Steam propulsion presented such a problem. To ignore it would encourage others, particularly the French, to commence a programme that would leave the huge sailing Royal Navy outdated. To recognise it, and to instigate a British programme, would have much the same effect but, at least, give the Royal Navy a lead.

The 1840s thus proved to be a decade of intense activity, both in the construction of new steamships and in the conversion of existing vessels, too numerous to be discarded. Even before the various trials between paddle and propeller-driven ships, the Admiralty appeared to show a clear preference for the propeller. That there was little time to lose was evidenced by the knowledge that both the Americans and the French were constructing experimental screw-propelled ships, the *Princeton* sloop and the *Pomone* frigate respectively.

For fighting ships, the Admiralty favoured propulsion machinery sited below the waterline. In paddlers, this was not possible, with machinery and vulnerable paddle boxes also inhibiting the length and layout of gundecks. Such ships tended to be fitted with smaller numbers of individually larger pivot guns, which could be trained on racers to fire through one of several ports. With their obvious weaknesses and slow rates of fire, they compared badly with screw-propelled two or three-deckers which combined the advantages of auxiliary propulsion with a full broadside.

This period also saw one of the frequent states of high tension between Britain and France. The former saw merit in the conversion of a number of older sailing warships, 74s and 44-gun frigates, into mobile batteries for use in European waters. These, commonly called 'blockships', were usually poor under sail because the installed machinery dictated the siting of their masts.

A major conflict lay between the full after lines, or 'run', required by a sailing ship and the finer run necessary to give a propeller a reasonable performance. With the science of ship modelling still in the future, incomplete ships gained machinery while on the stocks while others were cut in two to have a new section inserted. Others again were cut a second time to enable the after run to be lengthened and fined. In a few cases the really difficult course of increasing the beam was adopted. As major longitudinals were, in any case, fashioned from shorter lengths of timber such surgery did not appreciably weaken the structure.

Horizontal engines fitted surprisingly well into existing hold spaces but the flanking coal bunkers must have been difficult to fill. Even a converted 74 was fortunate to be powered by more than 500 ihp and the best speed could be anything between six and nine knots. The Admiralty quickly began to bemoan the cost of coal and to restrict the time spent under steam. Oddly, despite mutual friction, British firms built much of the machinery for French ships, due to that nation's yet underdeveloped manufacturing base.

New machinery and old ships

Even a two-bladed propeller exerted considerable drag on a ship which still progressed mainly under sail. Screws could be declutched to revolve freely or aligned with blades vertical in the wake of the sternpost, but lifting screws were commonly fitted. These were installed in a rectangular frame which

Below: This section, of the French wooden First Rate *Louis XIV* as converted for steam screw propulsion, represents the intermediate step between those shown on pages 51 and 61. Note how the two-cylinder, single expansion machinery gains protection from the coal bunkers.

could be hoisted by tackles into an overhead trunk once the propeller itself was disengaged.

Improvements in the stiffness of wooden hulls introduced by Seppings' diagonal framing had been further refined by John Edye yet, now burdened with up to 120 guns, they were still too flexible. Alignments of long propeller shafts were impossible to maintain, resulting in enormous wear in stern bearings. This, in turn, lowered efficiency through extra friction, increased vibration and accelerated rot due to leakage.

Only the British and French were major players in this phase of the warship's development, modifying 49 and 29 respectively. In new construction, the British outstripped the French by 18 to nine.

With the *Napoleon*, completed in 1852, the French produced the first purpose-built steam battleship, beating the British *Agamemnon* by some three months. For a little more than a decade the two major seapowers would measure their strength in terms of old-fashioned wooden broadside ships fitted with modern machinery. Their shortly forth-coming alliance in war against Russia (1854–6) would, however, change all that with the re-intro-duction of the previously discredited metal hull, together with armour plate and the gun turret, and a reversal of the importance of sail relative to power.

Top: Paddle-propelled warships had short life spans, having many dis-advantages compared with screw propellers, introduced at much the same time.

Above: As gun positions on broadside ships were spread along their lengths, charges were equally widely distributed. The potential for mishap was considerable.

PADDLE *versus* PROPELLER

Above: The advantages
of screw propeller
propulsion were obvi-
ous well before the
showpiece tug-of-war
between the *Rattler*
and the *Alecto*
in 1845. Paddle
propulsion was
manifestly unsuitable
for warships and had
a life of less than
a decade.

THAT EARLY STEAMSHIPS WERE propelled by
paddles rather than by screw propellers was more
from engineering expediency than lack of mechani-
cal awareness, for the principle of the helical screw
had been described by Archimedes and illustrated
by da Vinci. As we will see later in the feature on
early submarines, Bushnell used it for his *Turtle* craft
in 1776, 25 years before the *Charlotte Dundas*
demonstrated the practicality of the sternwheel.

From the engineering point of view, the fact that
all shafts and bearings for a paddle wheel were
above water level was an asset. Its rather inconve-
nient layout was of little consequence to small craft
serving as passenger ferries or tugs in ports and
estuaries, although low-speed manoeuvring characteristics were poor.

Once the principle was applied to deep-sea
vessels, however, other problems became apparent. The earliest paddles, with fixed floats, were
inefficient, dissipating energy in throwing water
about, but the introduction in 1829 of a feathering
mechanism enabled it to develop useful thrust

throughout the submerged part of its cycle. Some
of the submerged section of a paddle wheel must,
however, always be travelling more slowly than the
speed of advance of the ship and, therefore, detract
from the developed thrust.

It was also soon apparent that there existed a
critical depth of immersion for a paddle wheel to
develop optimum efficiency. It was an unfortunate
fact of life, however, that the draught of a merchant ship varied constantly with the consumption
of its bunkers, and also between its laden and ballast condition. Heavy rolling or a press of wind if
the ship were also under sail would immerse the
leeside paddle wheel too deeply while bringing
that on the weather side almost clear of the water.
The resulting asymmetric thrust then greatly
affected steering.

The bluff hull forms of the time, still based on sailing ship practice, also generated wave patterns that
adversely affected the flow into the paddles, but the
consequent need for finer forward entries reduced
cargo-carrying capacity, a trend not enhanced by the

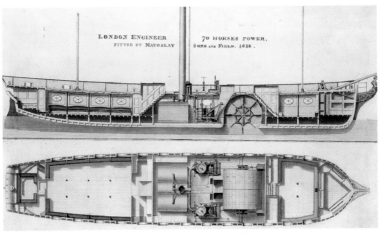

Left: These sections of the 1818 paddler *London Engineer* show the tall funnel for natural draught, the low-pressure box boiler, the centreline paddle assembly and a plan profile still that of a sailing ship.

Development of screw propulsion

Following Cummerow's lead, Francis Pettit Smith patented an Archimedean screw arrangement, which the Screw Propeller Company was formed to exploit. Scale experiments, carried out on a launch, were sufficiently encouraging for the company to built a 125 ft (38.1 m) merchantman, appropriately named *Archimedes*. Completed in 1838, she quickly proved her ability to go deep-sea and, in organised trials, was able to hold her own with some of the best paddlers of the day. In so doing, she caught the attention of the British Admiralty and the celebrated engineer Isambard Brunel.

Advised by both the company and by Brunel, the Admiralty modified one of a class of paddle sloops for screw propulsion for the purposes of direct comparison. Her after-run was fined and lengthened, both to improve flow into the propeller and to allow space for its aperture. Machinery was still very much auxiliary to sail, so the hull remained a compromise shape and the screw (soon refined to a two-bladed design) was either aligned vertically for sailing or lifted completely from the water. For the latter case, it was accommodated in a sliding frame which could be hoisted vertically into the ship's overhung counter. Another, and later, means of reducing drag was through a variable pitch mechanism to feather the blades into the flow, first patented in 1850.

Completed in 1843, the propeller-driven sloop *Rattler* was exhaustively trialled against her sister paddler *Alecto*, the tests including a celebrated tug-of-war in 1845. Her superiority was not so much in higher speed as in improved layout, important for British naval development in influencing the conversion of the sailing battle fleet to screw propulsion.

Below: Launched in November 1838, the *Archimedes* was the world's first seagoing screw propelled ship. She was built on behalf of the Ship Propeller Company to evaluate and promote Pettit Smith's designs.

requirement of the paddles and their machinery to be located in the prime amidships section.

For warships still reliant on broadside batteries, paddle machinery reduced the number of gun positions considerably. Understandably, paddle boxes were thought to be vulnerable to action damage (in practice, less than expected, although they were little tested), while a propeller and its shaft line would be safely below the waterline. The first successful commercial exploitation of a steam-driven paddle craft is credited in the United State to Fulton's *Clermont* of 1807 and, in Great Britain, to Bell's *Comet* of 1812. Inception of the screw propeller principle was the business of the British Ship Propeller Company, incorporated in the late 1830s. Early inventors had proposed various means of supporting a revolving propeller shaft that projected through a ship's counter but, in 1829, Cummerow first proposed locating the propeller in an aperture cut in the deadwood, forward of the rudder post. Here, it would be protected and, by directing its thrust directly into the rudder, improve steering characteristics.

THE AMERICAN CIVIL WAR (1861–65)

ALTHOUGH THE ISSUE was inevitably settled by armies, the Civil War saw much activity afloat. Being more developed and industrialised, and with the greater part of the population, the northern states of the Union held the advantage. Its considerable merchant fleet was immediately preyed upon by privateers, bearing letters of marque issued by the southern Confederacy's president, Jefferson Davis. President Lincoln countered by declaring a blockade of the 3,500-mile (5,600 km) southern coastline, which stretched from the Potomac River to the Mexican border. To be recognised in International Law, a blockade must be effective, so the Union commenced an emergency building programme of the so-called '90-day gunboats' and the purchase of any vessel capable of bearing arms.

Before the blockade began to bite, blockade runners, many of them British, made huge profits from the supply of luxury goods, no longer available in the South, the sale of whose staple produce, cotton, had been badly misjudged. Because many states had outlawed privateering through the 1856 Declaration of Paris, Confederate raiders found it increasingly difficult to take prizes into port, so most Northern ships were destroyed when captured.

Two of the most successful raiders were purpose-built in Great Britain. The *Alabama*, under Raphael Semmes, took 69 prizes before being brought to book in a celebrated duel with the USS *Kearsarge* outside Cherbourg.

Increasing Union naval strength was used to seize, either by bombardment or by amphibious attack, key points for tightening the blockade. Thus the taking of Port Royal put a clamp on the ports of Charleston and Savannah, and that of Ship Island, the ports of New Orleans and Mobile.

From the outset, the Union sought also to move southward down the huge Mississippi river system, the control of which would split the Confederate states. A flotilla of 'sidewheelers' (as paddler steamers were known) was quickly built. Of shallow draught, they were well protected by iron plates and stout timber. Weakly opposed by the few Southern ships this flotilla, under the flag of Andrew H. Foote, and often accompanied by transports loaded with troops, bombarded and reduced fortifications and raided towns for military stores. In April 1862, two of its gunboats intervened decisively in the bloody battle of Shiloh, preventing Federal troops being overrun by the 'rebels'.

To complement this slow southward advance New Orleans, at the river's mouth, came under attack from the Union base on Ship Island. David Farragut's ungainly fleet of gunboats and sea-

Right: The Battle of Mobile Bay of 1864 is interesting in showing an action of the era of transitional warships. Visable are both broadside- and turret-armed ironclads, paddle-and screw-propelled steamers and ramming tactics.

going vessels had been augmented by mortar schooners, capable of high trajectory bombardment and first cousins to the bomb ketches that had served the Royal Navy well in the past. Farragut forced the defences below the town in a chaotic night action, defeated the intervention of an inferior Confederate flotilla and entered New Orleans, where everything that could be of military or commercial value had been put to the torch by its retreating garrison.

'Damn the torpedoes!'

Foote's flotilla continued its slow advance southward, now joined by eight wood-built rams, which were prominent in the defeat of the Confederate stand off Memphis, in June 1862. Moving northward to effect a junction, Farragut was held up at Vicksburg, where the river was commanded by heavy artillery sited on high ground. As a military operation was necessary, and his deep-draught ships were experiencing problems with dropping water levels, Farragut pulled back to New Orleans.

To take Vicksburg, General Sherman brought an army down-river from Memphis but, following an initial bloody repulse, had to invest the town, which finally capitulated only in July 1863. Once Farragut re-cleared the lower reaches the whole river, up to its confluence with the Missouri, was in Union hands, separating the Confederacy from its primary sources of foodstuffs.

Sherman, advancing on Atlanta, requested Farragut to stage a diversion by attacking Mobile. This port lay on a shallow bay, whose entrance was commanded by forts on outlaying islands. A brisk battle developed, the attack faltering as one of its ships ran onto an improvised mine and sank. Climbing into the rigging of his flagship, the *Hartford*, Farragut gained immortality by shouting 'Damn the torpedoes! Full speed ahead!'

The only major port remaining to the Confederacy was Wilmington, SC, through which passed supplies essential to the Capital, Richmond. The port was approached via the Cape Fear River, commanded by Fort Fisher. Following an initial repulse, Rear Admiral David Porter assembled a fleet of 62 ships which staged a protracted bombardment to cover the landing of 10,000 troops. With Fort Fisher's fall in January 1865 the final naval action of the war had been fought.

Above: William Overend's depiction of the same battle shows Farragut standing in the rigging of the *Hartford*, as she attacks the Confederate ironclad *Tennessee*. Farragut went on to become the US Navy's first Vice-Admiral and Admiral as these ranks were created.

PAX BRITANNICA

gions, some hopelessly incompatible. The inevitable result was the spawning of problems that ranged from straightforward insults to the Crown to full-blown insurrections. In times of such troubles the Royal Navy was the first line of reinforcement, and to 'send a gunboat' was rather more than a humorous cliché.

A high proportion of the fleet comprised small 'cruising ships', dedicated to preserving peace throughout the empire and, colaterally, much of the world beyond. Commissions were long, stations remote; communications were poor, captains and crews self-reliant. Even after the introduction of steam propulsion, machinery was inefficient and unreliable, while coal supplies were scarce and expensive. Long after the first- and second-line fleets at home had abandoned full rig, therefore, sail remained the primary motive power on distant stations.

Bluejackets were fully trained in military skills, and were regularly landed alongside the Marine detachment. A battleship of the era was expected to be able to field a self-supporting 'naval brigade' of 400 men, including four or five companies of infantry, artillerymen with two 3-inch (76 mm) guns and a machine gun, all on carriages, men carrying reserve ammunition (each 3-inch round weighed 12 lb/5.4 kg!), armourers, a medical team, signalmen and buglers, equipped to the last water canteen and puggaree. By virtue of their sailing rig, even corvettes carried crews sufficiently large to put ashore a balanced force of 215 men.

Quelling mutiny and insurrection

Large scale interventions by naval brigades ran from the Burmese Wars to the Boxer Rebellion, from the Sudan campaign to the Western Front of World War I. Most involvement, however, was on a fairly small scale. As an example of the flexibility and the long arm of seapower, at much the same time, brigades from the *Shannon* 51 and *Pearl* 21 were distinguishing themselves in the Indian Mutiny while British ships joined with others of the leading powers for the war in China. The four-gun screw gunboat *Lynx* was operating against the slave trade off Africa's east coast but finding time to land men in conjunction with others from the East India Company's ship *Assaye* to subdue the rebellious subjects of the Sultan of Zanzibar. The five-gun *Torch* captured seven slave-runners off the west coast of

Above: For a time the beauty of sail survived the onsalught of steam. This warship – her graceful clipper bow suggests that she is the *Warrior* of 1861 – is running under almost full sail, including studding sails.

'WIDER STILL, AND WIDER, shall thy bounds be set' ran the words of the patriotic song and, throughout the reign of Victoria, this was indeed the case. Additions to the British Empire were both significant and frequent, for instance Burma between 1824 and 1885, Fiji 1835, Hong Kong 1841, Egypt 1882, Malaya 1896, Nigeria 1900 ... Colonies and protectorates were scattered worldwide, bound by a web of British shipping that ceaselessly fetched and carried. Manufactured goods out, raw materials home. Foodstuffs – grain, meat and fruit – which the empire had the space and climate to produce more cheaply than in the home islands. Coal, which the United Kingdom regarded as a stock export, was being mined more cheaply elsewhere. Armies of administrators to apply British rule; they and their dependents, their servants and goods, endlessly rotated and relieved on the liners of companies that won fame and fortune on the business. The empire itself encompassed a wide range of peoples and reli-

Left: Slavers, bent on escape, might heave their human cargoes overboard, either to destroy evidence or to provide a diversion. Turner's painting captures such an incident with characteristic drama.

Below: Victoria's bluejackets were customarily trained in military skills and a small police operation ashore provided a welcome diversion from the routine of shipboard life.

Africa while the six-gun *Styx* caught more off Cuba. A detachment from the *Clio* 22 helped prevent the city of Panama being seized by a mob while protecting French nationals from 'infuriated Negro rioters'. In British Columbia the *Satellite* 21 marched a party up-country to 'overawe certain miners who were causing anxiety to the Government'. The *Pearl*, before her hasty diversion to India, was despatched to Peru to apprehend ships responsible for the boarding and plundering of a British merchantman during an insurrection.

The slave trade was well established, highly profitable and difficult to eradicate. Many slavers were Arab-crewed dhows, well-armed and prepared to fight. In 1887, as subjects at home celebrated Queen Victoria's Golden Jubilee, her 12-gun corvette *Turquoise* lay off Pemba. She sent away a pinnace to investigate the neighbouring coast. Crewed by a lieutenant, six hands and an interpreter, it made to board a suspicious craft but in the process was, itself attacked. In desperate hand-to-hand combat, outnumbered two-to-one, the boarders succeeded in despatching nine of their assailants for the loss of one dead and several badly cut about.

The dhow was run aground and abandoned by her crew, and 53 slaves were liberated from below. Severely injured, the lieutenant was sent home for treatment, and promotion. His name was Frederick

Fogarty Fegan, and who eventually retired a vice-admiral. Fifty-three years later in 1940, his son, Captain Edward Fogarty Fegan, was to earn a posthumous Victoria Cross in commanding the armed liner *Jervis Bay* in her hopeless, lone fight to protect a convoy from destruction by a German 'pocket battleship'.

IRON SHIPS AND THE INTRODUCTION OF ARMOUR

WITH IMPROVEMENT in iron-working techniques, it was a natural progression from ships constructed of wood, but with an increasing number of iron components, to iron hulls proper. These promised to end the problems of rot, and to give (what many found difficult to comprehend) a ship which, for comparable dimensions, would actually be lighter and, therefore, a more efficient cargo carrier. With engineering now developing as a science, rather than an application of rule-of-thumb techniques, it was also apparent that iron hulls could be built longer, wood construction having reached its limit.

Wrought iron plates were still of variable quality, but were used for canal barges as early as the 1780s. Credit for being the first iron-built, sea-going vessel is claimed by the *Aaron Manby*, constructed for a direct London–Paris service starting in 1822. Although later much modified, her hull lasted over 50 years.

Iron-built commercial shipping soon proliferated, a social consequence being the shift of the construction industry from the south of England to new yards in the iron and coal-producing centres of the North.

The Admiralty had long been experiencing problems with magnetic compasses as the iron content of hulls increased, and now hired-in iron-hulled ships for evaluation before committing itself. Credit for operating the first iron warship, therefore, went not to the Royal Navy but to the Honorable East Company, whose 1840-built iron paddle sloop *Nemesis* was considered a great success. Her design was important in its including, for the first time, truly watertight transverse bulkheads.

Within a year, and following favourable testing and reports, the Royal Navy put in hand several small inshore gunboats, the world's first regular warships built of iron. By 1845 confidence had advanced to the point where the first iron frigates, of about 2,900 tons displacement, were under construction.

Abroard, the Americans experimented with iron craft but still lacked sufficient industrial base. Better-equipped, the French sent their renowned constructor Dupuy de Lôme to study British processes. However, although Brunel was about to

Below: A further impression of the *Warrior*, funnels raised and under steam. Her innovative design included iron plating on iron frames, watertight bulkheads and a double bottom.

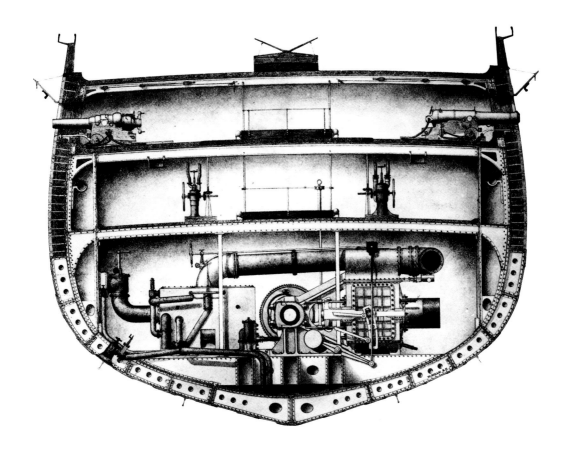

introduce his bold and innovatory iron screw steamer *Great Britain* as the world's first modern merchantman, the Admiralty's acceptance of iron warships was about to experience a setback.

The acceptance of iron ships

Since 1845, extensive firing trials had been conducted against targets representing ship sections. High and low velocity shot penetrated iron plates easily; all produced showers of splinters and, in the latter case, a jagged exit hole that was difficult to plug. Only backing by a substantial thickness of timber could prevent this. The only 'live' ship target available, against which results could be verified, was the *Ruby*, a fleet tender, poorly constructed of thin plating, already wasted by rusting. Not surprisingly, close range firing trials, conducted in 1846 by the gunnery training ship *Excellent*, reduced her to a shambles. Further influenced by political argument, the Admiralty took fright at these quite misleading results, cancelling the building programme and converting the existing iron frigates to troopships.

The case for iron warships was, nonetheless, hard to resist and, in them, the French sought a way to reduce the Royal Navy's predominence. Wooden ships, converted to steam-powered screw propulsion, had problems in accommodating machinery and bunkers, whose weight further stressed hulls already built to near maximum size. Improved artillery, firing explosive shells, threatened wooden ships with fire as much as penetration. Suitable timber was also becoming scarce.

In 1855, during action in the Crimea, the French proved the value of appliqué armour on floating batteries constructed of timber. Extending the concept to a full-sized ship they took the standard, screw-propelled *Gloire*, cut her down to a single deck and clad her overall in 4¾-inch (120 mm) wrought iron plate. She was completed in 1860, but the British response was already taking shape.

Further experiment had convinced them of the merits of iron plating, suitably backed, on an all-iron frame. Commenced in 1859, the *Warrior* was half as long again as the *Gloire*, and adopted a central battery arrangement, concentraing heavy protection amidships. Here, a 4½-inch (114 mm) belt, closed off by two heavy transverse bulkheads, formed an armoured box that enclosed 26 of her designed 40 68-pounders. It is an interesting point that, where her 'box' armour was backed by 18-inches (457 mm) of teak, the thin plating at her extremities was unbacked, an arrangement that would have been unacceptable only a few years earlier.

Above: This cross-section of the *Warrior* contrasts nicely with that of the Rodney on page 51. Note how the iron construction generally copies that of wood. There is only one gundeck, with 68- and 110-pounders on more advanced carriages. The Penn single-expansion trunk engine, of 5000 ihp is sited fully below the waterline.

DEVELOPMENT OF THE NAVAL GUN

DURING THE WAR IN the Crimea the French developed the concept of wood-built shallow-draught floating batteries, whose sloping sides were covered in iron plate. Their function was to approach the Russian fortifications and, in exchange for a battering from solid shot, reduce them with 56-pounder shell guns.

It was 1855, and the explosive shell was still no more than a hollow, cast-iron ball filled with powder. Its invariably off-set centre of gravity resulted in strange trajectories, which limited its use to close ranges. The invention of the French General Paixhans had first been used at Vera Cruz in Mexico, some 17 years earlier. Subsequently, at the battles of Eckernförde and Sinope, in 1849 and 1853 respectively, wooden warships were subjected to explosive shellfire for the first time. While they proved to be surprisingly resistent, the potential of the weapon was obvious.

Standard naval guns were still massive cast cannon, very heavy in comparison with their weight of shot, an 18-pounder, for instance, weighing almost three tons and a 68-pounder nearly five. Their range was short. Resulting from Crimea experience, the British engineer Armstrong developed a new method of construction, built up from wrought-iron tubes, shrunk over each other and reinforced as required. The innermost tube, comprising the bore, was rifled with spiral grooves, borrowing a principle already proven effective in small arms. The projectile was elongated and coated in a softer metal which, on travelling along the bore was intended to bite into the grooves to impact a stabilizing spin. This, together with its improved aerodynamics, resulted in greater accuracy and range.

Armstrong also re-introduced the centuries-old concept of breech-loading, although it would be some time before a reliable, gas-tight breech mechanism was developed. A great advantage of the design was that, in the event of a misfire, it was not easily possible to ram home another shot and charge, the firing of which would probably burst the gun.

Breech loading also enabled gun barrels to be made longer, increasing muzzle velocity by giving the projectile time to accelerate along the bore, propelled by the expansion of the gases produced by firing the charge. Early black powder caused huge stresses in the gun by virtually exploding on ignition. It had been supplanted by more scientifically-based formulations which burned rapidly, but in a finite time. The increased muzzle velocities that resulted improved both range and accuracy, besides being critical to the penetration of armour plate, which made its general appearance in the 1860s.

Longer barrels and revolving turrets

Guns were now growing rapidly in terms of both size and weight. For centuries they had been mounted on simple carriages, still light enough to allow training with handspikes and recoil restraint with tackles. The popular 7-inch (178 mm) weapon, which threw a 110-pound (50 kg) projectile, weighed over ten tons all up. A central battery ship, with a dozen or more of these monsters, each served by 15 men and all confined in a single armoured box, was possible only through the guns being accommodated on sliding carriages. These were arranged so that the gun's recoil moved it up an incline, bringing it to rest by gravity before sliding back into the reload position. The carriage itself could be manhandled on pivots and racers to serve more than one gun port. It will be appreciated that the tendency to longer barrels conflicted with the speed of muzzle loading, while increasing the distance inboard that the gun required to be withdrawn for loading, both of which problems were solved by breech-loading.

Following the lead of Cowper Coles and Ericsson, it was obvious that the way forward was to

Below: Guns firing explosive shell were usually referred to in terms of barrel diameter (or 'calibre'). Here, an Armstrong 7-inch weapon is seen aboard HMS *Black Prince*, the *Warrior*'s sister ship.

mount one or two large guns on a common turntable. Sited correctly, these could command considerable arcs of fire, thus necessitating fewer weapons than in the central battery layout. It was also a matter of expediency, for improvements in armour protection were leading to guns of a size that could no longer be manhandled, and of which only limited numbers could be carried.

As we have already seen, revolving turrets were introduced in the early 1860s but, when the concept was translated to very large guns (up to 17.72-inch/450 mm bore by 1880) the combination of adequate protection and height of command gave stability problems to the ship itself. An interim solution was to mount the guns on a turntable, sited so as to be fired over the edge of a vertical armoured tube known as a 'barbette'. As many were still short-barrelled muzzle-loaders, they could be loaded by depressing the muzzle to deck level, aligned with apertures in an armoured 'glacis' below which was the loading mechanism.

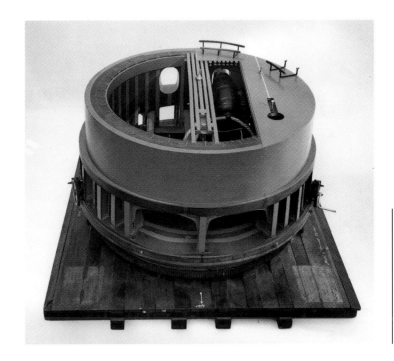

Left: A model of Cowper Coles' turret with only a single gun mounted. Only the solid part of the structure projected above decklevel, the roller path being protected below.

Below: On the ironclad ram HMS *Hotspur* (1870) the turret structure was fixed. Within, a revolving turntable allowed the single 12-inch muzzle loader to be fired through any one of four embrasures. The track (or 'racer') on the deck permitted the gun to be trained through about 45 degrees at any of the firing positions.

EARLY TURRET SHIPS

IN ORDER TO APPROACH HIS TARGET more closely Captain Cowper Coles of the Royal Navy had a 32-pounder cannon mounted on a raft and towed across shallow waters. During his bombardment, he was impressed by the ease with which the gun could be trained, simply by revolving the raft.

It was 1855 and the Crimean War was in progress. Coles then enthusiastically designed a steam-powered raft with heavier cannon protected by fixed, bee-hive shaped cupolas. As the raft would be trained on the target, rather than the individual guns, the gunports could be made smaller and safer. The craft was meant for direct attack on fortifications, but the war ended in 1856 and the Admiralty then had no interest in the project.

These were the days when warships still relied on broadside gunfire, and Coles realised that a few heavy guns, mounted in revolving, protected turrets, would be far more effective than a gun-deck lined with virtually fixed cannon. He patented a design for a turret in 1859 and, following persistent lobbying, persuaded the Admiralty to build and test a turret on a floating battery. The results, in 1861, were completely successful. This same year saw the outbreak of the American Civil War, in which great use was made of waterways and estuaries. The combination of turret-mounted guns and shallow draught was invaluable, spawning generations of flatiron craft called 'monitors'. The term derived from an eponymous craft designed and built in a great hurry by the inventor John Ericsson to counter the depredations of the steam-powered Confederate armoured battery *Virginia*, which had destroyed two wooden frigates with impunity.

The *Monitor* displaced some 1,200 tons, her shallow and flat-bottomed iron hull overlaid and overlapped by an armoured raft with only about 2 ft (610 mm) freeboard. Beside a small armoured pilot house and funnel, the only real feature was the 20 ft (6.1 m) diameter turret. This housed two 11-inch (280 mm) muzzle loaders, run back into the turret for loading.

Monitor's opponent, the 3,500-ton *Virginia*, is often still referred to as the *Merrimack*, as she was built from a frigate of that name, razed to the waterline and fitted with a long, armoured deckhouse. This house had sides that sloped at 45 degrees, and it was pierced conventionally with gunports for 10 cannon of various sizes.

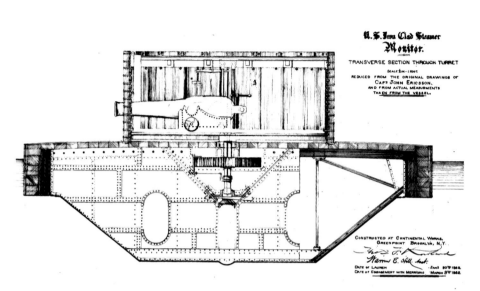

Above: A contemporary illustration contrasting the *Thunderer* with the conventional sailing fleet.

Above left: Little more than a steam-propelled armoured raft, the USS *Monitor* of 1862 carried her two 11-inch Dahlgren guns in an Ericsson-designed turret. Normally resting on the deck, the whole assembly had to be lifted to revolve on a central column.

Below: This view of the *Devastation*, laying at Malta, shows well the low freeboard and central superstructure (or 'breastwork') at either end of which is a circular turret housing a pair of 35-ton muzzle loaders.

The fabled duel of 9 March 1862, was a drawn action in that the armour of each proved more than equal to the hits received. Inasmuch as the *Monitor* had only one fifth the number of guns and displaced only one third as much as the *Virginia*, however, the turret principle was vindicated.

Low freeboard – the dangers

While the US Navy went on to build considerable numbers of single- and twin-turreted monitors, their characteristically low freeboard made them very uncomfortable and not a little dangerous in anything but coastal waters.

More conventionally-proportioned turret ships were constructed for several navies, the best-known British example of the time being the 8,300-ton *Monarch* of 1868. As the firing arcs of her two amidships-mounted turrets would be greatly curtailed by permanent standing rigging, much of this was attached to a light flying deck. This compromise posed a laborious task to get into action and attracted high-profile criticism from the indefatigable Cowper Coles, who was campaigning to get a turret ship built to his own ideas. He succeeded, the result being the 7,770-ton *Captain*, completed early in 1870. Her two central turrets were mounted on a low-freeboard armoured hull, built up with a light forecastle, poop and central house, with a flying deck over. Much heavy standing rigging was obviated by adopting tripod lower masts.

Just nine months after completion, the *Captain* capsized in not-unreasonable conditions in the Bay of Biscay. Among the many lost was Coles himself. It had not been understood at the time that the heeling moment of the heavy rig would quickly submerge the deck edge of the low-freeboard hull, following which the restoring moment would diminish rapidly.

Low-freeboards persisted, however, in the unrigged coastal defence craft known as 'breastwork monitors'. Conventional monitors always risked flooding through the likes of hatchways and ventilation trunks. Through the addition of an elongated armoured deckhouse, or breastwork (which, importantly, did not extend quite to the deck edge) turrets and apertures could be raised with advantage.

The Pre-Dreadnought Age

SINCE THE LATE SIXTEENTH century, attempts to build a practical submersible craft have been many and, often, ingenious. Until comparatively recently, however, they failed through limitations in technical knowledge and materials.

The first known to have undertaken a mission was the *Turtle*, a wooden, egg-shaped craft constructed by David Bushnell in 1776, and designed to attack blockading British warships during the American War of Independence. The *Turtle* operated with its major axis vertical, her one-man crew admitting water to submerge, thence controlling depth with a hand-cranked propeller. By means of a second propeller for forward motion, the craft was intended to position itself against the underside of its target, following which the crew would use a sheathed auger to attach a screw and explosive charge.

On 6 September 1776, Ezra Lee made history by thus attacking Lord Howe's flagship, HMS *Eagle*, off New York. Unable to properly attach the screw, Lee was detected and pursued. He submerged and escaped, jettisoning the charge, which exploded harmlessly., soon afterward, British warships similarly invested French bases, Robert Fulton persuaded Napoleon to finance construction of his *Nautilus*.

Distinctly 'submarine shaped', she was completed in 1801 and was about 21 ft (6.4 m) in length and capable of diving to 25 ft (7.6 m). Contemporary accounts speak of her undertaking dives of one hour's duration, although her progress still depended upon the muscle power of her four-man crew. Despite her blowing up a stationary target ship with a detachable charge, her concept was progressed no further by the French. A disillusioned Fulton therefore crossed the Channel to enthuse the British instead, but when this, too, failed, he returned to his native United States to pursue other projects.

The American Civil War (1861–65) saw a variation in the development of the so-called 'Davids', small, cigar-shaped craft that could be ballasted down until only a vestigial topside casing protruded above the surface. Although steam-propelled, they had a lowering funnel to minimise their profile prior to an attack. Their weapon was the spar torpedo, a canister of gunpowder, fitted with an impact fuse and mounted at the tip of a long, forward-pointing spar, by which it was to be thrust against its target. In October 1863 the first Confederate 'David' attacked the Federal ironclad *New Ironsides* off Charleston, SC. Minimal damage was sustained by the target but the 'David' herself was swamped and sunk by the backwash of the explosion.

One Horace L. Hunley then built a series of true, shallow-diving submersibles powered by propellers cranked by up to eight men. The third of these craft successfully attacked the Federal ship *Housatonic* off Charleston in February 1864. Both vessels were destroyed.

EARLY SUBMERSIBLES

In common with many Victorian clerics, the Reverend George Garrett of Liverpool was enthused by matters technical. In 1878 he built a 45 ft (13.7 m) submersible, optimistically named *Resurgam*. Constructed of boiler plate, its cylindrical midbody terminated in simple, conical ends. Garrett ingeniously employed a principle used by the 'smokeless' locomotives of the first London underground railway. A boiler generated steam for surfaced propulsion, but also heated separate tanks of water which, for submerged use, yielded their latent heat to develop low-pressure steam.

Electric propulsion

Although the *Resurgam* was lost on trials, Garrett succeeded in interesting the Swedish armaments manufacturer Nordenfelt. The latter saw the craft as a potential platform for the deployment of the new Whitehead torpedo and, in 1885, completed the *Nordenfelt No. 1* to Garrett's principles. Some 64 ft (19.5 m) in length, she mounted a torpedo launch tube in the forward casing and a Nordenfelt machine gun aft. Several of these pioneer craft were sold but all suffered from lack of power and a system for submerged stabilisation and control.

In 1886 the Spaniard, Isaac Peral, first employed the idea of using an electric motor for submerged propulsion, its power being drawn from accumulators. This important advance went unheeded by Peral's government and it was left to the French, who sought an inexpensive torpedo carrier, to progress it. Following their prototype, *Gymnote* of 1888, they went on to the then-giant 159 ft (48.5 m) *Gustave Zédé* in 1893. All-electric, this craft's contribution was to adopt hydroplanes for depth-keeping, rather than the earlier, and ineffective, vertical propellers.

So promising was the *Zédé* that in 1896 the French Government staged an open competition for designers. It was won by one Maxime Laubeuf, whose Narval concept combined oil-fired steam propulsion for surface navigation with rechargeable electric propulsion for when submerged. It also introduced the double hull idea in which the enclosed annular space accommodated both water ballast and fuel. She was completed in 1900 and set the trend for future French development.

Great Britain was closely monitoring their progress but, when she eventually acted, it was to be with American assistance.

Above: This Nordenfelt submarine, sold to Germany, used steam power for surface propulsion and incorporated pressurised hot water reservoirs to derive energy for submerged navigation.

Below: Stranded at Charleston in 1865, the *David* was captured by Union forces. The picture gives a good idea of how little would protrude above the surface when trimmed down for attack.

TORPEDOES, TORPEDO BOATS AND DESTROYERS

EARLY DEVICES TO HOLE A SHIP below the waterline included towed explosive charges and the previously mentioned spar torpedo, but such suicidal weapons were quickly discarded when the Austrian, Luppis, invented a mechanically-propelled 'locomotive torpedo' in about 1865. A further couple of years of cooperation with the engineer, Whitehead, resulted in a prototype vehicle which could run several hundred yards at about six knots, powered by a compressed-air engine and carrying the equivalent of an 18 lb (8.2 kg) warhead. Within four years, Whitehead had added a depth-keeping mechanism, coupled to the necessary control surfaces.

To sink a ship her hull must, ultimately, be flooded with water. Armour, recently introduced, was an antidote to gunfire, making submerged attack even more attractive. Of the means to achieve this, the also newly-developed moored mine was a passive device, dependent upon the target coming to it. Understandably, therefore, Luppis' invention created a considerable impression and rights to manufacture were soon purchased by the British Admiralty.

From this point the Whitehead torpedo sold widely, shrugging off competition from rival designs employing wire or flywheel devices. Its next major improvement was by another Austrian, Obry, who added a gyroscope to give it directional stability. By the end of the century, it had become a reasonably reliable weapon, capable of carrying a 220 lb (100 kg) charge for a half-mile at 28 knots.

Having acquired the weapon the British established a Torpedo Committee in the early 1870s to examine the best means of deploying it. Its recommendations included launching from major warships (both directly and from the ships' steam launches) and building specialised inshore and seagoing craft.

Known simply as a 'torpedo boat', the inshore type was intended primarily to defend bases from close blockade by an enemy fleet. Its origin may be traced to the design of a Thornycroft fast river launch, with few concessions to adequate seakeeping. The popularity of the weapon was such, however that, by 1873, the firms of White and Yarrow were also building large numbers of craft for service with foreign flags.

In 1877 the British Admiralty purchased an 84-footer (25.6 m) from Thornycroft. She carried two

Below: Typical of early destroyers, the 330-ton Italian *Nembo* of 1902 was later converted from coal to oil firing. Note the high proportion of hull volume devoted to boilers and machinery.

above-water torpedo tubes and could make 18 knots in the deep loaded condition. Initially named *Lightning*, she was joined by eleven more, whereupon the class was known by the more prosaic 'Torpedo Boats 1–12'. Their weapons were carried in a mixture of tubes and dropping gear.

The birth of the destroyer

In continental Europe, literally hundreds of equivalents were joining the fleets of France, Germany, Italy and Russia. Of these, both France and Germany also built extensively for export, some of their craft exceeding 25 knots. Fearing a massed torpedo attack on a battle line, the British took appropriate countermeasures. Battleships acquired four-barrelled Nordenfelt guns, which fired solid one-inch

(25 mm) calibre shot at 150 to 200 rounds per minute, capable of riddling a torpedo boat at up to 500 yards (450 m) range. Torpedoes were already comfortably exceeding this distance, however, and heavier quick-firing (QF) guns, firing fixed ammunition (i.e. projectile and cartridge combined) soon made their appearance.

Working on the ancient principle that attack is the best form of defence, the Admiralty also specified craft capable of both attacking an opponent's battle line with torpedoes and destroying his torpedo boats with gunfire. Thus, in 1885, was laid down the first Torpedo Gunboat or TGB, HMS *Rattlesnake*. A 550-tonner, she carried four tubes and a medium-calibre gun. Within seven years, 33 TGBs of four classes were in the water, their individual displacements having grown to 1,070 tons, and armament to five tubes and two guns. Because

of their 18/19-knot speed, they were deemed failures but, although they would certainly have proved vulnerable in torpedo attack, their size and freeboard meant that they could maintain speed and use their armament in weather conditions that would leave opposing torpedo boats helpless.

A second line of development was the First Class Torpedo Boat, sometimes known as a Division Boat. Soon developing to 160 ft (48.8 m) in length, these could interchange torpedo tubes with three-pounder QFs and twin Nordenfelts. Their stems were also strengthened for ramming.

Service use showed the theory to be correct but the craft were, as yet, too small. In 1892, therefore, 'Jackie' Fisher, then a Rear-Admiral and Third Sea Lord, requested specifications from a half-dozen suitable builders for a Torpedo Boat Destroyer, capable of a 27-knot continuous speed and carrying a suitable gun armament. The result was the rapid ordering of the six 'A' class boats, usually known as the '27-knotters', from Yarrow, Thornycroft and Laird. Armed with three torpedo tubes, one 12-pounder and three 6-pounder guns on a displacement of only 260/280 tons, these were the first true destroyers.

Left: The Yarrow-built *Hornet* was one of the Royal Navy's first class of Torpedo Boat Destroyer. Typical features included the turtle-decked forecastle and the 12-pounder gun over the recessed conning tower.

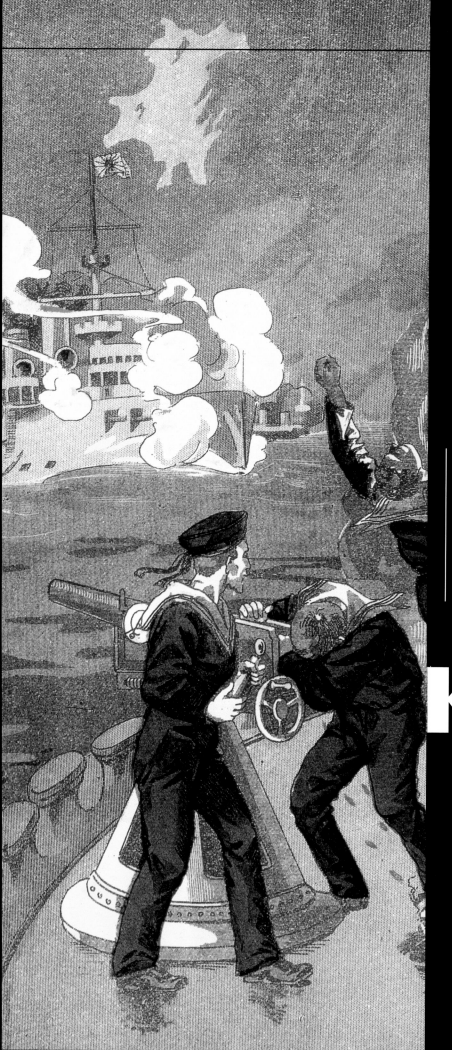

Left: **This popular Japanese impression of Tsushima suggests a much closer (Tsushima) engagement than it actually was. Far too many guncrews were, however, still exposed to fire.**

EFFECTIVELY A PROTÉGÉ´ of the British Royal Navy, the Imperial Japanese Navy was already, in 1904, both skilful and confident. Upon Japan becoming embroiled in war with Russia, its task was to establish sea control over neighbouring waters in order that military operations could be safely conducted on mainland Asia. During 1904 the Russian Far Eastern fleet suffered a series of reverses and allowed much of its surviving strength to be bottled-up in the beseiged base of Port Arthur.

To restore the naval balance the Russians had been leisurely overhauling ships of their Baltic Fleet to form a Second Pacific Squadron. Sailing in October 1904, it was a scratch collection of new capital ships, vintage coast defence ships, modern cruisers and armed auxiliaries. It took until the following May to reach the Far East, by which point most of its ships were in considerable need of dockyard attention.

Port Arthur had long capitulated and the Russian admiral, Rozhdestvensky, was obliged to make for the more northerly base at Vladivostok. In order to do this, he had to cross the virtually enclosed Sea of Japan, which he intended to enter by its widest access, the Tsushima Strait. Here he was intercepted by the Japanese Fleet whose commander, Admiral Togo, had had adequate time to prepare. On paper, the two fleets were not so very different in strength

Key
BATTLE
3 TSUSHIMA

but, where the Russians were jaded and far below par, their opponents were honed and exercised.

At first light on 27 May 1905 Togo's scouting forces reported Rozhdestvensky's approach. The Russians headed northeast, between the island of Tsushima and the Japanese mainland, as Rozhdestvensky detached his auxiliaries under escort and formed his heavy ships into two columns.

At 13.29hr the Russians were sighted from the bridge of Togo's flagship Mikasa. The Japanese were on a virtually reciprocal heading, holding it until 14.08hr, when Togo swung 16 points to parallel his opponent. In the process he tested the standard of Russian gunnery for, by ordering his ships to turn in succession, each had to pass in turn through a single point well registered by the opposing gunlayers. For the age the 7,500-yard (6,900m)range was long and the ships suffered only superficial damage from medium-calibre projectiles.

All recently docked, the Japanese ships were the faster and slowly drew ahead. As they did so they concentrated their fire on the three Russian divisional leaders as the latter tried to form a single battle line. Togo pressed across the Russians' bows and, both to keep his broadsides bearing and to avoid his 'T' being crossed in classic fashion, Rozhdestvensky was obliged to pull round slowly to a more easterly heading.

During this stage Togo was accepting damage in order to be able to inflict more. At about 15.00hr the Osliabya, leading the Russian Second Division, was badly holed by a succession of heavy-calibre hits and foundered. It was a severe blow to Russian morale, particularly as it was obvious that the flagship, Kniaz Suvorov, was also in a bad way.

Togo, however, had now drawn so far ahead that Rozhdestvensky was able to haul around to a point west of north and cut through his opponent's wake to head back toward the Sea of Japan. Realising his error, Togo ordered two successive eight-point turns together, which reversed both his heading and his line order, but setting him on a northwesterly course to again threaten to cross the Russian 'T'.

Again Rozhdestvensky was obliged to turn away, his flagship being literally shot to pieces at this juncture and himself gravely injured. His deputy, Vice-Admiral Nebogatov, assumed command and regained a measure of control over the disintegrating Russian line.

Doggedly, he tried to re-assume the course for Vladivostok but the head of his line attracted a continuous storm of Japanese fire. At the Russian rear, meanwhile, the growing number of injured, straggling ships was being savaged by Togo's armoured cruisers. As the long day drew to its close, Nebogatov made a further fruitless attempt to break through but, as dusk deepened, Togo was able to pull his capital ships back, leaving it to his destroyers to worry his adversary with torpedoes through the night. Dawn on the 28th found Nebogatov still heading northward with a small group of survivors. As the Japanese closed to renew the battle, the Russian commander accepted the hopelessness of his position and surrendered. Elsewhere, his stragglers either capitulated or were sunk, several electing to fight it out against overwhelming odds.

Tsushima had been a battle of annihilation. The Russians suffered 12 major units sunk and four captured. The Japanese lost three destroyers. The defeat brought the war to an end within four months, Japan gaining considerable territorial concessions and emerging as the predominant naval power in the western Pacific.

Above: At the outset of the war with Russia, and without a formal declaration of hostilities, Japanese destroyers attacked Port Arthur, torpedoing the battleships *Tsarevitch* and *Retvisan*, together with the cruiser *Pallada*.

Bottom: Bottled-up in Port Arthur, much of the Russian naval strength in the Far East was destroyed by Japanese siege artillery. Here, sunk in shallow water, are the *Pobieda* and *Pallada*.

DREADNOUGHT – THE ALL-BIG-GUN BATTLESHIP

AT THE TURN OF THE NINETEENTH century, battleship designers, notably Cuniberti, were moving toward the concept of overwhelming firepower. They appeared to be vindicated by engagements of the Russo–Japanese War of 1904–5, in the course of which battleships were scoring hits at ranges hitherto thought impractical, while other ships were smothered in medium calibre fire. In the Royal Navy, however, the standard heavy gun, the 12-inch (305 mm), was still regarded more for its smashing power than its potential range.

Gunnery experts such as Sims in the United States and Scott in Great Britain, were nonetheless thinking along slightly different lines. Battle exercises, customarily conducted at under two miles' range, put a battle line within the theoretical range of an opponent's torpedoes. Admiral Sir John ('Jackie') Fisher, while C-in-C Mediterranean Fleet had already demonstrated that twice that range of engagement was possible and, with proper control, probably more.

Battleship design was suffering through having been refined over 40 years without the harsh experience of major battle to prove its validity. For instance, the British 'King Edward VII' class carried four 12-inch, four 9.2-inch (234 mm), ten 6-inch (152 mm) and 14 12-pounder/3-inch weapons. In an all-out engagement, this arsenal would be controlled by several directing officers but, such would be the confusion of shell splashes, particularly from a squadron, that correction for range and bearing would be very difficult. Matters were exacerbated by the poor quality of gun sights.

Protracted trials to determine the best method of gunnery control produced no clear-cut solution with the procedures and systems then current, but both Americans and British concluded that Cuniberti was correct in proposing a main battery comprising guns of just one calibre. What was required in addition were procedures to fire them together, in salvoes or broadsides, to observe the fall of shot and to correct for error. This would best be effected by a single observer, sited as high as possible. Such a control had only recently been made possible through the introduction of electrical and telephonic communication.

Fisher claimed that he had been pondering the concept since 1900 and, on being appointed First Sea Lord in 1904, immediately set up a Committee on Designs to re-define important categories of warship. It first met in January 1905. It is not known what it knew of American plans but it was in that same year that Congress authorised the two 16,000-ton 'Michigans'. Their design broke new ground in having a homogeneous main battery of eight 12-inch guns, disposed in four twin turrets of which one superfired another at either end, in what would become the classic disposition. Secondary armament was limited to 22 3-inch quick-firers (QF), while spotting tops were mounted on two lofty cage masts. In no hurry, the Americans laid down both ships in December 1906.

Below: Without superimposition, the *Dreadnought* required ten guns for an eight gun broadside. As can be seen, the claim for an axial fire of six guns was very much limited by adjacent superstructure.

Inset: A contemporary rendering conveys at least the essential features of the USS *Michigan*'s sister, *South Carolina*.

WILLS'S CIGARETTES.

Setting new navy standards

The British did not favour superimposed turrets, because of anticipated blast effect, but Fisher (the self-styled 'apostle of end-on fire') wanted maximum chase fire. Of 10 proposals formulated by his committee, that chosen for a new-style battleship mounted five twin 12-inch turrets. One was sited on a narrow forecastle with high freeboard. Flanking it, but sited one level lower, were two more, giving a theoretical axial fire of six guns. Two more mountings were sited on the centre line aft. Five turrets thus gave a broadside of eight guns, the same as the Michigans, which had one mounting less. Similarly, the secondary battery was limited to 3-inch QFs, most of the 20 being very exposed.

An equally important innovation was steam turbine propulsion. Effectively sea-trialed to date in only a pair of destroyers, this machinery's planned major test platform was the light cruiser *Amethyst*, then still under construction. Both the Committee and the Navy thus took a huge gamble in adopting a new form of machinery in what represented a very considerable design extrapolation.

Fisher was in a hurry. The new ship, HMS *Dreadnought*, was laid down by Portsmouth Dockyard in October 1905, launched in February 1906 and commenced trials a legendary year-and-a-day after keel laying. Final completion was actually in December 1906, even as the 'Michigans' were being laid down. The latter, therefore, although the first of the genre to be conceived, were beaten to completion by more than three years. The *Dreadnought*, as a prototype, had limitations. Her powerful, homogeneous main battery was an undeniable step forward, although its layout was poor and the lack of a credible secondary armament was a drawback. The spotting platform, upon which her shooting depended, was sited atop a sturdy tripod, but in such proximity to the forward funnel that it was often untenable through heat and exhaust gases. The protection scheme was thought deficient by later standards. A speed of 21 knots and good seakeeping however, set new standards which were enthusiastically adopted by the world's navies.

Above: John Arbuthnot Fisher, first Baron Fisher of Kilverstone was the greatest combined innovator and administrator who ever served in the Royal Navy. Ever controversial, he converted a tradition-bound Victorian service into a modern, fighting fleet.

THE ANGLO-GERMAN NAVAL RACE

GERMANY WAS CREATED as a nation as recently as 1871 through the unification of many disparate states. Its voice was that of Chancellor Bismarck, backed by substantial and experienced military power. Such fleet as there was acquired the title of the Imperial Germany Navy, but the Chancellor regarded seapower in Germany's case as an expensive irrelevance and that the nation should be content with 'second rank' maritime status.

In 1888, however, Kaiser Wilhelm II succeeded as emperor. One of his grandmothers was Queen Victoria, whose empire and influence he viewed with a blend of admiration and envy. An avid reader of the then-fashionable writings of Mahan, he believed that such riches and status resulted from, and depended upon, the understanding and exercise of sea power. Germany was undeniably prospering but for her to acquire significance beyond the confines of continental Europe she needed, he believed, to create a credible fleet.

Wilhelm's character was weak and volatile, and he was much influenced by a small coterie of advisers. His rather extreme ambitions quickly brought him into collision with the cautious statesmanship of Bismarck who, in 1890, he dismissed. The German Admiralty, hitherto run by army officers, was given a naval head and the first incumbent, although he died soon after taking office, had already put in hand a first group of four small battleships, the 'Brandenburgs'. Completed in 1894, they presaged the emergence of the German Navy from its limited role of coastal defence and formed an impressive centrepiece to the international naval presence that gathered in 1895 for the opening of the strategically-important Kaiser Wilhelm (or Kiel) Canal, which allowed the rapid transfer of ships from the Baltic to the North Sea.

Work commenced immediately on a class of larger battleship, the five-strong 'Kaiser Friedrich IIIs' and, before they entered service, Wilhelm appointed Rear-Admiral Alfred Tirpitz to head the Imperial Navy Office. Responsible for the direction of naval development, Tirpitz, like the Kaiser, had a passionate belief in German destiny and the role that sea power would play in it. Both developed elaborate, idealised plans which became merged with official policy as Tirpitz, who held parliamentary status as a State Secretary, proved adept at influencing the members of the Reichstag.

Ten months from assuming office, Tirpitz had steered through the First Naval Bill which, over a six-year programme, would expand the fleet by seven battleships and nine assorted cruisers.

Germany overtly supported the cause of the Boers in the South African War and the infamous Kruger telegram (in which Wilhelm pledged his support) went far to reduce British public opinion to a level similar to the virulent Anglophobia generated by the German popular press. The latter was empty rhetoric, however, for the nation yet lacked the means to intervene either here or in the Boxer Rebellion, then occupying the attention of the major colonial powers in China. To rectify this assumed impotence Wilhelm rode the wave of public enthusiasm to have the by now ennobled von Tirpitz pilot through a Second Naval Bill in 1900. With no apparent restriction on cost, the Navy would, by 1916, be doubled in overall size to 38 battleships, 20 armoured and 38 light cruisers, supported by an appropriate number of light units. Tirpitz spoke of even 45 or 48 battleships.

Facing up to the German challenge

More than the anti-British baying of the German press, it was the latent challenge of twelve battleship keels laid in five years that finally obliged influential British naval opinion to take notice. Britain's tradition-bound army had not fared well in the unorthodox war in South Africa and it was realised that, in any future confrontation, the Royal Navy, grown comfortable on decades of Pax Britannica, might perform equally badly.

As is so often the case there appeared the man for the moment. Admiral Sir John Fisher served as Second Sea Lord in 1902–3 and as First Sea Lord from late in 1904. He gathered reformers about him, abolished out-dated procedure, scrapped obsolete tonnage, improved conditions for personnel and pushed through the 'Dreadnought' concept.

Compared with the German fleet, the Royal Navy enjoyed an overwhelming superiority in 'pre-

Below: Typical products of the pre-Dreadnought era, the four 11,800-ton German 'Kaisers' were built 1895–1902. Their small main battery calibre of 9½-inch, was offset by a powerful secondary armament of eighteen 6 inch weapons.

Dreadnoughts', but the 1906 completion of the revolutionary ship herself rendered both fleets obsolescent. Wilhelm's stated objective had been to build a navy strong enough to deter even the most powerful foreign fleet from tangling with it, implying that a rival power would be expected to grant concessions rather than risk a clash and unacceptable losses. Germany, essentially a continental power, had no need of a large fleet, and the British were now fully alive to the threat.

Starting with a new datum, defined by the *Dreadnought*, British wealth and industrial capacity was more than able to outstrip Tirpitz. Supplementary Naval Bills were passed by the Reichstag in both 1906 and 1912, saddling the nation with crippling debt but, by the end of 1914, 22 British battleships and ten battle cruisers had been completed, against 17 and five respectively.

Above: The Grand Fleet lays off its base at Rosyth. In the foreground are light cruisers, and the presence (centre distance) of both *Renowns* dates the picture as after September 1916.

Left: Resplendent in their Victorian livery, *Royal Sovereign*-and Majestic-class battleships are seen at the 1897 Diamond Jubilee fleet review at Spithead.

75

BATTLE CRUISERS

Main picture: Battle cruisers and armoured cruisers together off Portsmouth. Note the absence of any visible armoured belt along the hull. The prominent booms and anti-torpedo nets were removed early in the war.

Below: The *Courageous* was one of Fisher's notorious trio of 'tin-clads'. Officially 'light cruisers', they mounted 15- and 18-inch guns and were intended for shallow-draught work in the Baltic. All were later converted to aircraft carriers.

'THE ESSENCE OF WAR is violence. Moderation in war is madness. Hit first! Hit hard!! Keep hitting!!!' 'Jackie' Fisher unequivocally believed that a combination of superior speed and the largest guns would be unbeatable. Having gestated the *Dreadnought* his Committee of Designs re-focussed on the concept of a fast armoured cruiser.

Existing armoured cruisers had grown to displace much the same as battleships but were longer and narrower, exchanging armament and protection for speed. Fisher wanted a ship that could run down the best of these, and destroy them from an unanswerable range. They would also need to accomplish more – to approach and report on an enemy battle line, to support friendly scouting forces, to dispose of stragglers or damaged enemy ships or to hunt down the fastest commerce raider. What the First Sea Lord wanted was the marriage of the all-big-gun armament of a 'Dreadnought' to the fastest practical hull.

Italian and Japanese designers had already moved halfway to the concept but their ships under construction were limited by triple expansion machinery to only 21/22 knots, less than contemporary armoured cruisers and only three knots or so better than the battle line. Equipped with the new 'secret weapon' of the steam turbine, Fisher sought 25 knots. Combined with a 12-inch main battery, such a speed would allow the ship to force or decline action as appropriate.

Design was hardly straightforward. Thirty-one boilers were required, competing for space with the lower structure of four heavy turrets. For driving hard in adverse conditions a generous freeboard was essential. The result was a hull with huge vertical and horizontal area but with very little spare displacement to allow the armour necessary to protect it. While it would thus be vulnerable to heavy-calibre fire at both long and short range,

Fisher considered it acceptable as it was not intended to engage directly with anything larger than an armoured cruiser.

In order to slow a quarry, powerful chase fire was imperative. One turret was, therefore, mounted on the centre line forward and aft, while the other two were sited *en echelon* in the waist. In theory this permitted six guns to fire axially in a chase but, practically, blast overpressures made this impossible. Six guns could fire in broadside again, in theory, increased to eight over a limited arc by the waist turret on the disengaged side firing across the ship.

Built quickly, and under conditions of great secrecy, the three 'Invincibles' – dubbed 'battle cruisers' rather than 'fast armoured cruisers' – made a great impact when completed in 1908. Germany was following suit. After a faulty start with the *Blücher*, her first example was the *Von der Tann* of the 1907 Programme. At 19,000 tons, she displaced some 2,000 tons more than her more extreme British peers, and was the better for it. She was only marginally slower but the smaller size and weight of her 11-inch (280 mm) armament allowed for better protection and a layout that permitted a genuine eight-gun broadside.

Battle cruisers – pros and cons

Following three improved ships of the 'Indefatigable' class the British moved up to a 13.5-inch (343 mm) armament for the 'Lions' of the 1909 Programme. Speed was also increased to 27 knots, which ambitious combination demanded an overall length of 700 ft (213.4 m), an increase of 23 per cent over the 'Invincibles' of just three years previously. Their 42 boilers could burn either coal or oil and the large stoker complement accounted for the crew of 997, as compared with the 752 of the

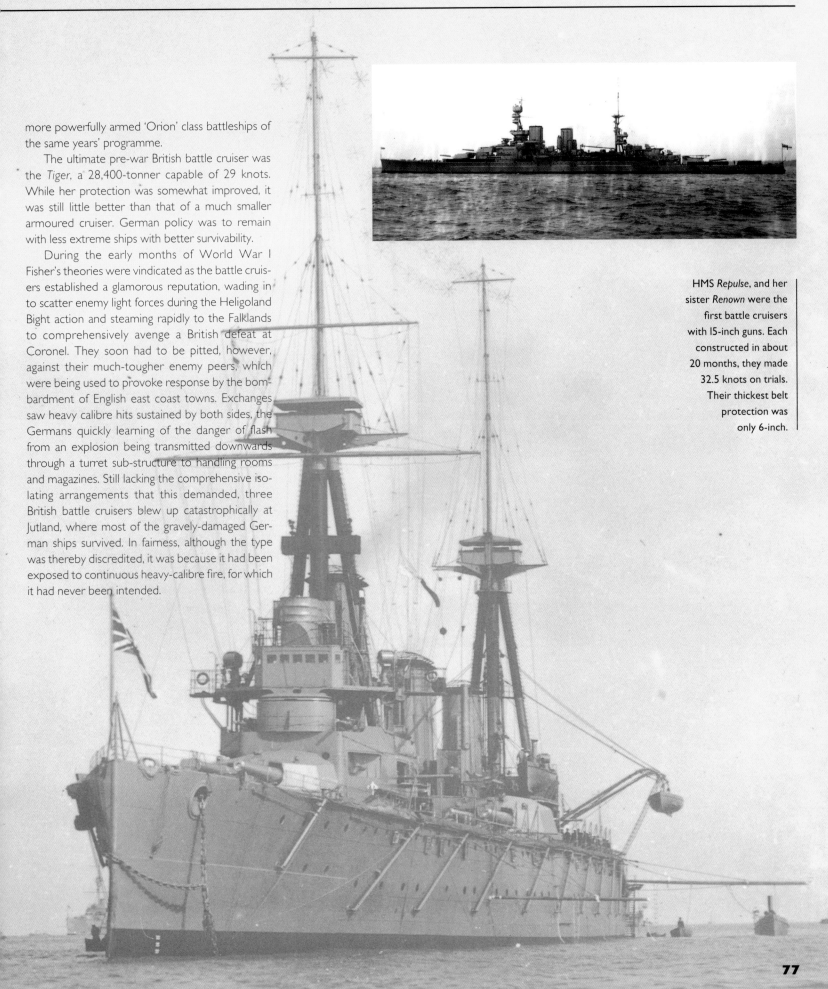

more powerfully armed 'Orion' class battleships of the same years' programme.

The ultimate pre-war British battle cruiser was the *Tiger*, a 28,400-tonner capable of 29 knots. While her protection was somewhat improved, it was still little better than that of a much smaller armoured cruiser. German policy was to remain with less extreme ships with better survivability.

During the early months of World War I Fisher's theories were vindicated as the battle cruisers established a glamorous reputation, wading in to scatter enemy light forces during the Heligoland Bight action and steaming rapidly to the Falklands to comprehensively avenge a British defeat at Coronel. They soon had to be pitted, however, against their much-tougher enemy peers, which were being used to provoke response by the bombardment of English east coast towns. Exchanges saw heavy calibre hits sustained by both sides, the Germans quickly learning of the danger of flash from an explosion being transmitted downwards through a turret sub-structure to handling rooms and magazines. Still lacking the comprehensive isolating arrangements that this demanded, three British battle cruisers blew up catastrophically at Jutland, where most of the gravely-damaged German ships survived. In fairness, although the type was thereby discredited, it was because it had been exposed to continuous heavy-calibre fire, for which it had never been intended.

HMS *Repulse*, and her sister *Renown* were the first battle cruisers with 15-inch guns. Each constructed in about 20 months, they made 32.5 knots on trials. Their thickest belt protection was only 6-inch.

CRUISERS

Main picture: Cruisers are intended to be able to remain at sea for considerable periods on individual missions. Here, the 14,600-ton armoured cruiser *Shannon* contends with heavy conditions. Note the dazzle-painting and the rangefinding baffles on the funnels.

THE TERM 'CRUISER' DERIVES from 'Cruising ship', a command independent of the battle fleet and engaged on duties such as imperial policing or trade route protection. Carrying marine detachments and bluejackets trained by custom in military skills, the timely intervention of such ships could often contain a local insurrection before it flared into something more serious.

Such commissions, before the introduction of telegraphic communication, were usually remote from higher authority, and commanders were truly 'captains under God'. Self-sufficiency was of paramount importance. Although these vessels, commonly sloops or corvettes, were fitted with steam machinery, this was not very efficient, while coal was expensive and scarce. They consequently spent much time under sail, being among the last warships to finally abandon full rig.

The American Civil War (1861–65) in which, at sea at least, the British were not entirely uninvolved, demonstrated that fast ships could not only make fat profit through blockade running but also could act in a privateering role. Such raiders caused huge losses and disruption, necessitating disproportionately large forces to hunt them down. The United States, France and Russia all went on to build large raiders. Great Britain, alive to the vulnerability of her scattered trade to the attentions of such ships, responded with what may be regarded as the true antecedents of the modern cruiser. These included the 16-knot, iron-built *Inconstant* of 1868 and the 18-knot steel *Mercurys* of 1877. Although their main batteries, ten 64-pounder muzzle loading rifles (MLR), were considerable, they were still arranged for broadside fire. French practice was to increase chase fire by mounting some upper deck pieces in protruding sponsons, with their field of fire increased by giving the hull tumblehome, the degree of which became a French hallmark.

British ships of this type grew to about 3,750 tons displacement and, while unarmoured, derived some protection by flanking the extensive machinery spaces with deep coal bunkers. A full bunker could stop a medium-calibre projectile and, even if holed and flooded, its contents still maintained two-thirds of its potential buoyancy.

From 1876 some cruisers gained a protective deck. Such 'Protected Cruisers' were built around a continuous deck, sited mainly below the waterline and arched both fore and aft, and to the sides. Usually 15 in (38 mm) in thickness, it was broken only in way of the machinery. Beneath it the ship was greatly sub-divided into watertight compartments, while many of the more irregularly-configured spaces above it were coal-filled. The curvature of the protective deck was designed to deflect flat tra-

jectory projectiles while blocking splinters from those bursting above.

During the late 1870s and early 1880s, several ships were built with their protective deck flanked by a shallow vertical armour belt. The extra weight increased the size of the ships, however and, as British ships had a greater need for bunkers and stores for long endurance, the type was discontinued.

The Naval Defence Act, 1889

The late 1880s saw the Royal Navy acquire much new tonnage, a process accelerated by the Naval Defence Act of 1889. Clear distinctions began to emerge between cruiser types, now rated First, Second or Third class depending upon their designed roles. These could range from reconnaissance in force to fleet support, from trade protection to policing the empire.

First class cruisers required significant firepower and speed. As both of these design ingredients increased size, this soon equated to that of contemporary battleships. Two of the largest, the 14,200-ton 'Powerfuls', were built in direct response to potential raiding cruisers constructed in France and Russia. As the threat did not materialise,

this pair, which had a voracious appetite for coal, never found a true role.

In parallel again appeared the 'Armoured Cruiser', incorporating both vertical belts and protective deck on the assumption that it was preferable to keep projectiles out rather than to merely survive the damage that they caused. Improved heat-treated armour now had greater stopping power and could, therefore, be incorporated more sparingly. The type nonetheless proved popular, and successive classes increased from 12,600 to 14,600 tons displacement, their extra speed requiring hulls longer than those of the contemporary battleships. It was such ships, being built during the early years of the twentieth century, that Admiral Fisher rendered obsolete with the introduction of the battle cruiser.

Four decades of rapid development produced large numbers of ships which, by 1905, had little or no fighting value. Fisher deleted no less than 154, many of which were cruisers. The run-up to World War I thus saw the emergence of new classes of 'Light Cruiser', designed for fleet support. Built for both British and German fleets, their size increased in successive classes from 3,300 to 5,500 tons. Smaller light cruisers, including the short-lived 'Scouts', found employment such as leaders to the large flotillas of destroyers.

Top: HMS *Hampshire*, built in 1905, was one of the six Devonshire class armoured cruisers. Just four days after Jutland she was mined off the Orkneys. Among those lost was *Lord Kitchener*, travelling to Russia.

Above: HMS *Warrior*'s heavy plating allowed only one gun deck. Technically, she could be termed a 'frigate', a sailing ancestor of the modern cruiser. Her weight of armament and its protection, however, made her an early battleship.

79

SUBMARINES BEFORE 1914

SUCCESS, IT IS SAID, HAS MANY fathers but, if one parent has to be selected for the modern submarine, it would be the American, John P. Holland. At the turn of the century it was he who combined the essential elements of longitudinal stability, depth control and electric propulsion into a practical craft some 63 ft (19.2 m) in length. A prototype, built by his company, was purchased for evaluation by the US Navy. It was quickly followed by an order for a class of seven. The British Admiralty, moving as ever when it considered the time to be right, ordered a further five, to be built in Great Britain under licence.

The attraction of the submarine was its combination of stealthy approach and its ability to deliver a torpedo. This weapon was already capable of running some 1,200 yards (1,100 m) at a reliable, gyro-controlled depth. Craft so inexpensive (the British Hollands cost £35,000 apiece) were attractive as a means of protecting harbours. The Royal Navy had not yet abandoned its long-effective strategy of close blockade, and required to know whether submarines had rendered the concept obsolete. It was well known that the French *Jeune École* favoured swarms of cheap torpedo craft to offset the advantage of a powerful enemy battle line.

French engineers had been innovative in the design of prototype submarines, building both single and double-hulled types. The former incorporated all tank spaces within the pressure hull; the latter gained useful volume by siting ballast and fuel tanks within a conformal outer hull, which could be lightly built as it remained open to external pressure. Double-hulled varieties tended to have high length to beam ratios and were intended to stay on the surface, diving when required. They were usually termed 'submersibles' and had topside casings to improve seakindliness when surfaced.

All types used battery-powered electric drive when submerged with, usually, petrol engines for surface navigation. The French, particularly, favoured steam propulsion for high surface speed, but the system made for very slow submerging. French boats tended to be large and to carry more torpedo tubes but, although they participated in exercises as early as 1898, they inclined to a series of 'one-offs' rather than classes.

In Germany, Admiral von Tirpitz was single-mindedly producing a battle fleet and viewed submarines as an irrelevant distraction. A private-venture, Holland-style boat was, however, built by Krupp and sold to Russia, which returned quickly with an order for three 131 ft (39.9 m) double-hulled submersibles. These owed much to French and, increasingly, Italian design. Their potential for coastal defence led the Imperial German Navy to

Above: Looking like a British X-craft of World War II, the *Holland* (SS-1) was built by John P. Holland to his own account and purchased by the US Navy in 1900 as its first submarine. The aperture in the bow is for an 8-inch dynamite gun!

Right: The concept of the submarine appealed particularly to the followers of the French Jeune École, who proposed a mass of inexpensive torpedo-armed craft as an antidote to large battle fleets.

Above: To John P. Holland goes the credit of creating the first practical submarine, incorporating essential features and utilising dynamic control. His facility became the modern Electric Boat Company.

order a near-copy. In 1906, the boat was commissioned as the U-1. The U-boat was born.

With von Tirpitz relenting somewhat, funding allowed for the slow development of a U-boat service. Early boats used paraffin engines on the surface. They were safer than petrol units but emitted dense clouds of tell-tale smoke. Although the newly-developed diesel engine was identified as preferable, it proved difficult to adapt. It was first fitted to a German craft, the U-19, in 1911, although another boat, *Atropo*, building to Italian account, was

the recipient of the first unit.

Driven by a combination of fine hull shape and the dimensions of essential internal elements (notably torpedo tubes, space to store and reload spare rounds, in-line engines and generators, and battery space) the submarines grew rapidly to what might be termed a 'modern' configuration. By 1914 submarines were already quite potent platforms but research into the means for detecting and destroying them had made little progress.

Above *Left*: Launched in 1893, the French *Gustave Zédé* was not only of greater size than her predecessors but also among the first to eventually feature depth-keeping hydroplanes and a raised conning tower.

A comparison of pre-war submarines:

Nationality	UK			Germany		USA	France
Class	*Holland 1-5*	*C1-C18*	*E1-E8*	*U1*	*U23-U26*	*K1-K8*	*Admiral Bourgois*
Commissioned	1902–3	1906–9	1913–14	1906	1913–14	1913–14	1914
Displacement*	113/122	287/316	655/796	238/283	669/864	392/521	555/735
Length x beam	63.9 x 11.8	142.3 x 13.6	178.1 x 15.1	139.1 x 12.5	212.3 x 20.7	153.5 x 16.8	84.4 x 18.
Speed§	7.4/6	12/7	14/9.5	10.8/8.7	16.7 x 10.3	14/10.5	3.9/8.7
Range+ (surfaced)	235/–	1300/9	3000/10	1500/10	7600/8	-/-	2500/10
Range+ (submerged)	20/5	14/7	65/5	50/5	85/5	-/-	100/5
Torpedo Tubes	One	Two	Four	One	Four	Four	Four
Torpedoes	3.18 in	4.18 in	8.18 in	3.45 cm	6.50 cm	-x 18 in	-x 45 cm
Complement	8	16	30	12	5	8	25

* Tons surfaced/submerged

§ Knots surfaced/submerged

+ Sea miles/knots

NAVAL BLOCKADE IN THE TWENTIETH CENTURY

Above right: Traditional close blockade was made impossible by the introduction of the submarine. On 22 September 1914 the U9 sank the 12,000-ton armoured cruiser *Cressy* and her sisters *Hogue* and *Aboukir* off the Dutch coast.

MARITIME WAR WAS NOT CONFINED to trials of strength between battle squadrons. Over centuries during the sailing era, the British had developed the art of blockading an enemy's coast, with the dual objectives of confining his forces to their bases (which slowly corroded their morale and fighting efficiency) and putting a stranglehold on his trade (debilitating his ability to wage war and undermining public support for it). The development of submarines and mines had made the earlier practice of close blockade impracticable, however, and a new approach was required in World War I.

German-flagged shipping virtually disappeared from the seas during the first few days of hostilities but it was necessary for the British to control the extensive German trade which flowed in neutral bottoms, mainly Dutch and Scandinavian, through both German and neutral ports.

To avoid blockade being simply a form of legalised piracy, international law must be observed. This divides cargoes into three categories, viz. absolute and conditional contraband, and a free list.

Of these, absolute contraband comprises purely military articles, which may be seized. Conditional contraband includes those articles, such as clothing or fuel, which could benefit either the military or civil population. The free list details many items such as raw materials, including rubber and cotton, which primarily benefit the populace and are immune from seizure. Britain, however, had never ratified this agreement and, not being bound by it, quickly 'upgraded' many commodities to become contraband.

U-boat retaliation

Control of shipping in the English Channel was effected simply through laying a vast mine barrage, that obliged traffic to pass through the Downs, off the Kent coast, where it had to submit to examination. To the north of the British Isles, however, lay the 600-mile gaps between Greenland, Iceland and Scotland. Enforcement of blockade in these dark and hostile seas was, initially, entrusted to a squadron of elderly cruisers but these proved

totally inadequate to the conditions. They were replaced, very successfully, by two dozen armed passenger liners which, as the 10th Cruiser Squadron, based its operation on Kirkwall and Lerwick in the northern islands.

Although in the gloom of winter many ships slipped through unchallenged, the scale of the enemy's loss may be gauged by the monthly average of 280 interceptions, together with about 150 fishing craft and coasters.

The British Foreign Office was very nervous of offending neutrals, particularly American, by these activities. To the fury of the Navy many ships, brought in at considerable effort and risk, were allowed to proceed with suspect cargoes. Some German ships, such as those belonging to subsidiaries of the Standard Oil Company, were re-flagged under the American banner of their parent company. Others, released by the Navy on orders, included the American ship *Greenbrier*, which promptly diverted to Bremen with her contraband cargo, released 14 of her crew as German nationals, and had interned a British engineering officer.

The Norwegian passenger liners *Bergensfjord* and *Kristianafjord* gave endless problems, delivering many enemy personnel and cargoes. On one search at Kirkwall the authorities discovered and interned 473 Germans.

By 1916, the slow process of blockade was causing the enemy shortages in staple commodities. Lack of sufficient bulk fertiliser was already resulting in shortfalls in harvest yields. Priority was enjoyed by the military, the civil population experiencing rationing in such as bread, meat and milk. Substitutes were introduced for leather and wool. From January 1916 the British operated a Ministry of Blockade to further increase the effectiveness of the squeeze. Its senior naval representative was Vice Admiral de Chair, lately in command of the 10th Cruiser Squadron but relieved by his deputy, Vice Admiral Tupper.

Germany's military leaders recognised and argued that, if allowed to continue, the blockade would bring about their defeat. A rapid decision was thus required, for which the only possible weapon was the U-boat arm. Unrestricted submarine warfare had brought about earlier, vehement American protest but this again had to be risked. It proved to be one risk too many. The remorseless destruction and loss of innocent life inflamed American opinion and was a major factor in President

Wilson declaring war in April 1917. From this point, Germany's ultimate defeat was certain.

The direction of the British Grand Fleet drew heavy criticism, from within and without, for failing to bring about a decisive showdown with the enemy. What went generally unnoticed was the crucial influence exerted on the war by the weatherbeaten liners of the 10th Cruiser Squadron. With the entry of the United States, the source of most contraband cargoes disappeared, and the squadron was stood down in December 1917. During its lifetime it had made nearly 13,000 interceptions (95 per cent of all movements), of which one in three were sent in for examination. Always vulnerable to enemy submarine and cruiser attack, it lost eight ships to enemy action and two to stress of weather.

Above: Long commissions were usual, with patrol ships in particular spending long periods at sea. General participation in amusements, such as this ship's concert party, was important for morale.

Left: The boarding of intercepted ships necessarily involved the use of small boats. In northern waters this could be very hazardous and Newfoundlanders were particularly valued for their seamanship.

CONVOY REVISITED

ALTHOUGH FEW IN NUMBERS and still primitive in design, German U-boats had demonstrated by the outbreak of World War I, that they could operate independently in British waters. From the outset of hostilities in 1914 the British exerted a seaborne blockade on Germany that became progressively tighter. Claiming that this constituted war against her population Germany saw the submarine as a means of retaliation against British trade.

Submarine operations were governed by international law, and only warships could be sunk on sight. The so-called 'prize rules' demanded that a merchantman could be sunk only once she and her cargo had been thoroughly checked out, and then only if she could not be taken into port as a legitimate prize of war. Sinking could be effected only after every effort had been made to ensure the safety of those aboard.

A submarine's own strength and safety, however, lay in her invisibility. She could carry no spare personnel to form prize crews, and neither space nor provisions for survivors. In short, a submarine could sink a target outright or let her proceed; half measures hazarded her own existance.

In February 1915, therefore, the Chief of the German Naval Staff declared all waters bordering the British Isles to be a war zone. Within it, all merchant ships could be destroyed, with obvious risk to neutral-flagged tonnage, crews and passengers. U-boat commanders were instructed that their first consideration was toward the safety of their own craft, and that surfacing to examine merchant ships was to be avoided.

Thus began the first period of unrestricted submarine warfare, with ships torpedoed without warning. Loss rates increased rapidly, as did viola-

Above: Seamen are seamen the world over and most U-boat crews derived little satisfaction from the destruction that they caused. This Claus Bergen impression sums up the mood of the moment.

Right: A later generation U-boat surfaces in heavy seas. This could be an anxious moment as the stability was always suspect until the upper casing drained of water.

tions of neutral immunity. Firm diplomatic warnings came from the United States, with matters coming to a head in May 1915 through the sinking of the liner *Lusitania*. Fierce American reaction to the loss of many of their citizens resulted in the Germans again applying restrictions to their U-boats. Although sinkings per boat decreased, however, their rapidly-increasing number maintained overall losses at a high level. Despite this, results still disappointed the German High Command which, also perturbed at complications with neutrals and the steady improvement in British countermeasures, eased off the campaign in September 1915, the war at sea being waged primarily by the High Seas Fleet.

Convoys – the fors and againsts

During the summer of 1916, following Jutland, there was great dissent in high naval circles regarding the overall conduct of the maritime war. In December of that year the new Chief of the Naval Staff, Admiral von Holtzendorff, issued a fateful memorandum. It argued that Britain's allies were war-weary, maintained by a Britain that could be knocked out only by a full-bloodied onslaught on her vital shipping. Germany, starved by blockade, needed, he argued, to end the war by the autumn of 1917. While a further period of unrestricted U-boat warfare would probably result in the United States declaring war, the time for their effective intervention would be too protracted to affect the outcome.

It was a huge gamble but, accepting the argument, the Kaiser authorised an all-out submarine campaign to commence on 1 February 1917. Its objective was to destroy 600,000 grt monthly and to deter neutrals from shipping for the British. It succeeded all too well, with monthly average sinkings in 1917 rising to an unsustainable 740,000 grt.

Submarines at this time had easy pickings, with shipping proceeding independently along 'safe routes', patrolled diligently but ineffectively by the Navy. Convoying shipping in escorted groups had a successful provenance dating back to the thirteenth century yet its suggestion was quashed by a general belief that the introduction of power had changed everything. A convoy, it was believed, would serve merely to give a U-boat commander a larger target, while its formation would waste an inordinate amount of time, thereby making available shipping less efficient.

The latter point would be exacerbated by a convoy being restricted to the speed of its slowest vessel. In addition, the Navy did not like it, viewing escorting as 'defensive' and patrolling (though demonstrably unproductive) as 'offensive'.

Oddly, the important French coal trade, and then the food and timber traffic to and from the Netherlands and Scandinavia, had already been successfully organised into convoys, greatly reducing losses but without resultant large-scale disruption. The actual degree of resistance to the general adoption of convoy at the Admiralty and, indeed, by the Merchant Service, remains a matter of dispute, as does the effect of the personal intervention of the Prime Minister, but the 831,000 grt lost in the awful month of April 1917 virtually forced the issue.

Commencing the following month in the Mediterranean, convoy was an immediate success, although losses among 'independents' remained high. Now obliged to approach convoys and their escorts, U-boats could be more easily found and destroyed.

Below: Contemporary submarines needed to spend most of their time surfaced. Aerial patrols, such as by this non-rigid 'blimp', were valuable in extending the convoy's visual horizon.

Left: Admiral Scheer had sought to isolate and destroy a squadron of the British Grand Fleet. Instead, he encountered Jellicoe's whole strength, resulting in one of the greatest of sea battles.

INFERIOR IN NUMBERS to the British Grand Fleet, the German High Seas Fleet's strategy was directed at reducing British strength by attrition rather than by pitched battle. As part of a continuing policy, therefore, Admiral Scheer sailed up the west side of the Jutland peninsula at the end of May 1916. His purpose was to draw elements of Admiral Jellicoe's forces out and into a pre-set 'submarine trap'. The German plan went awry in that the British put to sea in full strength, missing the submarines. On the afternoon of 31 May the two fleets, neither suspecting the other, were on a collison course.

Each fleet was proceeding some 60 miles astern of its respective scouting battle cruiser squadron and, drawn to investigate the same neutral ship, it was these squadrons that made first contact. The time was about 15.30hr, the day already far gone. Six British battle cruisers, under the courageous but impetuous Vice Admiral Sir David Beatty came in sight of five commanded by Vice Admiral Hipper. In accordance with general policy the latter immediately turned and headed southeastward in order to entice Beatty to destruction by the guns of Scheer's battle fleet.

Beatty did not wait for the four fast new 'Queen Elizabeth' class battleships that he had in support. Despite his numerical advantage, however, his ships were unsure of target allocation and came under a

Key
BATTLE
4 JUTLAND.

deliberate fire that, during the pursuit that followed, sank the British *Indefatigable* and *Queen Mary* by catastrophic magazine explosions.

Still in hot pursuit of Hipper, Beatty suddenly came in sight of Scheer's battle line. It was about 16.30hr and, with the positions reversed, it was now Beatty's duty to draw Scheer on to Jellicoe's yet-unsuspected Grand Fleet.

Beatty's supporting battleships had caught up but, by reversing course in succession, he caused each to come under heavy German fire. Nonetheless he drew Hipper well ahead of his support and, for an hour, punished him heavily. Jellicoe, to the north, now knew that the High Seas Fleet was closing him but, in the confusion of radical manoeuvring and generally indifferent visibility, scouting reports gave him little firm indication of its position and course. He was in cruising formation of six columns, each of four battleships. To give battle, he needed to deploy into a single line on either the port or starboard column, depending upon Scheer's bearing.

Jellicoe was given a little extra time by the intervention of Rear-Admiral Hood's three old battle cruisers which, also attacking Hipper, forced him back on the German van which, in turn, steered more to the east. With action imminent Jellicoe made the correct decision, at 18.15hr, to deploy on the port division, forming a battle line heading eastward. This, in textbook fashion, crossed Scheer's 'T'.

Fierce encounters were taking place between the two battle lines, and further magazine explosions accounted for Hood's *Invincible* and an armoured cruiser. Scheer, however, was faced with the daunting sight of a horizon-long line of British battleships which, even before completing their deployment, were subjecting his van to a deluge of fire. At 18.33hr, he ordered a simultaneous reversal of course and, in the general haze, his fleet melted from British sight.

Rather than order 'General chase', Jellicoe was content to steer a course that put him between the High Seas Fleet and its base. Scheer, realising his danger, tried to break through the British line at about 19.00hr but, under unendurable pressure, was obliged to execute another battle turnaway, covered by an almost suicidal charge by Hipper's sorely-tried battle cruisers and a destroyer torpedo attack. The latter caused the cautious Jellicoe to turn away, even though he was hitting Scheer hard and a 'turn towards' would have carried little more

risk. The result was loss of contact and, indeed, except for a brief clash involving Beatty, there would be no further major exchange between the capital ships.

Darkness fell and the Grand Fleet held its formation and course, intent on resuming the fight at daybreak. Incredibly, the significance of a series of vicious close-quarter skirmishes during the night was not appreciated and, indeed, went largely unreported. What they in fact indicated was Scheer slipping through Jellicoe's wake while the latter, poorly served by British signal procedures and subordinates who lacked initiative, steamed on. The Grand Fleet was untrained in night fighting and its careful commander was, understandably, not willing to risk a disorganised mãˊlãˊe, in which discipline and numerical advantage would have counted for nothing. Although confident of being able to renew the battle, Jellicoe found only empty sea as the light strengthened.

Faulty ship design features and poor heavy projectiles (which tended to break up when striking armour) caused the British to suffer a material defeat, losing 14 ships of 155,000 tons against 11 ships of 61,000 tons, together with over 6,000 dead against 2,500. It was, however, a strategic success for, considering their losses insupportable, the Germans turned predominantly to submarine warfare.

Above: **A heavy calibre hit on *Invincible*'s Q-turret blew off its roof and detonated the magazine. She broke in two with the loss of 1026 men. Three battle cruisers and one armoured cruiser were similarly destroyed.**

Left: **Before the battle. While the original caption of this picture suggests that this is part of Hipper's force en route to bombard Sunderland, the distinctive cranes and tops on the distant capital ship point to her being the *Nassau* or *Westfalen*.**

AVIATION AT SEA BEFORE 1918

Main picture:
A Curtiss biplane
with Eugene Ely at
the controls, makes a
second ascent from
the USS *Pennsylvania*,
November 1910.

Below: Several British
cross-channel packets
were modified to
serve as seaplane
carriers. The
Engadine, shown
here, provided the
first-ever aerial
reconnaissance in
a naval battle, at
Jutland in 1916.

FOR LONG, fast sailing frigates had been used as the military used cavalry, to throw out an advanced screen for the provision of early warning, or to reconnoitre for information on an opponent sufficient for an admiral to assess a situation accurately prior to ordering deployment for battle. With the machine age, however, there began an interest in developing the means to put an observer aloft at a commanding height. By the opening of the twentieth century there had already been widespread experimentation with operating man-lifting balloons and kites from shipboard.

It was an ascent in a tethered balloon (or 'aerostat') in the United States that fired Count Ferdinand von Zeppelin with the concept of an 'air cruiser'. His first model was the 420 ft (128 m) L.Z.1, whose maiden flight was in July 1900. It had a rigid framework and was powered by petrol engines. Its commercial and military applications were immediately obvious to the Germans and von Zeppelin went on to produce a series of eponymous airships, used militarily both for long-range reconnaissance and offensive bombing missions. They were to exert a powerful influence over aviation development in the Royal Navy.

By 1903, pioneers such as Langley, Curtiss and the Wright brothers were making short hops in powered, heavier-than-air machines, an option that both American and British fleets were to prefer to the airship. In November 1910 the American pilot Eugene Ely became the first to fly from a warship, using a temporary platform erected on the cruiser *Birmingham*. He followed it two months later with the first landing, a far more difficult undertaking, on to the heavy cruiser *Pennsylvania*. It was unfortunate for continued progress in this direction that the floatplane made its appearance at this juncture.

The French, noted builders of early aircraft and aero-engines, were quick to explore the possibilities of putting aircraft afloat but, having converted the torpedo boat carrier *Foudre* to deploy both deck- and water-launched aircraft, they failed to move the process further. In Russia, where another promising start had been made, all came to a halt with the revolution of October 1917.

In a bid to establish the relative merits of the German-style rigid airship and powered aircraft, the Royal Navy's only example of the former was completed in 1911. The experience was disastrous in that, being of over-light construction, the airship broke in two before its first flight. Fortunately the Royal Aero Club had, the year before, generously loaned two aircraft for the purpose of teaching young officers to fly. Their base, at Eastchurch on the Isle of Sheppey, thus became the Royal Naval Flying School. Its senior officer, Commander Samson, became, in December 1911, the first British pilot to fly from a warship, in this case the battleship *Africa*.

The US Navy, too, was examining every option. Setting a seaplane afloat and recovering it involved a warship heaving-to for a considerable period, during which she was a sitting target. To eliminate one of these operations, Captain Irvin Chambers, of the Office of Naval Aviation, developed a compressed-air catapult, which successfully launched its first aircraft in November 1912. Catapults continued to enthuse the Americans but the British, while continuing to experiment with them appeared more interested in pursuing the use of shipboard platforms.

hangar in what would become standard form, was first incorporated in the *Argus*. Converted from the hull of a passenger liner, she was the first true aircraft carrier, but was completed just too late to see service in World War I.

The Royal Navy successfully converted several cross-channel packets for the deployment of seaplanes. These pioneered procedures for spotting for ship-to-shore bombardment, reconnaissance and successful attack with both bomb and torpedo.

Innovators such as the American Curtiss and the Briton, Porte, developed flying boats, such as the Large and Small Americas, and the Felixstowe which, working from Naval Air Stations, proved invaluable in support of fleet operations.

The first aircraft carriers

Only wheeled fighter aircraft had the performance necessary to intercept a fast-climbing reconnaissance Zeppelin whose procedure, on being approached, was usually to dump ballast and ascend vertically. Biplanes enjoyed considerable low-speed lift, sufficient to get airborne from short platforms built over the forward ends of ships that could steam fast into the wind. To those fitted to destroyers and light cruisers were added others on the gun turrets of capital ships, which could train them on to the most appropriate bearing.

The large cruiser *Furious* was the first to be converted with a permanent flying-off deck forward and a landing-on deck aft. These were separated by the ship's original bridge structure and funnel, which created powerful and unpredictable eddies, making landing impracticable. This failing led directly to the concept of the through flight deck which, laid over a

Above: Being the weaker fleet, the German navy had to make best use of modern technology to remedy the shortfall. Submarine and floatplane are seen against the gaunt cliffs of Heligoland.

Left: Close relationships between the British and German fleets lasted to the outbreak of war. For Kiel Week in June 1914 the Royal Navy sent the four King George V-class battleships and the 1st Light Cruiser Squadron.

THE WASHINGTON TREATIES

THE CONCEPT OF THE 'decisive battle' was, if anything, strengthened by the disappointing outcome of Jutland. This fuelled the arguments of those who wanted larger, better protected and more heavily-armed capital ships. Although it was late in the war the principal allies all embarked on ambitious building programmes. The British wished to retain their traditional pre-eminence at sea; the Americans sought a fleet 'second to none', Japan wanted to reinforce her status of principal naval power in the western Pacific, while France required only to stay ahead of her neighbour and rival, Italy.

The end of hostilities in 1918 thus found the late allies facing no conceivable maritime threat, yet saddled with hugely expensive projects, which may be summarised as follows (see table below):

At a time when the nations, except perhaps Japan, were recovering financially from the late war such rivalry and expenditure were totally unjustifiable. It was the United States that grasped the nettle, inviting all, plus Italy, to a disarmament conference in Washington. Three months of hard bargaining, commencing in November 1921, were to have far-reaching effects on the limitation of capital ship tonnage and on future design.

It was agreed that all of the above programmes would be abandoned. The total allowable tonnage of capital ships would be 525,000 tons each for Great Britain and the United States, 315,000 tons for Japan, and 175,000 each for France and Italy. This created a fixed ratio of 5: 5: 3: 1.75: 1.75, which Japan accepted only under extreme pressure, see-

Right: The only unit of her class to be completed, the 'Mighty 'Ood' (HMS *Hood*) encapsulated the spirit of the Royal Navy between the wars. Her loss in battle in May 1941 came as a profound shock.

	Class	Type	No. off	Displacement	Armament	Speed (kts)
UK	Un-named	Battleship	Four	48,500	9 × 18-inch	31.5
	Un-named	Battle Cruiser	Four	48,500	9 × 16-inch	n/a
United States	South Dakota	Battleship	Six	43,200	12 × 16-inch	23
	Lexington	Battle Cruiser	Six	43,500	8 × 16-inch	33.3
Japan	Tosa	Battleship	Two	38,500	10 × 16-inch	26.5
	Owari	Battleship	Four	41,100	10 × 16-inch	29.8
	Amagi	Battle Cruiser	Four	40,000	10 × 16-inch	30
France	Normandie	Battleship	Five	24,800	12 × 13.4-inch	21.5
	Lyon	Battleship	Four	29,600	16 × 13.4-inch	23

ing herself being relegated to the second rank of naval powers.

To actually achieve these ceilings was no mean undertaking and scrap yards were glutted with discarded capital ships. In the first instance, the British had to scrap 583,000 tons, leaving 22 ships of 580,000 tons; the Americans 845,000 (a notional figure, much of it planned but not yet commenced), leaving 18 ships of 500,000 tons; the Japanese 449,000 tons, leaving ten ships of 301,000 tons. France and Italy retained ten ships apiece, totalling 221,000 and 182,000 tons respectively.

The aircraft carrier gains importance

There were concessions. The United States and Japan were each allowed to convert to aircraft carriers two battle cruiser hulls that, otherwise, would have been scrapped. Great Britain, whose retained ships were all prematurely aged by protracted war service, was permitted to build two new units – but only in exchange for four older ships being sent to the breakers.

Both new British ships had to conform to the agreed new limitation of 35,000 tons (as defined in standardised 'Washington' measurement) and have a main battery not exceeding 16-inch (406 mm) calibre. No existing ships could be replaced within 20 years of their completion date, while any modernisation could not increase unit displacement by more than 3,000 tons.

Carriers, still very much an unknown quantity, were also governed by the general ratio, the total allowable tonnages being 135,000; 135,000; 81,000; 60,000 and 60,000. Except in approved cases, individual ships should not displace over 27,000 tons.

The lower limits of warship governed by the agreements were 10,000 tons and guns not exceeding 8-inch (203 mm) calibre. This had the unintended effect of starting a 'cruiser race', with the signatories all building up to these standards, with no limit on numbers. Great Britain, so nearly defeated by the U-boat, worked to have the conference abolish submarines internationally. The attempt failed, mainly through French insistence on their retention as a concession for accepting their proposed quota of capital ships. Since 1902 Great Britain had been in alliance with Japan. The United States, sensitive to the balance in the Pacific, was aware of the threat, however unlikely, of facing a superior Anglo-Japanese fleet. Japan, still looking aggressive, had been rewarded for her recent support with mandate over ex-German island groups in the Pacific. Deeply suspicious of Japanese intentions, the Americans scored something of a diplomatic coup at the conference by having agreed a ban on fortification of all such islands, and also having the Anglo-Japanese Alliance, due for renewal, diluted to a Four-Power Pact by the inclusion of both the United States and France.

Due to run until 1936, the Washington agreements, although later weakened by Japanese renegation, were effective in curbing proliferation in construction. They marked the beginning of the end of the pre-eminence of the battleship, and its supersession by the aircraft carrier.

Above: The design for the American Lexington-class battle cruisers was modified continuously. To achieve a speed of over 33 knots about 180,000 shaft horse power was required.

Below: Eventually completed under Treaty rules as aircraft carriers, the *Lexington* and *Saratoga* proved to be very successful.

Merchant Shipping in the Heyday of Steam

Main picture:
Isambard Brunel, seen suitably with his massive creations, typified the confident Victorian engineer, whose accomplishments were bounded only by the limitations of contemporary technology.

Right: The launch of the Great Britain was a gala occasion for Bristol. This impression shows the ship with her original six-masted rig, later reduced to five.

IN 1835, THE 29 YEAR-OLD Isambard Kingdom Brunel, then chief engineer of the new Great Western Railway, proposed to the directors that, instead of considering the line to terminate at Bristol, they should build a great steamship for passengers' onward transit to New York. Enthused, they floated a subsidiary concern, the Great Western Steamship Company (GWS Co.) which, in June 1836, laid the keel for a 236 ft (71.9 m) wooden paddle steamer. Constructed conventionally, and named Great Western, she left Bristol just 14 months later under sail for London, where she was to be fitted out. At Blackwall, the ship received a 750 ihp two-cylinder engine from the noted firm of Maudslay, Sons & Field, together with berths for 128 passengers, 'exclusive of those for servants ... '

Trials began in March 1838 in certain haste, as others were also intent on making the first transatlantic passage under power alone. The largest of these contenders, the 275 ft (83.8 m) British Queen, was awaiting completion of her machinery and, anxious not to be beaten, her owners chartered the 320 ihp Sirius. As advertised, this little ship sailed from Cork for New York on 4 April 1838, carrying 40 passengers.

The Great Western had arrived at Bristol two days earlier, having suffered an engine room fire in which Brunel himself was injured. Delayed a further day by a gale, her passenger list reduced to just seven because of the mishap, she sailed on 8 April. Both ships used sail to assist their speed but the more powerful Great Western, despite stoppages for small repairs and adjustments, slowly overhauled her rival. However, the Sirius, with its bunkers empty, arrived at New York at about midday on 23 April 1838, the Great Western just three hours behind having covered 250 miles more, and at an average speed of 8.75 knots com-

BRUNEL'S GREAT SHIPS

pared with *Sirius*'s 6.70 knots. Although the chief engineer was lost in a further on-board accident, the *Great Western* sailed again on 7 May with 68 passengers and a cargo of cotton.

Noting the likely regular service offered by steam propulsion, the British Admiralty invited tenders for the Atlantic mail contract. Unfortunately for the GWS Co. its bid was beaten by that of Samuel Cunard and, already having difficulties with an intransigent Bristol Docks Board, it gradually transferred operations to Liverpool.

Although making five or six voyages annually, the *Great Western* was soon outdated. Sold in 1847 for further service, she was scrapped in 1856. She had been joined, in 1845, by the *Great Britain*. Using his railway engineering experience, Brunel built her of iron. In 1840, he had hired the Screw Propeller Company's trials demonstrator *Archimedes* to evaluate the possibilities of screw propulsion, which he also adopted.

Also built at Bristol, the *Great Britain*'s 322 ft (98.1 m) hull was the largest that could be eased from the basin, and she could accommodate 360 passengers and 1,000 tons of cargo. Trials commenced in July 1845, resulting in drastic modification of the propeller and a reduction in rig from six masts to five.

Hardly into her career, she ran hard aground on the Irish coast in September 1846. The cost of the eleven months' salvage operation and subsequent repair broke the company, which was wound up in 1847.

Bought cheaply and converted to, primarily, a cargo carrier, the *Great Britain* traded until 1876 when outmoded, she was converted to a pure sailing ship. In 1886 she was partially dismasted rounding the Horn and made for the Falklands. Beyond economical repair, she was sold locally and languished as a store for wool until salvaged in 1970 and returned to Bristol for restoration.

'The Great Eastern' – a great ship

In 1852, Brunel joined John Scott Russell in the conception of a giant ship for the Eastern Steam Navigation Company, which wanted to compete with P&O, which had just scooped the far-eastern mail contract. Their projected 692 ft (210.9 m), 19,000-tonner was four times the size of anything yet built and, with no single system powerful enough to drive her, she acquired both paddle and

propeller propulsion. Construction costs were hugely under-estimated. The size of the machinery caused many expensive failures in manufacture. Her hull, built for sideways launching into the Thames at Russell's Millwall yard, refused to move. Worn out by worry, his health broken, Brunel finally got the ship, named *Great Eastern*, waterborne on 31 January 1859.

Grossly over budget, she was sold to a new concern, the Great Ship Company, who fitted her out opulently for 4,000 passengers. She had six masts and five funnels, could carry 6,000 tons of cargo and, on military service, 10,000 troops.

On 9 December 1859, having commenced her trials, the ship suffered a serious boiler explosion, which killed five of her crew. Brunel, already incapacitated by a stroke, was devastated, and died on the 15th, aged just 53 years.

His monstrous creation was unable to make a commercial profit until, in 1864, when sold for conversion to a cable layer. The ship's size enabled her to load some 2,700 miles of submarine telegraph cable and she successfully laid four cables across the Atlantic and another between Aden and India.

Again obsolete, she was sold in 1874 as an exhibition ship and then sold again, this time for scrap, in 1888. Beached at Liverpool, she proved almost beyond the demolition methods of the time, virtually bankrupting a further company.

Above: Impressive rather than elegant, the *Great Eastern* was conceived on a scale that pushed available technology to the very limit. As a 'one-off' she was unable to fit into any trade.

TRANSITIONAL STEAM CARGO SHIPS

Right: Fresh Wharf, Billingsgate, seen in about 1900. Ships of the day were small enough to use rivers to penetrate to the heart of major cities. The bustling scene contrasts with the sad ditch that the Thames has become today.

AS WITH WARSHIPS, early powered cargo vessels were essentially sailing ships with added auxiliary power. Rig was simplified to that of a brigantine or a barquentine but the long, narrow sailing-ship hull was retained. This tended also to be deep with respect to its beam, resulting in a tenderness when in the loaded condition which accorded badly with some types of bulk cargo. Again, like pure sailing vessels, they were equipped with only vestigial (and flimsy) superstructure on a flush-decked hull. Unlike sailing ships, however, they could now be driven into wind and sea, with the result that many suffered damage and casualties, or were simply overwhelmed, by heavy seas sweeping the upper deck.

Sailing ships were usually single-hold vessels, their interior a large space undivided by transverse bulkheads, although often featuring a tweendeck. Once badly holed, there was little to keep such ships afloat. Their hatches were small, necessitating an army of dockers to manhandle and stow cargo in the wings. Stowage, especially for such as sawn timber, was encumbered by the ship's structure and numerous internal supporting pillars. In the sailing age, passages were long and labour was cheap, so time spent alongside was of comparatively little

consequence. With the greater investment represented by steamships, however, there came more pressure for this to change.

Power extended its influence in parallel with iron displacing wood as the principal material of construction, with the result that size grew rapidly. Even before 1860 the industry had the example of Brunel's 680 ft (207.3 m) *Great Eastern* to illustrate possibilities, but she remained freakish, with the typical 1870 cargo ship, the backbone of the British merchant marine, still of only 220 × 28 ft (61 × 8.5 m). On a gross registered tonnage (grt) of about 750, she could lift some 1,100 deadweight tons of cargo. Machinery comprised a simple, two-cylinder compound engine taking steam from a boiler at about 65 lb psi pressure. In port, this boiler would be shut down, with steam for cargo winches, domestic purposes, etc., being drawn from an auxiliary, or 'donkey', boiler. Safety features had begun to make their appearance with watertight transverse bulkheads, double bottoms and, from 1876, load lines.

Uncomplicated vessels such as these involved an initial capital outlay of some £14,000 and, under a succession of owners, would often go on to give 50

years of service. Improving techniques and the economies of size saw the average length of traders grow to 290 ft (88.4 m) by 1885, and to 320 ft (97.5 m) by 1900.

An experimental steel ship had been built by Laird's of Birkenhead as early as 1865 but, even as late as 1890, only one ship in five was of mild steel, which lacked the longevity of iron but which was 25 per cent stronger. Its obvious advantages saw it make rapid progress, however and, by 1910, three quarters of the fleet were steel-built.

Superstructures grew slowly to an open bridge spanning an amidships house that gave some cramped accommodation for the engineers while, importantly, elevating skylights and access to machinery spaces, previously vulnerable to water entry. Traditional berthing patterns were maintained, with the deck officers and master quartered aft, and the remainder in the forecastle. Here, the boatswain and the carpenter, seamen, firemen, cook and lamp trimmer shared quarters with spare cargo gear and, often, the chain cable. Surfaces were of painted metal and drying facilities were limited to finding a warm corner of the machinery space by the good offices of the engineers. Lighting was by oil lamp. A crew of 32 was shipped on a vessel that, today, would equate in size to a small coaster with a crew of four.

Varying loads and improving designs

Safety was enhanced by increasing freeboard forward and aft through the introduction of raised forecastle and poop. This also improved accommodation and, on some designs, increased cargo space by the extension of the poop forward to the bridge structure. This was the basis for the popular 'raised quarterdecker', whose forward well was left to compensate for a normal tendency to trim by the head.

The majority of ships operated on the tramp market, accepting cargoes and charters as available. Loads could vary widely from, say, bulk ores and concentrates that were very dense and occupied little volume, to such as baled esparto grass, so light that full holds and a towering deck cargo would not take her to her marks. 'Breakbulk' cargoes of varying types or for more than one destination were best suited to ships with tweendecks.

The period 1890–1910 was the heyday for patent designs such as arcform, corrugated sides, turret and trunk deckers, all taking advantage of the measurement rules to improve self-trimming of 'difficult' bulk cargoes, to maximise cargo deadweight for a given net, i.e. taxable, tonnage, and to minimise that tonnage itself.

By 1890 the triple expansion engine and new boilers allowed owners to invest in a little reserve power to further take advantage of the spot market.

LIFE ON AN EARLY CARGO STEAMER

Main picture: Every image of dockside activity is a reminder of how labour-intensive the shipping industry was, providing employment for whole communities.

Below: Portsmouth's Camber in about 1900. Wooden barrels were required in huge numbers, supporting a thriving cooperage industry.

AN 1835 ACT DEFINED a ship as being adequately manned with one crew member per 20 tons of her registered tonnage, but this was abandoned in 1849 with the repeal of the Navigation Acts. Manning levels were then much at the whim of the owner, and many ships were badly undermanned.

Signing-on, for what could be a five-month round trip, was either aboard or in the shipping office. A Board of Trade representative read out the articles that were about to be signed. Fines of 5 shillings (25p) could be levied for bringing aboard 'spirituous liquors' or offensive weapons, or for striking anybody. A first drunkenness offence also attracted a 5 shilling fine, a second offence 10 shillings (50p). This at a time when an able-bodied seaman (AB) earned £3 10s (£3.50) monthly and an ordinary seaman (OS) just £1.

An AB's discharge book should prove experience of at least four years 'before the mast' and an ability to 'hand, reef and steer', which is to say to set, to take in and to secure sails and, in a blow, to reef them. Ordinary seamen claimed no skills.

Seamen and firemen signed-on separately, claimed a month's advance and settled into the forecastle. This was divided axially, the two groups having little contact. Each man had a bunk with a straw mattress ('donkey's breakfast') and a small locker. Hard wooden forms and a table that lowered from the deckhead completed the furnishings. Space was too constricted for sea chests, most men preferring to work out of kit bags.

Food in port attracted little complaint, but it deteriorated rapidly after a few weeks at sea. Regulation entitlement, at the outset at least, was a daily issue of 1lb of bread and about 1 ½lb (0.7 kg) of beef or pork. Tinned or pickled meat was served after a few days. Preserved and/or compressed vegetables made up the ingredients for meals whose appeal was very much at the mercy of the cook. Breakfast, particularly, required a seasoned digestive system, with Irish stew recommended for Mondays and 'bread scowse' for Thursdays. Water was precious, each man having a daily entitlement of three quarts (about four litres) for all purposes.

The cook, together with the bosun, carpenter and sailmaker worked days, the remainder being

divided between port and starboard watches. Especially smart ABs were appointed quartermasters who, for an extra £1 on their wages each way, were responsible for steering. Luxuries such as steam- or hydraulically-powered steering were still unknown in small ships and it was demanding work that required two men on the wheel in heavy weather. On an open bridge, a two-hour 'trick' at the wheel taxed the resources of the best.

Seamen's duties and pastimes

The junior hand of each watch, termed 'Peggy', collected duties like taking meals forward from the amidships galley, checking the reading of the patent log at the end of each watch (with the aid of a bull's eye lantern) and, on demand, heating coffee for the officer of the watch. For this, no appliance was provided and, with the galley shut down for the night, it involved clambering down into the stokehold for a shovelful of live coals.

All planked decks – fo'c's'le (fore-castle) head , well deck, upper bridgedeck and afterdeck – were scrubbed at daybreak (brooms held vertically, bristles pointing away from the sweeper!). On a 'pukka' ship, regular 'bible classes' were held, with the watch on its knees holystoning the wood to whiteness. Accommodation was scrubbed out conventionally, using a powerful caustic alkaline solution known universally as 'sujee'. Brass was burnished with a mixture of oil and brickdust.

Coal trimmers were recruited from what was seen to be the lowest social class, their disagreeable work often having to be shared by delegated seamen. The blackness of coal bunkers in the heat of the tropics was a terrible place, the men slaking their thirst from a bucket of oatmeal water upon which floated a rime of coal dust.

In contrast to the daily grind were the social bonds that developed between the crew, of whom one in six would likely be foreign. Many were surprisingly literate and read avidly. Others indulged in painstaking hobbies, endless spinning of yarns or sing-songs from the current music hall repertoire:

'You would gaze upon the spotted duff
With eager longing eye,
And the steam from orf the winders you would lick … '

Above: Refrigeration was successfully introduced in ships about 1880. As Britain produced insufficient meat for her burgeoning population, this opened a huge new trade with Australasia and Argentina, which produced it cheaply.

THE EMIGRANT TRADE

Above: Behind these European Jewish immigrants of about 1920 New York looms like the promised land. From this point on, however, their future was their own responsibility.

temperature, dampness and bad weather. For sailing ships, 'fast' was a relative term, with masters taking extended tracks to follow the wind. Twenty days, for instance, was the average between Liverpool and New York. Not surprisingly, mortality rates could be shocking, especially among infants and children. In at least one recorded case it exceeded 12 per cent, yet conditions aboard were in excess of those required by law.

Passages did not come cheaply. An average transatlantic clipper could accommodate 10 to 30 cabin passengers, 20 intermediate and 800 to 1,000 steerage passengers. First class tickets were typically £30 sterling, intermediate £8 and steerage £5 (or more if one required basic comforts, care of the steward). On average figures it will be apparent that at least 80 per cent of passenger revenue derived from steerage, mostly emigrants.

Numbers became considerable. Between 1783 and 1847 over one million emigrated to the United States yet, in 1854 alone, this figure had become 200,000. In the same year, over 40,000 went to Australia. Only in 1856 did the first steamship company, Inman, tap this new source of income. Unfortunately it was customary to lease spaces aboard to specialists in this trade, who employed agents to provide the maximum numbers to fill them.

Rights of the steerage passenger

For the most part, emigrants were rustic and unschooled. In unfamiliar surroundings, where the best berths had to be claimed and retained, where cooking facilities had to be shared, the atmosphere was soon ripe for violence. It was not uncommon for ship's officers and crew to have to contain a disturbance, even to the show of firearms.

In early days steerage passengers supplied their own bedding, their food and the means with which to cook it. Improvements by the White Star company encouraged the British government to introduce scales for minimum levels of uncooked food, of which 30 days' supply had to be carried. Supervised by the First Mate, food was then issued on a weekly basis with passengers, ill-supplied with receptacles, trying to cope with provisions from biscuit to tea, salt beef to potatoes.

By the end of the nineteenth century matters begun to improve. Married couples might travel together but, otherwise, sexes were segregated,

THE END OF THE EIGHTEENTH century saw both Australia and the United States emerge as virtual 'promised lands' for the hopefuls and the poverty-stricken of Europe. Owners of fast sailing ships found that there was good profit in packing-in would-be emigrants and making the maximum number of voyages. 'Steerage' (as opposed to 'cabin') passengers were crammed into communal spaces that rapidly became infested and unhygienic. Infectious illness was rife, worsened by extremes of

Left: Immigration buildings at New York's Ellis Island, gateway or barrier between the immigrant and a new life. Alongside are the tenders which shuttled human cargoes between ship and shore.

men sleeping 16 to a dormitory compartment. All areas were cleared daily for cleaning, subject to inspection. The compulsory provision of a ship's doctor, usually with permanent medical facilities, was well in excess of what most emigrants had previously experienced and it became common for women to embark in the final stages of pregnancy in the hope that the delivery would be on board.

As any would-be citizen unacceptable to US Immigration had to be returned at the company's expense, it behove the latter to take precautions. Many British companies simply refused to accept steerage passengers from Central Europe. The Germans, with an eye to business, assembled them 24 hours prior to sailing in a purpose-built facility where they were given a shower and a physical examination while their luggage was fumigated.

Successive British Merchant Shipping Acts tightened-up definitions and the rights of passengers of limited means.

A steerage passenger remained other than a cabin passenger, the latter now having to enjoy at least 36 square feet (3.3 square metres) allocated exclusively and pay at least £25 for a prescribed ticket (or at least the equivalent of £3.25 for each 1,000 miles of the voyage). An 'emigrant ship' had to carry at least 50 steerage-class passengers (or more than one to each 20 tons for a steamship, or 33 tons for a sailing vessel).

Hygiene facilities remained sparse. Five washbasins and one bath had to be provided in separate facilities for every 100 males and females. A washing trough was added for every 100 women, but a similar facility had to be shared by 200 men.

Steerage passengers could be accommodated on a single deck below the waterline but they must have been relieved to know that cattle, if carried, could not be accommodated either directly above or below them! Five square feet of open promenade space per steerage passenger was mandatory, increased to eight if it had to be shared with the cattle, which had to be cordoned off.

Each was allowed a gallon of water daily and, on pain of a £2 fine, the Master was obliged to inform passengers of their legally-entitled scale of provisions. In terms of weight this was some 5 per cent better than that prescribed for men of the Royal Navy!

Below: In the Great Assembly Hall at Ellis Island, immigrants are seen in 1911 awaiting processing. Their registration by ill-educated Immigration Officers resulted in American surnames being spelled with many odd variations.

MARINE LEGISLATION – RIGHTS AND OBLIGATIONS

RESPONSIBLE SHIPOWNERS and shippers have always sought some form of insurance against damage and loss. Regularisation of cover probably began with meetings, or 'clubs', of owners as early as the sixteenth century, starting in the Levant and spreading westward. Such clubs which, from the time of the Restoration, included Lloyd's in London, provided a service in establishing lists of reputable ships. Definition of scales of cover, however, meant also developing ground rules for the precise measurement of ships, the size of scantlings, provision of gear, etc. From such beginnings grew the world's great classification societies.

There remained, also a mass of ships and owners operating outside the 'Rules' which, despite their name, were backed by very little actual legislation. Cargo could be shipped more cheaply in unregulated bottoms, even more cheaply if they were overloaded. By the mid nineteenth century the loss rate of ships and human life was what, today, would seem unbelievable. Today's 'rust buckets' had their equivalent in the many 'coffin ships' of the period, and it was to eliminate these that the Liberal Member of Parliament, Samuel Plimsoll, launched his crusade in the early 1870s. His passion was vented in parliamentary speeches and behaviour best described as intemporate, reaching a crescendo when the government withdrew a bill on the subject. He won much public support, however, for homes across the land had first hand knowledge of loss and bereavement.

His continued agitation resulted in the establishment of a Royal Commission, which reported to parliament in 1874 on the subject of overloading. From this, the Load Line Bill emerged as law, with all ships having to be measured and marked with what was popularly known as a Plimsoll Line. This comprised a circle, placed amidships on either side, with a horizontal 'load line' passing through its centre, and bounded by scales showing the limits to which the waterline might be set for various seasons and zones, both for salt and for fresh water.

Maritime Acts

Between 1825 and 1849 the ancient Navigation Acts were repealed, exposing British shipping to greater competition. Its regulation was the responsibility of what, from 1854, was known as the Marine Department of the Board of Trade. This body's remit was very wide and included, inter alia, both the welfare and conditions for seamen and their obligations to their employers. The principal instrument through which the Board exercised its authority was the extensive legislation lumped under the heading of the Merchant Shipping Act, which has been regularly updated ever since.

Thus, from 1851, officers and engineers responsible for British ships had to hold certificates of competence, issued by the Board following examination. An official ship's log book had to be maintained, written up as soon as possible after the events that it described. The practice of undermanning was addressed by making it compulsory for foreign-going steamships exceeding 700 grt to

Below: The large crews of warships beween the wars were always available to keep the ship in top order. On a fine day in 1937 Jack has turned deck cleaning into an enjoyable occupation.

Left: It was P & O's practice to employ European officers and Indians from the sub-continent (known as 'lascars') as more cheaply-paid crews. The complexities of this 1930 fire drill reminds us of the problems posed by language differences.

Below: Board of Trade regulations demanded that crews, particularly those of passenger liners, be proficient in the launch and handling of lifeboats. Instruction is here being given aboard the Orient liner *Orford* during the 1930s.

have at least six deck hands in addition to the Master and two mates.

Except for small vessels engaged in the coastal trade, seamen could be supplied and procured only through agents licensed by the Board. All had to sign an agreement with the Master, in the presence of a Marine Superintendent. Thereafter, until signed off, they were bound by a code of discipline where, for instance, desertion or refusal to work were felonies. On the other hand, a Master was duty bound to hear a seaman's complaint, while that from three or more men had to be investigated officially. Seamen discharged abroad, or shipwrecked, had to be properly supported and repatriated.

Medical stores had to be carried on a prescribed scale, accompanied by a certified practitioner if more than 100 people were aboard. Injuries sustained in the service of the ship had to be attended at the owner's expense.

Ashore, seamen's lodging houses, long known for overcharging and exploitation, could be

inspected and licensed by local authorities, but this empowerment was still not backed by obligation.

Aboard any ship carrying passengers (i.e. 'persons other than the Master and crew, the owner, his family and servants') a certificate had to be displayed, with penalties for carrying excess numbers. A fine of £100 could be imposed for weighting a safety valve beyond its survey limits.

Interestingly, in those pre-*Titanic* days, foreign-going passenger ships of any size over 10,000 grt were required to carry only 16 lifeboats under davits. Their stipulated capacity was to be 5,500 cubic feet, sufficient to accommodate only 550 'statute adults'. Any shortfall was to be made up by such as collapsible boats and liferafts 'provided ... that no ship of this class be required to carry more boats or rafts than would furnish sufficient accommodation for all persons on board'. As these would be distributed along both sides, and the boats on the high side of a heavily-listing liner would not be able to be launched, this requirement was still deficient.

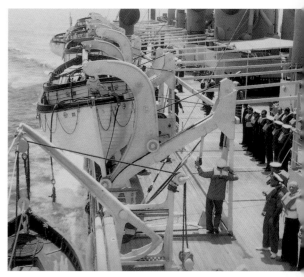

THE LATER DEVELOPMENT OF THE MERCANTILE STEAM ENGINE

Right: The Hon. Charles Parsons built the 100-foot *Turbinia* as a testbed for his steam turbine. She could make 34½ knots and famously did so at the Diamond Jubilee Fleet Review.

Below: At the battle of the Falklands, 8 December 1914, the cruiser *Kent* went in pursuit of the German *Nürnberg*. *Kent*, a poor steamer, could rarely attain her designed 23 knots but on this day was stoked to full speed for over eight hours, achieving over 24 knots.

AN EARLIER SECTION dealt with developments up to the side-lever engine which, despite its space-saving design, had the drawback of short connecting rods. In the course of their cycle these swept a large angle, which imposed heavy cyclic loads on the fixed structure, which had to be made heavier to cope. A refinement, with open-topped cylinders, allowed for an increase in rod length, but a better alternative was to allow the whole cylinder and piston assembly to oscillate, enabling the connecting rod to bear onto the crankshaft in a continuous straight line.

This 'oscillating engine', stemming from Maudslay's original patent of 1827, developed to considerable size and complexity. A large, but by no means the largest, example powered the paddle machinery for Brunel's 1858 *Great Eastern*. This engineer's difficulties in building his monstrous one-off are exemplified by this machinery's four cylinders of 6.17 ft (1,880 mm) diameter, with pistons having a travel of 14 ft (4,267 mm), the whole engine weighing 836 tons and developing 3,400 ihp.

Huge sizes resulted from low steam pressures. Boilers on seagoing ships ran on seawater and could

rarely better 25 psi. In 1860, Hall's 'surface condenser' allowed fresh water to be used in a closed cycle and, freed from excessive deposits and corrosion, boiler design could be improved.

Higher pressures were, however, not compatible with box-shaped boilers and cylindrical types, notably the Scotch boiler, came into use about 1870, giving eventual service until World War II. Early examples could deliver steam at 60 psi, but gradual improvement succeeded in pushing this to beyond 300 psi. With cylinders that were basically horizontal, Scotch boilers could be fired from either end and the water case, occupying the upper segment, was penetrated by the heating tubes. Once filled with water, it was a heavy item which needed to be supported by the main structure of the ship.

Higher pressure steam permitted 'compounding'. Earlier two-cylinder engines had both cylinders powered from a common steam source, both operating at the same pressure. In contrast, the compound engine injected steam into the primary cylinder only. Once expanded in driving down the primary piston, the steam exhausted into the secondary cylinder, to be further expanded to near atmospheric pressure in driving the secondary piston. In order to match the thrust produced by the two piston rods, it was necessary to make the secondary cylinder and piston of larger diameter than the primary.

Paddles were slow-turning devices, well suited to early forms of machinery. The marine propeller, however, required higher shaft speeds to operate efficiently. Warship machinery, often to be overlaid by a protective deck, or continuous gundeck, required to be of low profile, favouring horizontal, or near-horizontal, cylinders. These, however, suffered from out-of-balance forces which militated against higher speeds, resulting in the inevitable adoption of vertical ('cathedral') engines.

Oil burning and steam turbines

In order to extract the maximum power from higher pressure steam, secondary cylinders became inconveniently large in diameter, resulting in the low-pressure stage often being divided into two identical cylinders. This, in 1880, led to the dubious development of 'triple expansion'. With ever-more efficient boilers this cycle was repeated, i.e. the adoption of a two-cylinder tertiary stage leading to the introduction of 'quadruple expansion'. Engines of this size were, however, suitable only for larger ships.

During the 1890s the water-tube boiler made its appearance. It reversed the earlier arrangement by circulating water through banks of pipes set on the combustion chamber. This was more efficient and the boilers themselves were much lighter as they contained less water. To increase coal combustion rate, low pressure air could be injected into the furnaces, or the whole boiler room sealed and operated at higher than ambient pressure. This increased air flow was known as 'forced draught'.

From about 1890 experiments began with the burning of oil in place of coal. Being a solid, coal had to be accommodated in what was prime space aboard. Huge crews of stokers and trimmers were required, while 'coaling ship' was a frequent and disagreeable chore. Oil could simply be pumped aboard and around the ship, bunkers thus using odd-shaped spaces that, previously would have been void. In this area, warship practice led the way, some ships having transitional coal or oil firing.

In 1896 the marine engineering world was surprised by the steam turbine, in the form of Charles

Parsons' demonstrator *Turbinia*. The great naval reformer Admiral 'Jackie' Fisher, immediately recognised its value to the navy and, following brief experiment on smaller ships, used this machinery in his revolutionary *Dreadnought*.

Quiet, compact and vibration-free, the steam tubine was quickly adopted for high speed passenger ships. A disadvantage lay in its high output speed, necessitating complex gearing, and the requirement for a separate reversing turbine.

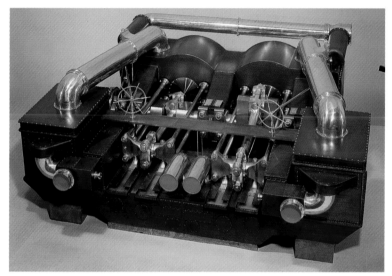

Above: Water tube boilers, introduced by the French in the 1870s, permitted more compact design, higher steam pressures and less weight, due to a smaller quantity of water in the system.

Above left: Completed in 1869, HMS *Monarch* was the Royal Navy's first sea-going turret ship, and directly comparable with the ill-fated Captain that followed a year later. Her return connecting rod engines, of 7840 ihp, made her the fastest battleship of the day at 14.9 knots.

Left: Brunel's *Great Eastern* had separate machinery for paddles and propeller. Her 58-foot diameter paddles were driven from four oscillating cylinders, each 74 inches diameter and 14-foot stroke, taking steam at 30 psi.

THE COASTAL TRADE

Main picture:
London's power
stations consumed
millions of tons of
Geordie coal, giving
employment to fleets
of colliers. Here
three of Cory's ships
lay on a tier down-
river, awaiting
discharge berths.

Below: Displaced one-
by-one by road and
rail traffic, companies
such as Clyde
Shipping, Tyne Tees
and Coast Lines once
ran fast passenger
and cargo services
that connected major
British ports.

BEFORE THEY WERE DISPLACED by the railways and door-to-door road transport, coasters were the major means of goods distribution. They fetched and carried cargoes for deep-sea ships in the great ports. From tiny Welsh inlets they loaded slate to roof the houses of fast-expanding cities. Fertilisers, cattlefeeds and grain moved in and out of muddy East Anglian creeks. From snug West Country harbours china clay for the Potteries. Livestock from Ireland. Raw steel products from the mills of Middlesbrough and Swansea. Cured herrings from East Scottish ports. Passenger services connecting the rivers Thames and Tyne, the Mersey, Clyde and the Forth. Above all, there was coal. Coal for ten million hearths and kitchens, coal for gas works, coal to fuel the machinery of a burgeoning industrial nation.

Figures for 1728 showed over 6,800 entries by coastal craft into the Port of London, over three-quarters of the port's total movements. Within 70 years this had soared to nearly 12,000. The tideway was unregulated and choked, leading directly to the construction of the great enclosed docks systems.

Between 1863 and 1913 the population of Great Britain almost doubled, 50 per cent of it set-tling within 15 miles of a port. Small wonder that 60 per cent of coastal movements were of coal.

Sailing coasters, because of their economy, lingered on in business until World War II but their replacement had begun a century earlier when, in 1841, the 214 grt *Bedlington* became the first screw collier, although employed only to move cargoes from the Tyne to larger ships laying in nearby Blyth. The east coast trade to London began with the powered, barque-rigged *QED* in 1844 and, in 1852, came the *John Bowes*, the first such with sail as an auxiliary to steam. Her nine knots permitted a passage in under 48 hours and a large hatch for the times and unobstructed hold allowed discharge inside 24 hours. She could do the work of two sailing brigs.

Coasters, like larger merchantmen, began their evolution from sailing ships with amidships machinery, raised forecastle and bridgedeck. With the twentieth century, however, the engines-aft, and raised quarterdeck became almost standard. Lacking a long shaft tunnel and gaining the prime amidships space, these could carry more within the same dimensions. The well deck forward prevented trimming by the head in the loaded condition.

A particular, and distinctive, type of raised quarterdecker was the London 'flatiron' collier. These were built with every possible fitting recessed, and with folding funnels, masts and even davits, to minimise airdraught in order to proceed up river to serve power stations as far as Putney, necessitating 'shooting' up to 16 fixed bridges.

Life on a 1920s' coaster

The availability of cheap coal resulted in British owners long neglecting the threat posed by the Continental diesel coaster, typified by the Dutch schuyt. With a tiny machinery space, half the crew strength and of shallow draught, these craft made rapid inroads into the British coastal trade, which was open to foreign-flagged ships. They, too, had masts that lowered to proceed up canals and rivers, and were able to operate over the full range of the British Home Trade Limits, which stretched from Brest to the Elbe River.

Life on British coasters in their 'twenties heyday was tough but companionable. Crew and firemen bunked and lived together in the forecastle, lit by paraffin lamps and heated by a single 'bogey' stove. Each provided his own bedding (a mattress tick and fresh straw), eating and cooking utensils – and food. This was cooked in the galley, aft, and was invariably cold by the time that it found its way forward and, in heavy weather, when the forward well deck was usually awash, could even be lost altogether.

Machinery drained down into a common hot water tank adjacent to the condenser, allowing a spot of clothes washing ('dhobying') or even a washdown oneself. 'Baths' however, were usually taken in the crew's WC, a four-by-four compartment immediately abaft the forecastle, by emptying the remains of a bucket of cold water over one's head to rinse off a soapy body, the water draining through the scuppers.

Many coasters still lacked an enclosed wheelhouse. On the entirely open bridge the sole shelter for the watch and the steersman was a canvas 'dodger' rigged on a taut wire across the bridge front. The wheel itself was very heavy in poor weather, sometimes necessitating a second hand. There was a steam steering engine but, for economy reasons, this was unpowered at sea.

A seaman's wages (paid weekly in the coastal trade, monthly for deep sea voyages) were about £2 sterling per week. If the ship was drydocked, he was often given the option of being paid off or working aboard for half-pay. This could involve anything from chipping and painting while sitting on a plank over a sheer drop to the task of entering the main ballast tanks (compartmented and with a 2 ft 6 in/760 mm headroom) with a candle and a bucket to ladle out the noxious muddy sediment that collected over time.

Above: Traditional British steam coasters could not compete with the diesel-propelled Dutch Schuyt. Known as 'paragraph ships', their design reduced chargeable tonnage and crew size.

MERCHANT SHIP DEVELOPMENT

Below: Although engaged primarily in the coal trade Cory ships, like many others, were available on the spot market for other cargoes mainly between the home trade limited of the Elbe to Brest. Cargo derricks, as carried here, are not required to handle bulk coal.

Opposite right: Royal Mail liners serving South America were designed to carry large refrigerated cargoes in addition to passengers. The 1926-built *Alcantara* (shown here) and *Asturias* unusually changed from diesel to steam propulsion in 1934 to improve their speed.

CERTAIN COMMODITIES require great care in stowage and, in time, gave rise to specialist ship types. In the era when steam was still the exception, such ships had not been developed and preparations to receive cargo could be elaborate in order to avoid subsequent damage, insurance claims or hazard to the ship itself.

The major British export was still coal which, in large quantities and over a considerable length of voyage, can be dangerous stuff. Freshly mined and loaded wet, it absorbs both oxygen and moisture, which combine to form unstable peroxides. These then break down again in exothermic, or heat-producing, reactions which readily cause spontaneous combustion. Fires could smoulder for weeks deep down in a cargo and, on wooden ships, could cause immense structural damage and even total loss.

Some types of coal, particularly Welsh, were noted for giving off explosive gases which, in pre-electric days of unguarded lanterns, frequently caused spectacular accidents. Ventilation at sea posed the problem that a flow of air flow that cleared accummulations of methane would also provide the oxygen necessary to convert a smouldering cargo fire to incandescence. Small coal, known as 'duff', was particularly dangerous in being liable to shift. Careful trimming was required to ensure that any tweendeck spaces were filled and, as ships tended to be loaded from a single point, they had to be moved regularly to ensure an even distribution of large and small coal, while maintaining correct trim and draught.

Familiarity, nonetheless, bred contempt and, in the period 1875–77, about 70 British ships with coal cargoes were lost each year, a number which increased to a staggering 100 annually by 1881–83.

Grain and pulses in bulk behave very much like a liquid and, again, regulation preparations had to be thorough to prevent shifting. Main hold spaces had to be divided up by 'shifting boards', supported by temporary wooden stanchions, and thorough trimming was required to ensure that the spaces between the frames and stringers were filled. Feeder trunks, resembling bulk oil practice, could ensure full holds without excessive free surface, but it was more usual to overlay loose grain with a temporary timber platform supporting several layers of grain in bags.

Often pressured by penny-pinching owners, officers were tempted to minimise such precautions. Even in 1896, for instance, elevators at the American Gulf port of Galveston could meter and load cargo at a rate of 700 tons per hour. A then-average cargo ship of about 3,000 tons deadweight capacity could load probably only 2,200 tons of such a low-density commodity so could be ready for sea in a forenoon. Bagging-up took time and, in any case, sacks cost ten pence (now about 4p) each.

Although equipped with a powerful refrigerating plant, a ship in the carcass meat trade would still need to carry general cargoes outward and require significant preparation for the return load. All shell plating and structural members were overlaid with zinc sheet over wood, covered by 6 in (150 mm) of lump charcoal retained by battens. The latter were spaced so that cold air could circulate within, fed from a sequence of overhead timber ducts radiating from a 'snow box'. This latter feature was fed directly from the refrigerating plant room and, every four hours, the disagreeable task for a junior engineer was to enter these ducts to clean them of hoar deposits.

Pouring oil on troubled waters

Another low-density cargo was sawn timber from the upper Baltic. To carry a full load, a deck cargo was required and while, in winter months, the height of this was limited by law to 3 ft (915 mm) it was, in summer, left to the discretion of the master. Gambling on fine weather, some would stow up to 11 ft (3.3 m) in the well decks.

In heavy weather, if loose water was taken aboard, this mass of cargo, although restrained by chains tensioned by bottle screws, would try to float, quickly loosening its fastenings. As the steering chains passed along the deck edge on either side of the after well deck, they could easily be jammed by such an occurrence, often with fatal results for the ship.

The North Sea, while capable of vile behaviour, is quite shallow and some old time masters of low-powered early steamers, on meeting exceptionally bad conditions, would unshackle both heavy anchor cables and trail 100 fathoms or so (say 200 m) of each along the bottom. With plenty of searoom, a ship would thus ride comfortably head to wind with a slow drift. To reduce the strength of a breaking sea, hoses were rigged down the hawse holes and crew members on the forecastle would pour colza oil through them onto the surface. It is recorded that crossing Sunderland bar in a gale was a 'four-gallon job'!

THE ORIGINS OF SOME GREAT PASSENGER COMPANIES

AS WE WILL SEE below, the North Atlantic mail contract was a major influence behind the Cunard and White Star lines and the subsequent great international rivalries on this route. Other companies, however, had similar origins. It was a privilege to prefix one's ships 'RMS', or Royal Mail Steamer, while the implicit image of reliability was attractive to prospective passengers.

One such concern had its modest beginnings in 1815, when Brodie McGhee Willcox began business as a shipbroker in the City of London. Within ten years his one-time office boy, Arthur Anderson, had become his partner in a joint interest in small sailing ships trading to Spain and Portugal. In the early 1830s they acquired a pair of small steamships, of which one was chartered to the Dublin & London Steam Packet Company, which had common interests in the Iberian peninsula.

Following an open competition in 1837, they were jointly successful in gaining the Government mail contact to the Peninsula. For £26,000 per annum (soon reduced by the Government to £20,500) the newly-styled Peninsula Company undertook to provide a weekly service.

They also took the India mail as far as Gibraltar, from whence it travelled to Alexandria in the Indian Government's ships, was then hauled overland to Suez and, thence, transported to its destination by the East India Company. To speed matters, the Government again tried open competition, which the company again won. For £34,000 per annum the renamed Peninsula & Oriental Steam Navigation Company would carry mail and Admiralty packages and, at concessionary rates, Service officers. In 1840 the 1,600-ton *Oriental* and 1,540-ton *Great Liverpool* opened the service to Alexandria, with the 1,800-ton *Hindostan* serving the onward leg from Suez to India and Ceylon (Sri Lanka). In 1845, when its fleet comprised 14 ships, P&O won the onward mail contract to the then Straits Settlements, Singapore and Hong Kong, their rate being barely half that charged by the East India Company.

Above: By the late 1890s, 80 per cent of shipping transiting the Suez Canal wore the British flag. In 1875 the British purchased the Egyptian interest in the waterway for £4 million. When this picture was taken the shares were generating that sum *per year.*

Right: Few artists evoked the sheer romance of ships better than Kenneth Shoesmith, depicting here one of the Highland-class passenger-cargo liners built for the Nelson Line, a subsidiary of the Royal Mail Line since 1913.

To discharge its responsibilities, the company needed to create coaling stations (90,000 tons in 14 separate locations), fresh water supplies, hotel facilities and repair yards. In 1859 the hideously uncomfortable or wildly romantic (depending upon one's point of view) overland route from Alexandria to Suez was eased by the commissioning of a rail link. Ten years later the Suez Canal was opened.

Since 1853 a service of sorts had been operated between Singapore and Sydney but, with the availability of the new canal, the company acquired new buildings suitable for through mail services – 16½ days to Bombay, 35½ to Melbourne and, later, 37½ to Shanghai. The convenience of the canal, the Post Office insisted, merited a cut in subsidy. When P&O refused to countenance this, officialdom required, for nearly two years, that mails be landed at Alexandria, travel overland, and be re-loaded by the ship at Suez!

A parallel experience was that of the appropriately-named Royal Mail Steam Packet Company which, in 1841, won the Government mail contract for the West Indies. For a handsome annual £240,000 the company dedicated its 14 ships to providing a fortnightly service on a time-consuming route which took in Corunna, Madeira, Barbados, St Vincent, Grenada, St Thomas, Port-au-Prince (Haiti), Santiago de Cuba, Port Royal (Jamaica) and Havana. From 1850 the company speeded up its service by 25 per cent and added a monthly call to Brazil. Five new ships were then added, the subsidy increasing to £270,000. Following lobbying and parliamentary action, this was reduced in 1874 to just £86,750! The service, later extended to the River Plate, was particularly difficult and seven of the company's ships, known for their powerful construction, were lost in the first decade of operations.

The Union Castle Line

The first regular mail contract to the Cape was agreed in 1857 by the Union Line. Founded five years previously as the Union Steam Collier Company, it had five ships with which, for a £30,000 annual subsidy, to guarantee a 37-day cycle to Capetown. On expiry, the contract was sought by Currie's Castle Line, founded in 1872. As a result the subsidy was cut to barely one fifth of its previous rate, and divided equally between the two companies on the understanding that the service would be speeded to 19 days.

The Union Line's 3,170-ton *Scot* was a good example of a transitional liner, with masts no longer crossed for sail. Launched in 1860, she was their largest ship, her dimensions of 500 × 54 ½ ft (152.4 × 16.6 m) being still of the very slender form typical of sailing ships. Although her best time from the Cape was under 14 days she was not up to the improved service and, in 1895, and at a mature age, she was lengthened by the insertion of a 54 ft (16.5 m) amidships section. Four years after the Castle Line's celebrated 1896 loss of the *Drummond Castle* on Ushant, the two rivals merged to form the Union Castle Line, synonymous with the South African service for the next three quarters of a century.

Below: Union-Castle operated magnificent motor ships on the Southampton-Cape Town service. The *Cape Town Castle*, a 27,000-tonner of 1937 here shows her characteristic Harland & Wolff stern.

Above: Off-season many passenger liners earned their keep by cruising. Here in unfamiliar near-Eastern surroundings is the 13,000-ton Cunarder *Lucania*, dating from the early 1890s.

THE BLUE RIBAND OF THE ATLANTIC

Below left: The powerfully modernist styling of the French liner *Normandie* of 1935 inspired a generation of poster images. One-time holder of the Atlantic Blue Riband, she was destroyed by fire in 1942.

Below right: An immense amount of literature, was produced by the shipping industry. Of typically high standard is this invitation to attend the launch of the *Mauretania* in 1906.

IN THE DAYS OF SAIL, the crossing of the Atlantic was not for the fainthearted, its duration depending as much on the weather as the qualities of ship and seamen. Power promised regularity (once reliability ceased to be a problem) and huge public interest was engendered by the unofficial 1838 race between Brunel's *Great Western* and the *Sirius*. Having set out four days earlier, the latter 'won' by a few hours, having crossed at an average speed of less than 9 knots. Their times, of 15 and 18 days respectively, were no better than those for good sailing passages but the British Admiralty, suitably encouraged, invited tenders for a Royal Mail contract. It was won by Samuel Cunard, a Canadian, who, with British partners, raised the capital to float a company bearing his name and to build four wooden paddle steamers. The first, *Britannia*, was of 1,150 tons and could carry 115 passengers. One of these, the novelist Charles Dickens, left a vivid, if unenthusiastic, account of life aboard.

Commencing their service in 1840, Cunard's ships linked Liverpool with Halifax, then Boston. The best of the original quartet, *Acadia*, recorded an average of 9.25 knots westbound and 10.75 knots eastbound. By 1848, his service prospering, Cunard had built six more ships, the *Asia* averaging 12.1 knots westbound.

The Americans then decided to compete, first with the Ocean Steam Navigation Company, which failed, then with the government-subsidised Collins Line. Four 3,000-tonners were built, their size enabling one, the *Arctic*, to make an eastbound crossing of 13.25 knots in 1852. Collins found that speed was ruinously expensive and, following the disastrous loss of two ships, his company folded.

Since 1848 the Blue Riband was accepted as a badge of distinction and the next to challenge Cunard's dominance was William Inman. His screw-propelled ships, notably the *City of Paris*, persuaded Cunard to change from paddlers but, by 1867, Inman had pushed the eastbound average to 14.7 knots.

In 1870 the newly-formed White Star Line entered the lists, its then-huge 3,700-ton *Oceanic* being quickly eclipsed by the *Germanic* and *Britannic* of 5,000 grt. Linking Queenstown with New York, these increased the east and westbound averages to 16 and 15.5 knots respectively in 1876–7. Cunard responded in 1884 with the *Umbria* and *Etruria* which averaged a very respectable 19.5 knots in either direction, but White Star and Inman then took advantage of government subsidy to build liners that could serve as fast auxiliary cruisers in wartime. Inman's *City of New York* and a second *City of Paris*, 10,500-tonners, pushed east and westbound averages to 20 and 21 knots but, in 1893, the company failed and passed into American hands. Cunard promptly struck back, with the *Lucania* making 21 knots in either direction.

Rise and demise of the Atlantic liner

Although hugely expensive, record-breakers attracted full and enthusiastic passenger lists and, much to international surprise, the German government then sought to improve national prestige by subsidising four vessels for Norddeutscher Lloyd (NDL). In 1898, their *Kaiser Wilhelm der Grosse* added about 0.8 knots in either direction.

The Germans, with various of their four ships, kept the record until 1907, successfully scooping a quarter of transatlantic passengers in the process.

Cunard again came back convincingly, this time with the impressive *Lusitania* and *Mauretania* which, from 1907, hiked both records to beyond 26 knots. It was a triumph for the new steam engine and the margin of the increase, (together with the disruption caused by World War I), saw the ships unchallenged for over 20 years. Germany, however, signalled her re-emergence as a maritime power in 1929–30 with the 51,600-ton *Bremen* and *Europa*.

Although the price of government subsidy was the merger of NDL with Hamburg Amerika (to form HAPAG Lloyd) the two modern-looking flyers took the crossings to 27.9 knots eastbound and 28.5 knots westbound.

Left: A sense of occasion well portrayed. The *Normandie* leaves her berth at Le Havre in May 1935 to take the Blue Riband with a time of 4 days, 3 hours and 2 minutes.

Below: The White Star Line's *Britannic* which, with the *Olympic*, was a sister to the *Titanic* served as a hospital ship until sunk in 1916.

Italy then successfully attracted much passenger traffic to southern Europe with the *Rex* and *Conte di Savoia*. Comparable in size with the earlier German pair, they had magnificent appointments and became great favourites although they increased the westbound average by only 0.4 knots. Their owner, the Italia Line, was formed by the compulsory merging of three other major companies.

France, never able to tolerate Italian supremacy, responded with the superb 79,000-ton one-off *Normandie*, 80 per cent subsidised it was propelled by turbo-electric machinery. Her 1935 achievement of 30 knots in either direction was, however, quickly displaced by the 31.7 knots eastbound and 31 knots westbound of the stately new British challenger, *Queen Mary*, for which Cunard and White Star had also to suffer amalgamation.

Again a world war ensured that the record stood for a considerable period but when, in 1953, the Americans came back with the functional *United States*, taking the honours with 35.6 knots eastbound and 34.5 knots westbound, it was almost irrelevant, for the passenger liner was already doomed, being displaced by cheap mass air travel.

LIFE ON A GREAT LINER

Right and below:
German style on the
North Atlantic. The
Bismarck was
launched in 1914 for
Hamburg-Amerika
but, awarded to
Britain as reparation,
was completed in
1922 as White Star
Line's *Majestic*. This
was her Palm Court.
Meals, especially in
First Class, were
occasions for
dressing-up,
for seeing and
being seen.

FOR THE MAJORITY of today's travellers the experience of flying is one of cramped conditions, confusion and anxiety, mercifully of short duration. Liner travel, which it displaced, offered by contrast a pleasurable experience, with each great company vying to impress and to cosset the passenger in equal measure. In short, it had a sense of occasion, now sadly lacking.

Over the first half of the twentieth century the European traveller was spoiled for choice for, to every continent, there ran comfortable ships of various flags. To South America by Pacific Steam or, say, Hamburg-Süd? To South Africa by Union Castle or, perhaps, United Netherlands for a change? To the Far East by reliable old P&O or enjoy some French flair with Messageries Maritimes? Or to Australia and New Zealand with Orient, or let's be adventurous, Danish East Asiatic? Even the names sounded romantic.

The 'Western Ocean' was different, for here the traveller was wooed. In the late 1930s they could go Cunard, whose fleet ranged from the crack Blue Riband holder *Queen Mary* to the stately old *Aquitania*. Or he could take the elegantly modernistic *Normandie*, backed by the refinements of the *Ile de France*. There were the German's utilitarian-styled *Bremen* and *Europa*. While the Dutch awaited with the *Nieuw Amsterdam*. With a little extra trouble, our traveller could avail himself of the neo-Roman glories of the *Rex* or *Conte di Savoia*. The Americans themselves, having scrapped the ex-German *Leviathan* in 1938, were still two years from commissioning her replacement, *America*.

Most liner tonnage serving routes to other continents was reliant to some extent on cargo carrying. Although their passages thus included several interesting ports of call, they suffered from hatches and cargo gear impinging on deck space. Recreational activities were therefore on a small scale while facilities and entertainment were also fairly basic, with passengers much left to their own devices. On the Atlantic, by contrast, each flag sought to inject some of its national flavour into the experience and to persuade each passenger that, in those aircraft-free times, theirs was the only company worth consideration.

The adventure commonly began with the cheerful chaos of the boat train whose tangle of steamer trunks and excited passengers eventually pulled in at an alongside terminal. Above it towered the looming mass of their ship, of what Kipling termed a 'monstrous nine-decked city'. Scattered along the quay, in endlessly-changing combination, were the vehicles of the contractors making last-minute deliveries – flowers, fruit, dairy produce, laundry. Vans of those making equipment repairs. Taxis, scores of taxis. The whole assemblage was a reminder of how much a port's economy depended upon its core activities.

Aboard, the foyer was abuzz with passengers sorting themselves out, mainly through non-stop quizzing of the purser's patient staff, whose problems were compounded by at least the same number again of visitors and well-wishers. Imperceptibly, the mêleé would subside, luggage and bodies disappearing as acquaintance was made of cabin stewards.

Dining and entertainment routines

If a voyage was to be enjoyed, one required a contented steward for, once satisfied with his charges, he became a combination of oracle and Mr Fixit. At home with a ship's timetable that miraculously expanded or contracted by one hour daily (depending on the direction of the passage) and with her labyrinthine geography, he was at once an indispensible source of knowledge and, passengers often prayed, a soul of discretion. Either way, his income swelled steadily with innumerable small considerations, that bane of the passenger's existance. For beside the cabin steward, there was the dining room steward (if one did not wish to dine alongside a serving hatch), the deck steward (for a steamer chair out of the permanent howling gale), the cabin service staff, the laundry staff, liftboys and bellboys, an endless procession of potential *faux pas* for the inexperienced passenger. Anxious to be on the safe side, unsure of shipboard protocol, he was permanently short of small denomination bills.

Setting sail was usually an evening event to allow time for passengers to travel to the ship which was ablaze with light. A band playing, passengers lining the rail and the quayside thronged, it all being an event in itself; it was carnival charged with sadness.

Passengers, officially, were restricted to their own class of accommodation but stewards needed

to be permanently vigilant to prevent the curious from straying. First class entertainment and, to the bold, cuisine were irresistible draws to the cash-strapped young of the lower classes. Conversely, the latter's public spaces, lacking the regimen of the *belle monde* existance above, proved to be havens for many anonymous darlings of society.

In the rather strange absence of professional cabaret, as agreed by operators jointly, passengers were encouraged to participate in fancy dress galas, sports programmes, 'race meetings', the much-dreaded ship's concert and in any one-to-one games that avoided the use of balls. The inevitable horrors of Immigration and the Customs would be tomorrow. Today was to be enjoyed.

Above and below: The surprisingly large swimming pool on the 1931-launched Italian record-breaker Rex. Appointments on the *Rex* and on her running mate *Conte di Savoia*, were particularly splendid, but the United States-Mediterranean route was the poor relation to the Northern Europe services.

Left: Basic deck sports persisted for a surprisingly long time to amuse passengers on British-flag ships. Here, on the Royal Mail's *Arcadian*, they are afflicted with the dreaded potato race, no less dreaded by the uniformed crew members detailed to assist.

TRAMPS AND CARGO LINERS

TRAMPING AND LINER operation are two of the broadest categories in ship management. Briefly, a liner is a ship, not necessarily passenger-carrying, that runs to an advertised timetable between specified ports. Her operation is entirely the responsibility of her owners, who will maintain the schedule even if the ship were temporarily lacking revenue-earning cargo or passengers. In contrast, a tramp, like the wayfarer of yore, will wander the world, directed solely by the dictates of her charterers.

Jealous of their reputations, liner companies may operate excess capacity in order to guarantee availability. Tramp owners often run just one ship. Liner organisations are larger and more complex, for they need to generate, and arrange for, cargoes. As with any sizable commercial undertaking they will support financial and planning departments, advertising, sales and legal departments, personnel and operations staffs in addition to the marine superintendent and marine engineer's departments.

Aggressive operations by variously-flagged liner companies in the same areas resulted in cut-throat competition that, ultimately, benefited nobody. The solution, as early as 1875, was for cooperation in the form of a 'conference'. Rules vary, but conference members will seek to harmonise rates to provide stability, and to pool ships to guarantee services. Profits are taken in the same proportion as contribution. Conferences are often accused of being monopolistic cartels, dictating terms to ships who lack alternatives. Shippers are, however, rewarded for loyalty by a range of special terms. One great advantage is that non-profitable services may be maintained, with losses shared by the conference members.

Designed for working specific routes continuously, liners will be fitted-out accordingly. Much of their freight will be 'break-bulk', smaller parcels of goods in crates, bales, sacks or barrels, for discharge at a range of ports. These parcels must be accessible without time-wasting re-arrangement of other cargo, so the ship is fitted with intermediate 'tweendecks' in way of the cargo spaces. Deep tanks, possibly with heating coils, may be built-in for the carriage of such as palm oil. They may have a refrigerated or insulated hold for seasonal produce. Some routes attract periodic heavy loads such as those of the chemical industry or railway rolling stock; these will require reinforced deck areas and, possibly, the provision of heavy-lift cargo gear. The machinery may well be under-rated so as to leave power in hand to 'crack on' and maintain a schedule following a delay. Cargo liners also frequently had comfortable appointments for a score or so passengers to whom a working voyage was, itself, a pleasure.

Cargoes and charter parties

A tramp, however, needs to be simple but versatile. Competing against seemingly unlimited cheap, second-hand tonnage the ship itself must be cheap to run. Crew costs must be minimised without adopting too much expensive automation but, above all, it must be economical in fuel.

Cargoes for tramps are often seasonal but the five staples are coal, grain, iron and aluminium ores, and phosphates. Scrap metal is common but timber, lumber and a range of what are now termed 'forest products' have tended to go to specialist carriers.

It will be noted that the freights mentioned are 'bulk' and tramps, as a result, are frequently 'single-deckers'. Some may have a tweendeck, but this increase in versatility will also close them to other freights and an owner will need to gauge carefully whether such expensive complications will pay for themselves over the lifetime of the ship.

Below: One of the once-thriving Royal group, the Royal Albert Dock is seen here in 1961. At left, on Berth 35, with its adjacent cold store is one of the Jamaica Banana Producers' ships.

Left: Far from the company's traditional type of ship, Blue Funnel's Priam class were of the final generation of cargo liners, already being rendered obsolete by the tide of containerisation.

Tramps operate by legal agreements termed 'charter parties', by which an owner consents to his ship being engaged for a single trip for a considerable period. Owner and charterer are brought together through the medium of the shipbroker, whose business is connnected in such as London's Baltic Exchange. Given an enquiry by a prospective shipper, a broker will match his requirements to a ship suitable in dimensions (particularly draught), capacity, speed and any specific cargo-handling gear.

The three major categories of charter party are voyage charter, time charter and demise (or bareboat) charter. While, of course, there is much small print, a voyage charter essentially pays an owner for conveying a described cargo between designated ports between specific dates. In a time charter the owner hires out his ship at an agreed rate per month, but usually bears all costs except those of cargo handling and port charges. Demise chartering gives the charterer full responsbility for the ship, together with all expenses.

Tramping was the way to see the world. One authority quotes the following consecutive movements for one vessel. Ballast, Middlesbrough-Baltimore, coal Baltimore-Alexandria, ballast to Gulf of Suez thence manganese ore to Dunkirk, ballast to South Wales thence coal to Perim, ballast to Durban thence four coal voyages to Perim, Port Sudan, Karachi and Colombo, ballast to Christmas Island thence phosphates to Fremantle, ballast to Bangkok thence rice for Hong Kong, ballast to Christmas Island, thence phosphates to Stockholm …

Below: Introduced in 1892, the turret decked ship was popular for about 20 years. With its narrowed weather deck it was able to profit from some reduced tonnage measurement.

FISHING TRAWLERS

THERE ARE MANY TYPES of fishing craft, as there are many types of fish. Scottish and Scandinavian boats pursue haddock and other flatfish with seine nets, suitable for sandy bottoms. Purse seiners catch herring and mackerel by surrounding a shoal with a net that can be drawn tight. Long lines, bearing hundreds of baited hooks, are used near the surface by Japanese seeking tuna, and near the bottom by Faroese wanting ling and conger. There are gill netters, scallop dredgers and fishers with bright lights, but most of the world's fish is caught by trawling.

A powered version of the weatherly 90 ft (27.4 m) sailing smack, the steam trawler originated in the mid-1880s. Towing a trawl net requires considerable power and vessels grew steadily to 140 ft (42.7 m) and 600 ihp following World War I, and 178 ft (54.3 m) and 950 ihp by 1939. Huge numbers of trawlers were requisitioned in both world wars for minesweeping, for which they were well suited. Oil firing replaced coal in 1946, resulting in a length reduction due to simplified bunkering. The adoption of diesel propulsion further reduced length through a more compact machinery space without a boiler room. Advantages remained in size, however, which steadily increased again. By 1957, big motor trawlers were of 185 ft (56.4 m) and 1500 shp. Even with powered assistance, shooting a trawl over the side of such vessels was heavy work, made the more dangerous by very low freeboard.

In the 1950s, the Scottish firm of Christian Salvesen instigated development of a new concept in the stern trawler. Being a whaling concern, Salvesen's idea was to use the established idea of handling gear over a stern ramp. On a 262½ ft (80 m) length, their prototype ship had a high free-board with space below for processing the catch while in perfect condition. Stern trawlers and associated fish factory ships, for the production of every conceivable product from fish liver oil to prime cuts, proliferated worldwide but particularly under the flags of what was the Eastern Bloc.

Processing the catch

Side trawling is still popular, however, with ships divided into near-, middle- and distant-water categories. Respectively, these are likely to be ships of 80–120 ft (24.4–36.6 m) with a 5–9 day endurance, up to 140 ft (42.7 m) and 14 days, and up to 185 ft (56.4 m) and 24 days. Big freezer stern trawlers may be up to 360 ft (109.7 m) in length and stay at sea for weeks. Older conventional craft packed their catch in ice, transferring it as quickly as possible to fast 'carriers', which accompanied each fleet to make regular trips to the nearest market. Today's factory ships are self-contained and waste nothing. 'Trash', earlier discarded to the gulls, is now mechanically processed to remove the last flesh, useful either as 'mince' for fishcakes or in fishmeal.

Equipment must take account of both fish type and depth of water. This results in the further categories of Demersal, or bottom, trawling, Pelagic, or middle-depth, trawling, and semi-Pelagic, where the trawl is kept just above the bottom.

Demersal trawls are of essentially irregularly conical form, with large open end forward. The net

Main picture and below: A Hull fish market. The auctioneer is taking bids from the crowd of buyers, who are agents for the wholesalers.

mesh size decreases as it progresses towards the apex, the closed 'cod-end'. Mesh size is controlled by law to prevent the waste of undersized and immature fish, and a major task of naval Fishery Protection Squadrons is the conduct of random checks to enforce such regulations.

The larger, leading end of a trawl is kept open horizontally by a pair of deflector plates, known as 'otter doors', and vertically by a headline supported by floats. On a ground trawl, the foot rope bears heavy rolling bobbins, which both carry the net over minor irregularities and stir up the fish. The latter, once inside the aperture, are herded inexorably via decreasing section and mesh size to the cod-end. A middle-depth net will be of lighter materials and have a foot rope that is weighted downward to maintain the aperture.

As the total length of a trawl and its towing lines ('warps') may be more than half a mile, the task of handling it over the side of a conventional vessel is considerable and, in really deep water, can be shared between a pair.

To avoid drifting into a net when handling it, a side trawler must lay athwart wind and sea, the gear on the weather side. An already risky process, with crewmen thigh-deep in green water, is thus worsened by heavy rolling. In contrast, a stern trawler heads slowly into the wind during these operations, her crew relatively dry and experiencing mainly pitch accelerations.

To give an easy roll for deckwork, side trawlers may have a small metacentric height and, thus, a reduced stability range. Ice accretion from wind-driven spray is thus hazardous, forming on masts, stays, rails and aerials, and all raising the ship's centre of gravity. Good design minimises such exposed features but safe practice is to move out of such conditions quickly.

Above: Newlyn Harbour, with a varied collection of near water and inshore craft. With the enforcement of internationally-agreed fishing quotas, this traditional industry has declined.

Left: For maixmum freshness, fish are auctioned alongside the ship. The seakindly hull form of a distant water trawler is here evident, the anchors recessed into pockets to reduce pounding in head seas.

Warship Development to 1945

Main picture: One of the four Myoko-class heavy cruisers, the *Ashigara* here shows her unusual sheerline. Japanese warships were unique in matching depth of hull to imposed stress levels.

Below: The US Navy's first 'Treaty Cruisers', the two Salt Lake City-class ships were launched in 1929. Armed with ten 8-inch guns, necessitating an combination of twin and triple turrets.

IN SATISFACTORILY HALTING a new naval race in capital ships, the five signatories to the Washington Conference of 1921–22 inadvertently created a new competition in cruiser construction. For the purposes of the treaty, a capital ship (other than an aircraft carrier) exceeded 10,000 long tons and carried guns of greater than 8-inch (203 mm) calibre. Simply, warships conforming to this definition would be subjected to tight regulation, lesser ships would not.

Large armoured cruisers, whose parameters greatly exceeded those above, had been discredited by World War I experience, and the largest current new buildings were the British 'Hawkins' class ships, whose 9,700 tons and 7.5 in (190 mm) armament greatly influenced the choice of parameters. The 'Hawkins' were also widely admired, increasing international interest in the creation of cruiser designs that would pour a quart of offensive power into the pint pot of 10,000 tons displacement. As with capital ships, however, the major qualities of speed, armament and protection were interactive, i.e. on a given displacement, any of them could be improved only at the expense of the others. In their efforts to squeeze the maximum capability from the limits designers inevitably resorted to cheating. The following table gives basic details of what might be termed 'first generation treaty cruisers': see *TABLE ONE*.

The comparatively modest specifications of the American and British ships were considered the best that could be achieved on the displacement, yet it will be immediately apparent that Italian and Japanese examples were, at the same time, larger, faster, better armed and better protected. Either Archimedes had been wrong or their official displacements were cosmetic.

Succeeding classes followed quickly. Interestingly, the Americans improved their protection by

THE CRUISER RACE

dint of losing one gun. Where the 'Pensacolas' needed two twin and two triple mountings for a battery of ten, the succeeding 'Northamptons' opted for three triples and nine guns. This standardised mounting design, saved the weight of one mounting complete, and improved topside layout. It was so successful that it set the pattern for all succeeding American classes. See TABLE ONE

Renewal of the Washington Treaties

From the 'Pensacolas', launched in 1929, to the 'Astorias' of 1933–36, the Americans built 17 cruisers in four closely-related classes without being able to effect a radical improvement on the displacement. The British experience with a dozen 'Counties' was much the same. Archimedes had been right.

To improve protection and to produce a cheaper cruiser, the British built two 'Kent' derivatives. These, *York* and *Exeter*, shipped only six 8-inch guns but had 3 in belts on a displacement of only 8,550-tons.

The Washington Treaties were due for renewal in 1931 and, in a bid to curb the rapidly-developing cruiser race, the three major signatories made a new agreement in London during April 1930. For the first time, distinction was made between 'heavy' cruisers, with guns of 6.1 to 8-inch (155–203 mm) calibre, and 'light' cruisers, with guns of 6.1 in calibre or less. See TABLE TWO

It will be noticed from the above that, in order to build their full quota of 12 8-inch cruisers, the Japanese would have to limit them to a unit average of only 8,370 tons. They skilfully circumvented this by building the six 'Mogami' and 'Tone' class ships with triple 6.1-inch mountings, i.e. as light cruisers, in which category they had spare tonnage. Later, with the treaties' lapse, they replaced these mountings with twin 8-inch gunhouses, which were designed with the same barbette diameter.

The British, who neither required nor could afford heavy cruisers, needed large numbers of smaller units, primarily for trade protection. To numbers of surviving C and D class ships were added, therefore, the 'Leanders' and 'Arethusas'. Peer competition also obliged them to build large light cruisers, in which category a new competition developed once the actual number of 8-inch hulls was prescribed. A comparison of these is also of interest. See TABLE THREE

Left: Heavy cruisers, which consumed much of the tonnage allocation, were not popular with the British. They were confined to the County class, one of which is seen here in white and buff Far-East livery.

TABLE ONE

	USA	UK	Italy	Japan	France
Class/No. off	Pensacola/2	Kent/7	Trento/2	Myoko/4	Duquesne/2
Standard Disp.(tons)	10,000	10,000	10,000	10,000	10,000
Length (oa)x breadth(ft)	585.7 × 65.3	630 × 68.3	646.2 × 67.6	661.8 × 68.0	626.6 × 62.3,
Speed, continuous (kt)	32.5	31.5	35.0	33.8	33.0
Armament, primary	Ten 8 in	Eight 8 in	Eight 8 in	Ten 8 in	Eight 8 in
Belt protection (in)	2.5	0	3.0	4.0	nil
Year	1926–27	1926–27	1926–27	1927–28	1925–26

TABLE TWO Agreed allowances for each fleet were:

	USA	UK	Japan
Heavy cruisers	18 ships, not exceeding 180,000 tons	5 ships, not exceeding 146,800 tons	2 ships, not exceeding 108,400 tons
Light cruisers	43,500 tons total	192,200 tons total	100,450 tons total ·

TABLE THREE

	USA	GB	Italy	Japan	France
Class/No. off	Brooklyn/9	Belfast/2	Garibaldi/2	Mogami/4	La Galissonniére/6
Standard Disp. (tons	10,000	10,000	9,400	10,000	7,600
Length (oa) × breadth (ft)	608.4 × 61.7	613.5 × 63.3	613.5 × 61.9	669.3 × 66.3	587.3 × 57.3
Speed, continuous (kt)	32.5	32.0	33.0	34.0	31.0
Armament primary	15 × 6 in	12 × 6 in	10 × 6 in	15 × 6.1 in	9 × 6 in
Belt, protection (in)	5.0	4.5	5.0	4.0	4.7
Year	1936–38	1938	1936	1934–36	1933–36

CONVOY ESCORTS (1939–45)

Main picture: Slower and more lightly-armed than fleet destroyers, the 'Hunt'-class were designed primarily as anti-aircraft escorts. Here, the *Holderness*, a Type I vessel, shows her seakeeping.

Below: Ahead-throwing weapons allowed escorts to attack a submarine while it was still in the Asdic beam. 'Hedgehog' fired a pattern of 24 spigot-mounted depth bombs, which exploded on contact.

DURING THE 1930s the major threats to convoys in a future war were assessed by the British naval staff as air and submarine attack. Escort types thus reflected this assessment but, themselves, also fell into two major categories. First were those built to full naval standards, fast and well-armed. These would be manned by regular naval personnel and employed on convoy routes likely to be heavily contested by the enemy. In support were large numbers of relatively simple little ships, built to relaxed mercantile standards by smaller yards not normally associated with naval work. Their crews would be drawn mainly from naval reserve and 'hostilities only' (HO) personnel.

Typical of the former category were the 'Black Swan' class sloops and the 'Hunts', effectively small destroyers. Both types were fitted with a full outfit of high-angle 4-inch (102 mm) guns with director control. The 1,300-ton sloops, of which 37 were completed, were powered for 19–20 knots, the 84 smaller 'Hunts' for 29–30 knots.

A general shortage of hulls, and recollections of how damaging mine warfare had been in 1914–18, led to the sloops being specified with minesweeping gear and to some being required to lay mines in addition. This, together with three twin 4-inch mountings and a steadily-growing battery of automatic weapons, meant that, initially, there was little space for depth charges. War experience soon showed that there were never enough of these weapons, and successive modifications of the 'Black Swan' design saw capacity increased from 40 to 110. This all added to topweight on what were already small and crowded ships. It also, however, gave them a long roll period, improving them as

steady gun platforms. The sloops were notable, however, as patient submarine killers, working in specialised groups in the Atlantic.

The faster, but generally more lightly armed, 'Hunts' were closely associated with the Mediterranean, where their services were valued in the face of unrelenting air attack, and in the defence of British east coast convoys, which were subject not only to routine attention from the air but also to sudden forays by German destroyers (usually after a mine lay), and E-boats.

Bitterly contested from the outset, the vital transatlantic convoy route will, forever, be associated with the 'Flower' class corvettes. No less than 135 of these tough little ships were built in United Kingdom yards and a further 79 in Canada. The design originated at Smith's Dock, Middlesbrough and the general profile, with its pronounced sheerline, reflected this company's experience in the construction of catchers for the whaling industry.

Mousetrap, Hedgehog and Squid

The 'Flowers' were intended originally for coastal duties and, again, many were equipped for minesweeping (and, indeed, were so used if they served in Malta during the seige years of 1941–42). They were supremely seaworthy but, when employed in the deep ocean, had a vicious motion that exhausted their already permanently wet crews.

The enormous contribution made by Canada to the Atlantic war is, all too often, overlooked but Canadian manned and built corvettes, in company with a scratch collection of armed trawlers and

superannuated destroyers, helped hold the ring throughout the darkest period of the battle.

An urgent parallel programme was pursued to produce a larger, twin-screw anti-submarine (A/S) escort, better suited to ocean conditions. This, the 'River' class revived the old category of frigate, and offered improved habitability, higher speed and more depth charge capacity.

With the rapid progress typical of wartime, the 'Rivers' were superseded by the 'Loch' (A/S) and 'Bay' (anti-aircraft, or A/A) class frigates, supported by the smaller 'Castle' class corvettes. The first two classes were notable in being the first to be assembled from prefabricated welded modules.

In the early days, the few available escorts needed to remain close aboard their convoys. More and faster escorts were gradually assisted by specialist A/S groups which could rapidly reinforce threatened convoys. Gradually, too, the northern ocean gained total coverage from especially-modified, very long range (VLR) aircraft, invaluable in keeping submarines down and in warning an escort commander of any others lurking ahead.

Slowly, the mid-Atlantic gap, a graveyard of shipping, was closed with the assistance of escort carriers which, with night-adapted aircraft, could give a convoy 24-hour coverage. British and Canadian-built escorts were boosted by increasing numbers of American-built 'destroyer escorts'.

Escorts detected submerged submarines with Asdic (later re-named Sonar), whose sonic pulses yielded range and bearing, and, rather later, depth. Because Asdic worked ahead of the ship and depth charges were released in patterns from the after end, the few seconds covering the actual attack

were 'blind'. This drawback was rectified by the development of ahead-throwing weapons, successively Mousetrap, Hedgehog and Squid. Mention must also be made of high-frequency direction-finding (H/F, D/F, or 'Huff Duff') with which escorts could gain a bearing on any surfaced U-boat which was transmitting and, often, mount a surprise attack.

Left: Sloops of the Black Swan classes proved to be admirable destroyers of U-boats. The *Starling* was leader of Captain Frederick 'Johnny' Walker's group, which had an unsurpassed record of kills.

Left: Many American-built 'destroyer escorts' were transferred to British colours, the turbo-electric driven *Holmes* being shown here. As a coastal escort, she has a 2-pounder 'bow-chaser' fitted.

WINTER, NORTH ATLANTIC — LIFE ABOARD AN ESCORT

Main picture: An open ship's lifeboat, with its cargo of desperately-grateful survivors, became symbolic of the convoy war in the Atlantic. Escorts could be overwhelmed with numbers rescued but near as many died from oil or exposure.

DURING THE FIRST LONG YEAR of the war, as the vital transatlantic convoy bridge became established, responsibility for its safety rested on a variety of craft, most of which had one thing in common — unsuitability. There were armed yachts, armed liners and aged destroyers, all too old for fleet work, and then there were the corvettes. Until the specialised frigate evolved and came on line the little corvette held the ring. Simple in detail, cheap to build, these were intended for the defence of coastal convoys yet, with politics once again overtaken by events, they were found in the deep ocean.

Able to be built seemingly anywhere, the 'Flowers' issued in a steady stream from British and Canadian yards. Formed into escort groups, usually with a destroyer carrying the senior officer, they were based on Liverpool and Londonderry, Halifax and Sydney, Nova Scotia. Even when numerous enough to offer coverage 'all the way' they were still too short-legged to cross the Atlantic, taking their charges to the Mid-Ocean Meeting Point (MOMP), before handing over to a group from the other side.

They were manned with personnel from all walks of life — hastily-trained 'HO' (Hostilities Only) hands, aged anywhere between 18 and 40, serving alongside men from the Reserves with, usually, only a small proportion of 'regulars' (often with men recalled from retirement) to leaven the mixture. Common tribulation soon bound them into an effective team. Ultimate pleasure became the distant prospect of a hot bath and unlimited sleep in a clean bed that remained both dry and steady.

Corvettes in a seaway could gyrate beyond belief. As the merchantmen ploughed stoically onward, seemingly steady as rocks, their short

escorts followed the contours of the long ocean seas, bursting through a breaking crest in a curtain of drenching spray before plunging sickeningly into the next trough. At a point that seemed, each time, to be too late, the bows would rise to the next, pointing at clear air. An occasional rogue sea, shorter than the rest, would catch the ship off-rhythm. Water at such a time appears to attain the consistency of concrete, bringing the ship to with a jarring crash, the structure whipping and the shaft racing momentarily as the screw, only half immersed, sought to regain its grip. A change of course, bringing the sea either onto the bow or the quarter, resulted in a wild corkscrew of a motion, each cycle of which had the cox'n fighting the wheel to avoid a broach.

A pin-prick on the ocean

The noise, like the movement, was unrelenting. Depending upon one's position the wind roared, whistled, shrieked or howled, but never gave up, lashing any exposed skin with an intensity akin to flaying. Add to this the crashing of the ship as she fought on and men could grow hoarse on the simplest communication. Through squinting, tired eyes and streaming binoculars lookouts swept sky and sea for an enemy who, thank heaven, was suffering to a like degree.

'Gaining one's sea legs' was mercifully quick for most, but many were habitually ill for the first day or two. Some could never cope, and were returned to depot, branded 'Unfit for service in small ships'. For the rest, watch on deck meant encasement in heavy weather gear — 'woolly long johns, all the jerseys

you could find, an overall suit, a duffel coat, all topped off by an oilskin coat, a couple of pairs of gloves, a balaclava helmet and a sou'wester … ' And the water still found a way in.

Life was passed wedged in space, legs braced against the nearest solid structure. Movement was a series of short dashes from one handhold to the next. To exist was to be fatigued. Cooks (or, more correctly in the Royal Navy, 'chefs') worked wonders in their reeling galleys but, all too often, for those who could contemplate food, the menu comprised soggy sandwiches.

End of watch meant a welcome return to messdecks made interesting by the contents of personal lockers, usually one's own, rolling, sliding and clattering around a deck which might, itself, be awash. Amid this squalor, men, still cheerful, lived their leisure in endless card games and 'uckers' (a form of killer Ludo with rules known only to the Navy), letter-writing, yarning or 'zizzing'.

On occasion, in the chill of February, a boardflat sea and the atmosphere combined to create the apparent brittleness of cut glass. In such stillness, the enemy seemed all-hearing, all-seeing. The steady throb of scores of marine engines could be felt through the deckplates. Columns of funnel smoke climbed vertically into the greyness above. From the escort on its flank, the ponderous mass of shipping seemed to stretch for ever. How could the enemy not notice it? In truth, the largest convoy was but a pin-prick on the immensity of the ocean, insignificant, virtually invisible. For all the slaughter and pain of convoy warfare, the individual tragedy and grief, the brunt of the fighting was against the elements themselves.

Above: The Flower-class corvettes served in large numbers. They were slowly supplemented by frigates – larger, with greater depth charge capacity and 'longer legs'.

Left: Liverpool was the home of Admiral Sir Max Horton's Western Approaches command. Escorts, including this pair of Black Swans knew the port as their base.

THE WAR AGAINST THE U-BOAT

Above: A depth charge plume marked the point where it was hoped that the target was. As Asdic contact had been lost perhaps half-a minute previously, this was usually not the case.

UNDER THE LEADERSHIP OF ADMIRAL KARL Dönitz, the primary task of the German U-boat arm was to break down the North Atlantic convoy system. The United Kingdom could remain in the war only if sustained by a continuous supply of food-stuffs and war materials from the United States. In the dour struggle that entered history as the Battle of the Atlantic both sides were aware that defeat for either would probably decide the overall out-come of the war.

Himself an ex-submarine commander, Dönitz had been appointed in 1935 as U-boat supremo and had created an elite force whose morale was maintained even to the final bitterest of ends. He was single-minded in his objectives; in simple terms, he needed only to keep sinking Allied merchantmen faster than they could be replaced and, eventually, victory would be assured.

Unfortunately for him, his Führer's impetuosity brought war earlier than his Navy had planned and, in September 1939, there were only 56 operational U-boats. Of these, just 26 were of types large enough to conduct ocean warfare. Germany was a signatory to the Submarine Protocol of November 1936, which expressly forbade unrestricted subma-rine warfare, this was rapidly adopted on the quasi-legal grounds that merchantmen were receiv-ing defensive armament and were proceeding in convoys protected by armed escorts. Of the Royal Navy's 176 destroyers, all the modern flotillas were reserved for fleet support. Many of the older ships, allocated for convoy protection, were of World War I vintage, too short on endurance, uncomfort-able and with inadequate depth charge capacity. Dedicated anti-submarine escorts began to be commissioned, however – first a trickle, later a flood, of corvettes and frigates.

Asdic sound-ranging equipment had been under development by the British for 20 years and had, fairly recently, entered operational service. Despite field experience during the Spanish Civil War, the Royal Navy had greatly over-opti-mistic expectations regarding its performance. In practice, although it was highly effective with trained operators in good conditions, it was sus-ceptible to false returns and signal degradation from external noise.

Dönitz, well aware of the equipment's exis-tance, ordered his commanders to attack convoys on the surface and at night. In darkness, lookouts were unable to spot the small profile of a surfaced submarine while the noise of its diesel engines was

Left: Heavily strafed by an attacking aircraft, a U-boat desperately tries to get under. The final swirl of her submergence, however, would usually be marked by the aircraft with a clutch of depth charges.

drowned by that of the convoy itself. Asdic could not detect surfaced boats. Easily slipping through the huge peripheral escort gaps, a U-boat commander could surface in the 'brown' of a convoy, create mayhem with a full load of torpedoes and be gone long before retribution could arrive. The eventual answer was to fit escorts with newly-developed, short-wave radar.

As his operational strength increased, Dönitz was able to introduce his long-desired 'wolf-pack' tactics. Any boat locating a convoy would desist from attacking it but would make every effort to stay in contact, acting as a beacon to concentrate a number of boats which, having reached maximum practicable strength, would be unleashed together at Dönitz's order. For all too long, a convoy's totally inadequate defences would be overwhelmed.

Aerial assistance

The system, however, together with Dönitz' obsessively centralised control, generated the means of its own defeat in the enormous volume of radio traffic that it generated. Escorts were, therefore, equipped with high-frequency direction finding (H/F D/F) equipment, enabling them to get an accurate bearing on a transmitting U-boat.

Submarines of the time had very limited submerged speed and endurance, and needed to surface to stay in contact with a convoy. If the escort could keep them down, they often lost contact. Aircraft, able to cover so much more area,

were even better at this. Coherent groups of destroyers (more of which were released by the fleet), corvettes and new frigates began to work from Canadian and British ports, handing over responsibilities at the Mid-Ocean Meeting Point. Coverage was greatly improved by the occupation of Iceland in mid-1940.

Long range maritime aircraft, particularly modified B-24 Liberators, gradually covered the mid-ocean gap where the U-boats congregated. From late 1942 auxiliary carriers, converted from mercantile hulls, became increasingly available to escort convoys and to act as the core of dedicated hunting groups. These exploited 'Ultra' intelligence to tackle both the operational U-boats and the specialised submarines that refuelled and re-supplied them.

Dönitz 's Atlantic campaign was based mainly on French Biscay ports and the 'Bay' became the focus of round-the-clock aerial operations to catch U-boats in transit. The Germans developed radar warning receivers but the British defeated these through the use of ever-higher frequencies. To avoid having to surface in transit the Germans developed the Snort air induction mast from a Dutch patent.

Until 1942 the U-boats were supreme, sinking nearly 7.8 million grt in that year alone. By mid-1943, however, the defence had their measure and, for the first time shipping tonnage built exceeded that lost. Despite the introduction of the new and fast 'electric boats' Dönitz faced ultimate defeat.

Below: U-boats transiting the Bay of Biscay proved to be so vulnerable to air attack that, at one stage, it was policy to remain surfaced to fight it out. Submarines became festooned with automatic weapons sited in galleries known collectively as the 'Wintergarten'.

AUXILIARY CRUISERS AND Q-SHIPS

Below: A Q-ship depended totally on an innocent appearance to entice a U-boat to approach on the surface. This coasting vessel certainly would not be worth a torpedo but offered her crew little protection in a gunnery duel.

BRITAIN HAS SUFFERED in wars over the centuries through her enemies specifically targeting the shipping upon which she depends. Although, during World War I, it was German and Austrian U-boats that wreaked the major havock (6.7 million grt of British shipping, from a total of 7.8 million grt was lost), surface raiders were also used to good effect. The initial wave of these raiders comprised a mix of armed passenger liners and regular navy light cruisers. Neither was successful, the liners being prodigious eaters of coal, which could not easily be supplied to them, and the cruisers proving too complex to operate for long without dockyard assistance. They were replaced, therefore, by innocent-looking merchantmen which carried powerful and carefully-concealed armament. These undertook extensive cruises, relying on their unremarkable appearance to approach an unsuspecting merchantman and subdue it either by threat or surprise

bombardment. Relatively easy to maintain and requiring small crews such raiders could, and did, remain at sea for extended periods, relying much on their captures for food and coal supplies. Their survival depended upon evading searching cruisers through frequent changes of operational area.

To put their depredations into context, regular and auxiliary raiders destroyed some 569,000 of a total of 12,800,000 grt of British, Allied and neutral shipping sunk by enemy action during World War I. As U-boats accounted for 11,100,000 grt of this total, the raider's contribution might appear small, but what is not readily apparent is the immense disruption and delays caused to vital trades by a raider's presence.

As in 1939, the German fleet was smaller in proportion to the Royal Navy than it had been in 1914, the contribution made by auxiliary raiders to cruiser warfare gained in significance. It was planned

bring them to port, and later by survivors, could number 400. Comprehensive machine shops permitted a high degree of self-maintenance. Considerable extra bunker space was necessary as, with ships now oil-fired, fuel was less likely to be captured. Stowage was provided for up to 400 mines. These were for planting in small and well-distributed clutches, usually at landfalls or chokepoints where a high density of shipping could be expected.

Warships in disguise

The raiders' fortunes varied widely but only two of the nine survived. *Atlantis* and *Pinguin* which, between them, had accounted for 50 merchant ships, totalling 280,000 grt, both fell victim to patrolling British cruisers. During a successful cruise, in which she had taken 11 ships of over 68,000 grt, the *Kormoran* encountered the Australian light cruiser *Sydney*. Both ships were sunk. The *Stier's* unlikely end was to blaze uncontrollably, having been hit by return fire from the single gun of the American Liberty ship that she had attacked. Most successful of the German auxiliary cruisers was the *Thor* which, in the course of two cruises, destroyed 23 ships of over 150,000 grt. This total included one of the three British armed merchant cruisers encountered. While refitting in Yokohama, she was destroyed by explosion. In all, German regular and auxiliary raiders sank 1,328,000 of the 21,570,000 grt of shipping lost during World War II.

Q-ships, like auxiliary cruisers, used disguise to achieve their objective. The British converted a number of small vessels for the purpose during World War I, their mode of operation capitalising on German U-boat commanders preferring to conserve their limited torpedoes for significant targets and using a deck gun to disposed of lesser fry. For this they needed to surface. The standard procedure when stopped was for the crew to 'abandon ship', leaving aboard gun crews, whose weapons were concealed behind a variety of temporary screens. If, to use her gun, the submarine closed on a favourable bearing the Q-ship's disguise would suddenly be dropped and, quite often, the situation reversed. As the enemy grew familiar with the ruse, the success rate fell off. Despite this, the Admiralty revived the idea in 1939, outfitting eight ships with heavy armament to tackle surface raiders, but none was ever encountered.

Left: One of the most successful German auxiliary raiders of World War II was the *Atlantis*, converted from the Hansa ship *Goldenfels*. Two of her 6-inch. guns are seen here with their concealing plating lifted.

Above: Remaining at sea for nearly 15 months the *Wolf* (ex-*Wachtfels*) was most successful Q-boat in World War I. During her cruise she captured 14 ships. Another 13 were sunk by mines that she laid.

to convert a total of 26 ships but, in the event, this was limited to only nine as work on them did not commence until after the outbreak of hostilities. Selected ships varied in size from the 8,736-ton *Kormoran* (formerly the HAPAG ship *Steiermark*) to the 3,287-ton *Komet*, previously the *Ems* of Norddeutscher Lloyd.

Usually, six 5.9-inch (150 mm) guns were carried, mounted singly and concealed behind hinged screens. About a half-dozen automatic weapons, 37 mm and 20 mm, were also carefully hidden. Four to six 21-inch (533 mm) torpedo tubes were sited behind ports cut into the ship's sides. Two Arado float planes were carried in the tween decks, put afloat and recovered by a ship's own cargo gear. The immense volume of the cargo holds was converted to a variety of uses. Extensive accommodation was required for a crew which, swollen at the outset by extra personnel to man prizes and

SMALL BATTLE UNITS

Main picture: Five 46-ton Type A midget submarines were transported to Hawaii by attack submarines as part of the attack on Pearl Harbor. Enjoying no success, all were lost, this one being beached on Oahu.

Right: The two-man crew of a British 'Chariot', or human torpedo. This was not a suicide weapon. Dressed in full diving kit, the crew were tasked with suspending the detachable warhead beneath the target's hull.

NAVAL WARFARE IS VIRTUALLY synonymous with activities on the High Seas, but it should be remembered that it is sometimes necessary to take the battle to the enemy in his own harbours. Throughout history, small groups of determined men have been landed to undertake urgent tasks beyond the reach of the fleet, and the ingenuity of twentieth century engineers increased the scope for this type of action, which still had its place despite the development of the strike aircraft.

Torpedo-armed coastal motor boats (CMB) were active during World War I. The Italians were particularly successful, sinking two Austro-Hungarian battleships, the *Wien* at Trieste in December 1917 and the *Szent Istvan* off Premuda in June 1918. A British CMB similarly penetrated the fortified Russian harbour at Kronstadt in 1919 to sink the cruiser *Oleg*.

Already showing a flair for the unorthodox, Italian rubber-suited swimmers entered the harbour at Pola in November 1918 and sank the flagship, *Viribus Unitis*, and an accommodation ship with limpit mines. Before this, they had made unsuccessful attempts to breach the defences with craft like amphibious tanks, fitted with tracks designed to negotiate floating booms.

Between the wars the Italian Navy continued to pursue this style of warfare with the development of very fast MAS boats and torpedoes modified for slow running. The latter were ridden by two rubber-suited personnel equipped with self-contained underwater breathing apparatus, the original 'frogmen'. Officially termed an SLC (unofficially 'maiale' or pig), the vehicle carried a detachable warhead and limpit mines, either being attachable to a target ship. The SLCs could be deployed either from specially-modified submarines or from surface craft, and enjoyed conspicuous success when, in December 1941, three of them sank the British battleships *Queen Elizabeth* and *Valiant*, and a tanker, in shallow water at Alexandria. At Gibraltar the Italians ingeniously constructed SLC facilities within the hulk of an ancient tanker 'interned' in Spanish waters. Between July and September 1943 they used this base to mount four separate attacks on the British base, sinking or damaging ten merchantmen. Two more merchant ships were similarly sunk at Algiers.

Midget submarines

Having captured specimen 'maiali', the British copied them successfully. In Janaury 1943 several penetrated the harbour at Palermo, sinking the new Italian cruiser *Ulpio Traiano*.

Just a month earlier, the British had tried a more precarious form of attack when Royal Marine Commandoes used canoes to enter the Gironde in order to disable serveral blockade-running merchantmen laying at Bordeaux. This style of raid was used later against Japanese shipping at Singapore. While the first was successful, the second resulted in the capture and execution of all personnel concerned.

It was the Japanese who, during the 1930s, invented the first true midget submarine. With a crew to two, and armed with two 18-inch (915 mm) torpedoes, these could travel about 18 miles submerged. Eight were lost in attacks on Pearl Harbor and Sydney, but they gained their first success in torpedoing the British battleship *Ramillies* and a tanker during operations to secure Madagascar. Again, however, three were lost. As the tide of war inexorably turned against them, the Japanese turned to mass production of midget submarines as a means of attacking the powerful American amphibious fleet. They accomplished little, most never seeing action.

During 1942 the remaining German heavy warships were based remotely in northern Norway. Apparently unassailable in their fjord anchorages, they menaced Allied convoys to North Russia. To tackle the huge new battleship *Tirpitz* the Royal Navy developed 51 ft (15.5 m) midget submarines known as X-craft. Two of their four-man crew could dress in diving suits and 'lock out' in order to attach two heavy explosive charges to a target's underside. In September

1943, six such craft, towed by regular submarines, succeeded in severely damaging the *Tirpitz*. Later in the war X-craft similarly disabled the Japanese heavy cruiser *Takao* near Singapore.

During an earlier raid on Bergen, the Germans captured a smaller type of British craft, a 16 ft 8 in (5.1 m) 'Welman'. This vehicle encouraged them to reverse earlier antipathy to small battle units and they commenced development of a wide range, from the 17-ton, two-man Type XXVII U-boat, which carried two torpedoes, to the 3-ton one-man/one torpedo Neger and Marder. As with the Japanese, the Germans planned production runs in hundreds for the purpose of destroying Allied invasion fleets. In conjunction with remotely-controlled explosive motorboats these small craft proved to be a minor nuisance off Normandy and in the Schelde but were vulnerable to the attentions of light surface forces and aircraft. So many were lost that the Germans themselves referred to as suicide operations. On balance, despite many individual acts of gallantry, it is doubtful whether the considerable resources devoted to these unorthodox operations were justifed by results.

Above: Type 127 (Seehund) small battle units in series production by Germaniawerft, Kiel. About 285 of these 15-ton craft were delivered, each being capable of carrying two torpedoes.

THE FINAL GENERATION OF BATTLESHIPS

Below: The two Japanese super-battleships, *Musashi* and *Yamato* each displaced over 69,000 tons and were armed with 18.1-inch guns. Both ships were destroyed by overwhelming carrier-based airpower.

Right: Still a new ship the British battleship, the *Prince of Wales*, is seen arriving at Singapore early in December 1941. Undeterred by her firepower, the Japanese sank her and her consort, *Repulse*, by massed air attack.

THE WASHINGTON TREATIES limited new capital ships to replacements for existing hulls. They should not exceed 35,000 long tons nor mount guns of greater than 16-inch (406 mm) calibre. Into these simple parameters, designers had to incorporate the experience of World War I and the means of countering newer threats. As ever, they sought to achieve a satisfactory balance between the demands of protection, hitting power and speed.

Because it had been expected that the actions of the early twentieth century would be fought at close ranges, where the shell trajectories would be flat, armour had been concentrated into thick vertical belts and bulkheads, with comparatively thin protective decks. Trials following World War I had shown, however, that even modern ships were vulnerable to bombing, while wartime advances in guns and fire control had increased ranges considerably. Armour, therefore, had now to be re-distributed to give both horizontal and vertical protection. Philosophies differed but usually took the form of thin 'bursting' decks (to detonate bombs or steeply-descending shells) overlaying a heavier deck, or decks, to prevent the resulting fragments from penetrating vital spaces.

Using whatever data that could be gleaned regarding foreign guns, their ranges, weight of pro-jectile, and penetrative power, designers developed the concept of 'immunity zones'. At short range, heavy projectiles would penetrate vertical armour but, beyond a critical range, would not. At long ranges, on the other hand, plunging shellfire would penetrate horizontal armour but, at shorter ranges, would impact at too shallow an angle, and would be deflected. With due allowance for bearing of attack and for ship movement, it will be apparent that there usually existed a range band within which the protection of vital spaces would not be penetrated. Using foreign gunnery data, designers thus sought to distribute protection to maximise this range band with respect to the capabilities of the most likely opponents. The usual solution was thick protection over the vital centre section of the hull and such spaces as the steering flat, leaving the ends of the hull 'soft', or protected sufficiently to prevent destabilising flooding following action damage. Superstructures, except for conning towers, gunnery control and turrets, remained largely unprotected.

Protection from torpedoes normally took the form of several watertight bulkheads running parallel to the sides of a ship over its vital central zone. The resulting voids were subdivided into spaces by occasional transverse bulkheads. Some spaces were liquid filled, some left void, the objective being to

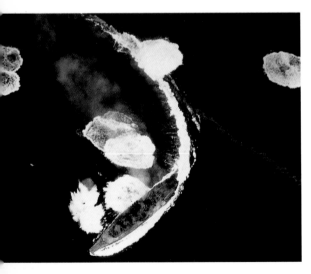

Left: Anchored in Tokyo Bay, the American battleship *Missouri* provides an appropriate setting for the signing of Japanese surrender document. Battleships had, however, already been displaced by aircraft carriers as primary capital ships.

provide sufficient volume for a warhead detonation to expend its energy without causing disabling damage or flooding.

With only eight to 10 barrels forming a main battery, the measure of hitting power turned more on weight of projectile rather than weight of broadside. Depending upon the type of shell considered, weight increased rapidly with diameter, or 'calibre'. Average figures were 1,550 lb (705 kg) for a 14-inch (356 mm) shell, 1,800 lb (818 kg) for 15-inch (381 mm), and 2,600 lb (1,182 kg) for 16-inch (406 mm). The monstrous 18.1s introduced by the Japanese fired 3,200 lb (1,455 kg) projectiles.

Earlier treaty restrictions fell apart in the 'thirties with their revocation by Japan, the bilateral Anglo-German Naval Agreement and a failure to renew revised Washington terms when they lapsed in 1936.

Gunnery revolution

Re-armament was in the air. Despite the French, Italians and Germans all opting for 15-inch main batteries (see table below), the United Kingdom alone pressured for a mutually-agreed reduction to a maximum of 14-inch. Wisely, the United States would not agree to this as long as Japan pursued her now-secret building programme. In the event, as the table shows, American 16-inch had to be weighed against Japanese 18.1s. Only Britain clung naively to the proposed 14-inch weapon, which armed the otherwise excellent 'King George Vs'. Four 15-inch twin mountings, discarded from earlier demolition, were later incorporated in the one-off *Vanguard* in a feeble attempt to recover ground lost by politicians during the lotus years.

Gunnery was to be revolutionised during World War II by radar, which particularly influenced the outcome of nocturnal actions, such as Matapan, the sinking of the *Scharnhorst*, the night action of Guadalcanal, and that of the Surigao Strait.

Speed was the design parameter that usually enjoyed lowest priority. Speed is always expensive as required power increases with it at an alarming rate, demanding in turn larger machinery spaces and greater areas to protect. Only the Americans, with the planned six Iowas, set out to create a truly fast battleship. While successful, the resultant significant increase in dimensions and displacement will be obvious from the table.

	Germany	**France**	**Italy**
Class/Number	Bismarck/2	Richelieu/2	Vittorio Veneto/3
Date completed	1940–41	1940	1940–42
Standard Displacement	42,300	38,500	41,200
Length x breadth (ft/m)	824x118/251x36	813x108/247.8x33	780x108/237.8x33
Main battery	8x15 in	8x15 in	9x15 in
Protection, vertical (in)	12.6	12.6	16.1
Protection, horizontal (in)	6.7	8.1	7.2
Speed (knots)	29	30	30

	UK	**United States**	**Japan**
Class/Number	King George V/5	Iowa/4	Yamato/2
Date completed	1940–42	1943–44	1941–42
Standard displacement (tons)	38,000	48,500	65,000
Length x breadth (ft/m)	745x103/227x314	888x108/270.6x33	863x128/263x38.9
Main battery	10x14 in	9x16 in	9x18.1 in
Protection, vertical (in)	15.0	12.2	16.0
Protection, horizontal (in)	7.0	13.3	9.0
Speed (knots)	29	33	27.5

AIRCRAFT CARRIERS – WASHINGTON TREATY TO 1945

Above: Inferno in 'Battleship Row' following the attack on Pearl Harbor. The *California* is seen listing from the effect of two torpedo and three bomb hits. She was repaired by January 1944.

Top: To attack Pearl Harbor in December 1941, six Japanese carriers put up 49 bombers with 1600-pound bombs, 51 dive bombers with 500-pounders, 40 torpedo aircraft and 43 escorting fighters.

THE AGREEMENTS SIGNED IN Washington early in 1922 allowed the signatories – the United States, Great Britain, Japan, France and Italy – to build aircraft carriers to a total of 135,000; 135,000; 81,000; 60,000 and 60,000 tons respectively. Except in the special case of the two 33,000-ton American 'Lexingtons', no individual ship was to exceed 27,000 tons, while any under 10,000 tons were not included in the total tonnage. As neither France nor Italy showed much interest, only the first three nations need concern us here.

The two big 'Lexingtons', carrying 80 aircraft apiece, soon showed the US Navy the value of large carriers, large air wings and high speed, although the long, lean shape of these converted battle cruisers made hangar and flightdeck operations excessively time-consuming.

Because this pair of ships consumed over half the Americans' permitted total (they were, in truth, even heavier than the official figure) later carriers would need to be designed to lower displacements. The 'Lexingtons', as in British practice, combined the flightdeck and the hangar walls into the main

'hull girder', i.e. they contributed to the ship's strength. Later ships would have a lower hull topped off with a protected hangar deck, above which a lightweight flightdeck and supporting structure would be erected. This open construction allowed more aircraft stowage space and saved much topweight, although the ships were more vulnerable to bombing.

All three fleets looked at hybrid 'flight-deck cruisers', as a means of adding non-accountable tonnage, but it was only too apparent that such ships would be of no use in either surface or air warfare.

A further requirement was a speed of 32.5 knots to operate with supporting cruisers and to permit independent operations beyond the screen of the battle fleet. Only with the lapse of the treaties in 1936 and the design of the nominally 27,500-ton 'Essex' class did the Americans have the size to operate in heavy seas and to possess the required speed and level of protection. Twenty-four 'Essex' class, together with the nine 'Independence' class (small carriers built on fast cruiser hulls) formed the bulk of the American Pacific carrier forces.

Unlike either the Americans or the Japanese, the British Royal Navy lost control of its aviation element, the Fleet Air Arm, with the formation in 1918 of the unified Royal Air Force. Funds were low, parsimony justified by the government's notorious Ten Year Rule. Further, as British carrier capacity was very limited, aircraft were invariably expected to be multi-role. All these factors conspired to produce a series of carrier aircraft with performance consistently inferior to that of their foreign peers.

Lessons learned at sea

The main inter-war British carrier strength lay in the three 'Courageous' class ships, also narrow-gutted conversions from large cruisers, and bulged for improved stability. American philosophy was to protect their lightly-built carriers with a powerful combat air patrol (CAP), their greater capacity allowing for more embarked fighters. To maintain strength in other directions, the British could deploy fewer fighters with their smaller air wings. The heavier, integral flightdeck, support structure and hull was, therefore, a tacit admission that damage was to be expected. Only the six large carriers of the post-treaty programme incorporated the so-called 'armoured deck', and experience in the Pacific War showed that they could survive damage that disabled or sank American and Japanese ships. The penalty was, however, their significantly smaller air wings.

Both the Americans and Japanese had appreciated the possibilities of an ocean carrier-based war and had trained and built accordingly. Their air wings were, in short, their main offensive weapons. Through conservatism, inferior material, and a lack of threat from other European carriers, the Royal Navy saw the role of the Fleet Air Arm primarily as one of observation and scouting, with offensive strikes aimed at slowing an opponent sufficiently to bring about a gun action, at which the aircraft would assist by spotting. Aviation was thus a subsidiary asset.

The coming war would furnish examples of these different philosophies – for the British, the pursuit of the *Bismarck* and the Battle of Matapan, for the others, the long series of carrier battles that ran from the Coral Sea to the Philippine Sea.

Carriers in the Pacific War proved highly vulnerable to dive-bombing, despite the emphasis on efficient CAPs. Carrying immense quantities of aviation fuel and explosive stores, their thin horizontal protection was insufficient. Often, a single bomb was sufficient to start a lethal sequence of fire and explosion.

Only with the acquisition of robust American aircraft did British carriers come into their own. Fighters like the Wildcat, Hellcat and the superb Corsair established air superiority over the Japanese Zero which, supreme at the outset, suffered by successive updates rather than replacement. Japanese reconnaissance was excellent, using either ship-based floatplanes or carrier aircraft. The latter, lacking such weight-consuming features as pilot protection and self-sealing fuel tanks, had consistently longer ranges.

By the end of the war the offensive power of carriers was under threat from bigger, and therefore fewer aircraft, together with the need to dilute the air wing with such as airborne early warning (AEW), anti-submarine (A/S) and communications aircraft.

Left: Most losses of carriers in the Pacific war followed fires, usually initiated by divebombing. After bomb damage sustained off Kynshu in March 1945, the *Franklin* survived only through the courageous effort of her crew. She was too badly damaged to be fully repaired.

Top and above: Leading in naval aviation in 1918, the Royal Navy fell badly behind between the wars due to government policies. The number and quality of the aircraft from HMS *Glorious* (top) compare poorly with those of the USS *Saratoga* (above).

AUXILIARY AIRCRAFT CARRIERS

Main picture: Too late the Italians discovered that land-based aircraft were inadequate to their fleet's needs. In July 1941 they commenced a rapid reconstruction of the passenger liner *Roma*. As the carrier *Aquila* she could have carried 51 aircraft, but she was never completed.

Below: Seemingly precarious, a Hurricane fighter mounted on the catapult of a CAM ship. The ships needed also to be fitted with early forms of air and surface search radar.

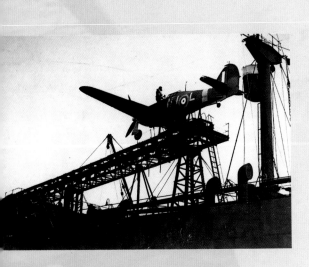

FOLLOWING THE FALL of continental Europe in mid-1940, British convoys were increasingly menaced by German long-range maritime patrol aircraft. These would attack unprotected stragglers directly, and also orbit a convoy out of gun range, reporting its content and position for the benefit of searching for U-boats. As the sight of a circling 'snooper' usually presaged a submarine attack, they were universally hated.

During World War I, the somewhat similar problem of the reconnaissance Zeppelin had stimulated the Royal Navy to ad hoc means of getting performance fighters to sea, promoting a sequence of developments that led directly to the introduction of the aircraft carrier. In 1940, however, carriers were too few to spare for convoy work and further stop-gap measures were called for.

The first of these was the fitting of catapults to a handful of the navy's auxiliary anti-aircraft ships. These, dubbed Fighter Catapult Ships, led to similarly equipped merchant ships, known as Catapult-armed Merchantmen (CAM). In these, of which only 35 of a planned 400 were converted, a

lightweight catapult was erected on the raised forecastle, allowing the full cargo capacity to be retained. Exposed to the elements, a fighter aircraft (usually an early mark of Hurricane) sat atop a cradle which was accelerated with rocket assistance. Once launched, the fighter pilot would need to carry out his attack speedily and fly on to an airfield ashore, if in range. Beyond this range, his only recourse was to return to the convoy, ditch and be rescued from the sea. The first CAM sailed in May 1941, with its first success being recorded in the August. Masters of CAMs were reluctant to launch pilots due to the risks and, of 170 sailings, only eight launches and six kills are recorded.

The CAM concept was, fortunately, overtaken by the introduction of the escort carrier but, as the entry into service of these ships proved to be disappointingly slow, a further temporary measure was necessary. Convoys required not only that reconnaissance aircraft were chased off but also that marauding U-boats were kept down or attacked. A small carrier could deploy aircraft for both tasks.

It was noted that merchantmen carrying bulk grain or oil could have their cargoes loaded and discharged by suction hose, hatch access being unnecessary. Thirty-two diesel driven tankers and dry cargo ships were thus selected to have a full length flight deck fitted, retaining their cargo capacity. Known as Merchant Aircraft Carriers (MAC), only two of the 19 actually converted boasted hangar facilities for their four aircraft, while some flightdecks were so brief that only the short take off Swordfish aircraft could be used. The first sailing by a MAC was in May 1943.

As already mentioned, auxiliary escort carriers preceded the MAC. Before hostilities, certain diesel-driven passenger liners had been earmarked for carrier conversions but, in the event, they were to prove more useful as troop ships. In the space of some four months, however, the British rebuilt a captured German freighter as the prototype escort carrier *Audacity*. With six aircraft and no hangar facilities, she first sailed in July 1941. By the time that she was sunk, just five months later, her reusable fighters had proved their worth in both patrol and attack.

Woolworths and Baby Flat-tops

Arriving at a similar solution by an independent route, the still-neutral US Navy commissioned its first escort carrier, *Long Island*, in June 1941. More elaborate than the *Audacity*, she was equipped with an elevator and a half-length hangar, while being able to operate a useful wing of 16 aircraft.

With their yards fully committed to repair work, the British converted only a handful of such ships, leaving the Americans to series-build for both fleets. Known variously as 'Woolworth' carriers, 'Jeeps' or 'Baby Flat-tops', 127 hulls were completed or commenced. Most numerous were those converted from standard C3-type mercantile hulls. Averaging about 16,600 tons, these could operate 24 aircraft. The larger 'Commencement Bay' type were of 23,100 tons and deployed 33 aircraft. A small group of tankers, the 'Sangamons', were also converted to 23,250-ton carriers with 27 aircraft apiece.

The austere nature of escort carrier conversions was reflected in their being equipped with what machinery was available. Diesel-drive was preferable, but many had steam turbines and even steam reciprocating machinery.

Although intended for duties such as convoy escort and anti-submarine operations, escort carri-

ers (CVE) could, as in North Africa and Italy, provide air cover for major amphibious landings. By the war's end, groups of CVEs, suitably supported, were acting in offensive roles but, being small and with little subdivision or protection for the large quantities of Avgas and explosive stores that they carried, they were vulnerable to severe action damage.

Both Germany and Italy had plans to convert passenger liners to carriers but only the latter actually did so, but neither of the two commenced were ever completed. Japan, however, converted seven, the largest pair each operating a respectable 53 aircraft.

Left: An interesting American concept was that of the conversion of heavy cruiser hulls into fast light attack carriers. This is the Princeton (CVL-23) in May 1943. Note the island and uptakes cantilevered out to avoid obstructing the narrow flightdeck.

Below: Escort carriers (CVE) were eventually produced in large numbers, using mercantile hulls. Their aircraft were vital to the protection of convoys sailing beyond the range of land-based air.

AMPHIBIOUS WARFARE

Right: Flooded down and with stern-gate lowered, the American LSD *Catamount* takes aboard an LCM and an amphibious engineer vehicle.

Below: In the Pacific War the Iowa-class battleships spearheaded the surface action groups. Five years later, in Korea, the enemy had no battle fleet, reducing the battleships' role to bombardment.

SOME FORM OF AMPHIBIOUS warfare has existed ever since armies have needed to cross water barriers but, in modern terms, it may be said to have started with the Gallipoli landings of 1915. Boldly conceived in strategic terms, the operation was dismally planned tactically, and the subsequent appalling and wasteful loss of life convinced many that opposed landings were not feasible.

The resuscitation of the concept was due largely to the Americans. Long suspicious of Japanese intentions, they recognised that the western Pacific territories, including the Philippines, were effectively indefensible against a major military campaign. Subsequent recovery would require a maritime-based force advancing westward against island-based opposition. Islands would require to be seized for advanced bases, necessitating a suitably trained and equipped assault force.

In the 1920s, savagely-reduced defence budgets threatened the very existence of the US Marine Corps but, under its then-commandant, Major General John A. Lejeune, it effectively re-invented itself around this role, convincing Congress that it should be funded as an element of national defence doctrine. It was a remarkably prescient move.

Amphibious exercises enabled the Corps to identify the essential requirements of a landing, these being enshrined in the Tentative Manual for Landing Operations, later to be the 'bible' of amphibious warfare. The six major ingredients were:

1 *Naval Gunfire Support.* Forego the surprise element in order to saturate the defences with as many naval guns as possible up to the moment of touchdown. Fire control officers should land with the leading wave in order then to direct deliberate shoots on demand. Fire support gave employment to many veteran battleships no longer fit for first-line duties.

2 *Aerial support.* Pilots had to be trained to work from carrier decks and, as directed by fire control teams, deliver pin-point support as required.

3 *Ship-to shore movement.* This quickly developed from being based on LCA-sized craft, slung under davits of Attack Transports, to LCMS and Tracked Amphibious Vehicles (LVT) carried in large numbers in the floodable wells of Landing Ships, Dock (LSD).

4 *Securing the beachhead.* During the critical phase of getting established ashore it was essential that the naval-controlled landing of supplies, and the military-controlled collection and distribution of them cooperated quickly and smoothly. Boundaries of responsibility had to be clearly defined.

5 *Logistics.* Assault Transport needed to be designed to task. Each had to accommmodate a battalion and its equipment, the latter 'combat loaded' so that it came ashore exactly in the sequence in which it was required.

6 *Command relationships.* As all services were involved, senior officers of each should be accommodated together in a Landing Ship, Headquarters (LSH) to facilitate close cooperation, quick decision-making and access to reliable communications. The landing operation was naval controlled, the military commander taking over ashore only after the assault phase had been declared complete.

In a parallel the British military establishment, chastened by the dark experience of Gallipoli, proceeded slowly. By the late 1930s, however, it had made progress in one area that the Americans had neglected, namely the ship-to-shore phase. Formed in 1938, the Inter-Services Training and Development Centre (ISTDC) developed its own doctrine and specialised craft. The original Motor Landing Craft (MLC) had, by the outbreak of war, spawned the Landing Craft, Assault (LCA) and Landing Craft,

Mechanised (LCM) for personnel and vehicles respectively.

The waterjet propulsion and flat bottoms of early craft soon gave way to more orthodox propellers (more vulnerable in shallow water but not liable to be clogged by weed) and keels with fore-and-aft curvature ('rocker') to reduce stiction and to simplify refloating.

Operation 'shoestring'

The British also recognised two classes of specialist vessel, viz. those capable of making an ocean passage but not necessarily of 'taking the beach' (Landing Ships), and those capable of making short passages, or of moving men and equipment from ship to shore (Landing Craft). Of the latter, the largest was the Landing Craft, Tank (LCT), which, with the larger Landing Ship, Tank (LST), passed rapidly through many marks and formed the backbone of the amphibious fleets.

Unlike the Americans, the British favoured a covert night approach and an unannounced dawn landing. To test theory in practice, Combined Operation Headquarters staged a frontal assault on the defended French port of Dieppe, in August 1942. In budget terms it was a disaster, with a great loss of men and materiel, but it taught invaluable lessons for future operations. By coincidence, the same month saw the first American landing in the Pacific, the 'Shoestring' operation to occupy Guadalcanal.

From here, the mass production of a huge range of landing craft was one of the war's major priorities. From cavernous LSDs to floating kitchens they were essential to the recovery of territory from the Pacific to the Mediterranean, and from Burma to Normandy.

Above: The LST became the maid-of-all-work but her prime function was the landing of heavy armour, such as this Sherman. Raised, the ramp formed an inner, watertight bulkhead behind the bow doors.

THE MOSQUITO FLEETS

BY THE FINAL QUARTER of the nineteenth century, separate international initiatives had produced the torpedo, the lightweight planing hull, the internal-combustion (petrol) and the compression-ignition (diesel) engine. High-speed small craft then developed quickly in the first decade of the new century, due to the popularity of 'speedboat' racing.

The early naval torpedo boats had, by comparison, been slow, being built as steel displacement craft wedded to boilers and steam reciprocating machinery. They had already been effectively superseded by the destroyer and an effectively new start was made by putting torpedoes and light armament aboard high-speed hulls.

Names such as Thornycroft, Yarrow and Fiat emerged as leaders in the field, with Thornycroft's 26ft (8m) racing motorboat *Miranda IV* of 1910, which had bettered 35 knots, being used as the basis for the British Admiralty's 40 ft (12 m) Coastal Motor Boat (CMB). This craft, soon joined by a 55 ft (16.5 m) derivative, proved its value in a multitude of functions.

The CMB's hull form was of flat V-section with a step but there soon developed clear preferences for either 'hard-chine' craft (very fast on the plane but quickly slowed by heavy conditions) or 'round-bilge' types (slower, semi-displacement boats, but more seaworthy).

Both British and Italian boats during World War I scored successes in torpedoing and destroying major warships but, between the wars, official interest lapsed, leaving development largely to private enterprise. With general rearming in the late 1930s, however, the British preferred petrol-engined 70 ft, hard-chine Motor Torpedo Boats (MTB) while Germany built round-bilge Schnellboote (S-boat) with diesel propulsion. Fast torpedo craft well reflected the dash of the Italian character, their navy having a range of hard-chine MAS boats, well-suited to lighter Mediterranean conditions. American PT (Patrol, Torpedo) boats came late, the result of fierce competition between British and home-produced candidates. Both Americans and Italians used petrol engines, whose low flashpoint fuel was a hazard in action. This was later offset by the adoption of aircraft-style, self-sealing fuel tanks.

The Royal Navy, like the US Navy, had little perceived peacetime role for mosquito craft and, at September 1939, possessed only a few flotillas of 70 ft MTBs and their first derivatives, the Motor Anti-submarine Boat (MA/SB, known unofficially as 'Masby'). With the outbreak of war the coastal convoy routes were soon attacked by S-boats (known to the British for some reason, yet to be satisfactorily explained as E-boats). More weatherly than their British opponents, and deploying cannon against machine guns, they proved difficult to counter until some MTBs were re-modelled as Motor Gun Boats (MGB), sporting a variety of automatic weapons in lieu of their torpedoes. In this mode, they operated in support of the standard MTBs.

Pre-war British boats had used the powerful Italian Isotta-Fraschini petrol engines but, after June 1940, and Italy's entry into the war, these were no longer available. Following a period of experimentation the Navy settled on the supercharged American Packard.

Fairmiles and Raumbootes

An interesting offshoot of the engine crisis was the Steam Gun Boat (SGB). This was of a steel-built, round-bilge form, 146 ft (44.5 m) in length. It lacked suitable armament for its size and, packed with high-pressure steam plant, it was very vulnerable to quite trivial action damage.

As aluminium, high quality timber and time all became short in supply, prefabricated marine plywood structures became the norm. The leading firm of Fairmile produced the drawings and masters for frames, bulkhead and planking. These could be produced in large numbers by firms skilled in furniture making, and sent to minor yards for 'screw and glue' assembly. Hard driving in heavy weather soon exposed weaknesses in structural design, which were rectified as developments proceeded.

Important standard designs included the Fairmile 'B', the 112 ft (34.1 m) Motor Launch (ML), produced in large numbers for a multitude of functions, and the Fairmile 'D' (popularly known as 'Dog' boats), the 115 ft (35 m) craft which was interchangeable between a four-tube MTB and an MGB equipped with a pair of 6-pounders, 20 mm Oerlikon cannon and 0.5-inch machine guns, a mixed armament that reflected the growing importance of Lend-Lease equipment from the United States.

The German equivalent to the ML was the versatile Raumboote (or R-boat), which was used for escort and patrol work, minelaying and minesweeping.

The narrow seas bordering the English east and south coasts became a general battleground

Below: Haslar Creek was home to both submarines and light forces. Seen here are Fairmile 'D'-types of about 115-foot length and capable of carrying interchangeable gun and/or torpedo armaments.

Left: An elderly 'four-piper' destroyer, USS *Gillis*, converted to a seaplane tender, hosts a trio of Higgins-type PT boats. The picture was taken in the Aleutians following the Japanese ejection.

Below: British Coastal Motor Boats (CMB) of World War I moved the concept of torpedo craft from a combination of steam and low-speed displacement hulls to one of petrol engines and high speed planing.

for British and German light forces. Narrow, swept channels, close in shore, were used by convoys which often became considerably attenuated and vulnerable to attack from shallow-draught craft crossing the seaward sandbars and minefields with impunity at high water. Both sides were actively engaged in the pursuance and prevention of minelaying.

American PT boats were not common in European waters but were active in the Pacific, interdicting Japanese supply craft which hugged the coasts of the theatre's myriad islands.

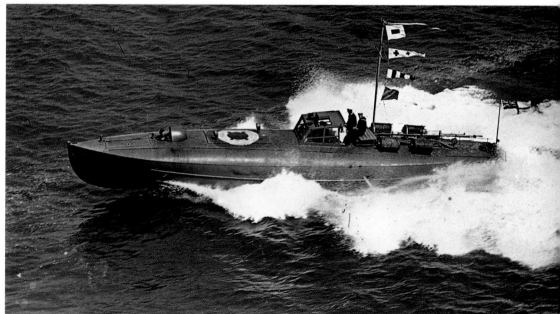

MINE WARFARE

Right: Destroyers proved excellent minelayers during World War II. While some of their armament needed to be landed as topweight compensation, the ships' speed facilitated overnight forays.

Below: Beautiful but deadly. The shock wave from an exploding ground mine can wreck a passing ship without even holing her.

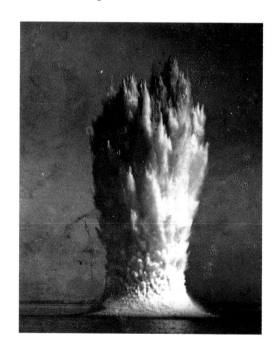

MINE WARFARE IS EXTREMELY cost effective, mines being simple to lay but very difficult to locate and sweep. Just one mine incident will bring traffic to a halt until a route can be declared clear. The resources absorbed in maintaining a minesweeping force are considerable and, as most minesweepers are auxiliary craft taken up from the fishing industry, the nation's food supply is also affected. By the end of World War I, 726 minesweepers were at work and, of these, no less than 554 were requisitioned fishing trawlers and drifters. Over 1.1 million gross registered tons (grt) of Allied and neutral shipping were lost to mines, of which 673,000 grt were British. Of the Royal Navy's 16 capital ship losses, five were caused by mining.

There is a clear division between offensive and defensive mining. Defensive fields are laid to protect one's own coastline and approaches, and their general area promulgated according to international law. Marked gaps allow shipping to pass safely and to be controlled, while secret channels exist for the purpose of one's own operations. Offensive fields are laid where they can cause an enemy the greatest loss and disruption, typical locations being port approaches and estuaries, choke points and popular landfalls.

Laying and sweeping

Most mines of World War I vintage were of the familiar horned variety, an explosive-filled buoyant body moored on a cable and sinker. In areas of great tidal range this type is impossible to moor at an optimum depth, while they frequently break adrift in heavy weather.

Controlled minefields were laid to protect access to fleet anchorages. The mines themselves were laid at a depth that allowed surface ships to pass freely but, surrounding them, was an energised cable loop, terminating in a hut ashore. The ferrous hull of any submarine attempting to steal into the anchorage distorted the magnetic field associated with the loop. This was indicated on a galvanometer ashore and the whole field detonated simultaneously by an electrical impulse.

This principle, involving magnetic field distortion, was then utilised for the first 'influence' mines, detonated by a target's signature rather than by contact, thereby extending their effective radius. British magnetic mines were used in 1918, but were unsuccessful. Interwar research, however, led to a practical weapon and, as importantly, to the necessary countermeasures.

During World War I, minelaying was largely by converted merchantmen (which had the capacity), modified destroyers (which had the speed) and specially-designed submarines (which had the stealth). By 1939, aircraft had been added but, being parachute-retarded, their mines were not too-accurately laid.

From the outset in 1939, the Germans used magnetic mines which, typically, would not hole a ship but do her catastrophic damage by shock. The disection of two examples found on an Essex mud-flat led to antidotes. Colliers were converted to Mine Destructor Ships through the installation of powerful electro-magnets in their forward holds. Minesweepers were equipped with 'Double-L' sweeps. Individual ships acquired either permanent protection by 'de-gaussing' (which used heavy currents passed through a cable girdling the hull) or short-term immunity through 'wiping' or 'de-perming' to reduce residual magnetism in their hulls.

By August 1940, the Germans were using acoustically-detonated mines. Fortunately, these reacted to wide-band noise and could be swept by equipping ships with pneumatic or hydraulic hammer assemblies, which were lowered over the bows. Magnetic mines were made difficult to sweep by the simple addition of counters, which inhibited their detonation until after a set number of stimuli had been experienced.

Four years later, off Normandy, the Germans introduced the pressure mine. In shallow water there will exist an accelerated flow between the seabed and the underside of a moving ship. Increased velocity means reduced pressure, here used to deflect a diaphragm as a triggering mechanism. They proved to be unsweepable and could be countered only by mine clearance teams, although ships could gain a degree of immunity by proceeding at dead-slow speed.

Enemy destroyers and E-boats made aggressive mining forays to the vital English east coast convoy route, while auxiliary raiders planted small fields to great effect at worldwide focal points. The British had six high-speed 'Welshman' class minelayers, which proved invaluable in several roles.

The Royal Air Force lost 533 aircraft in minelaying activities but claimed 762 enemy ships and 17 U-boats. In return, 534 Allied ships, totalling over 1.4 million grt, were sunk by mines, or to put it another way, about one ship in ten of those lost.

Above: Fitted with a cargo of empty barrels for emergency buoyancy this converted merchantman ploughs through a suspected mined area, streaming two sweep wires spread by paravanes. Note her lifeboats, swung out in case of emergency.

FLEET TRAINS

THE LOGISTICAL PROBLEMS of supporting the movement and operation of fleets have been around for as long as the fleets themselves, but the organisation that supplies the fuel, ammunition, foodstuffs and every last nut and bolt required thousands of miles from base invariably goes unnoticed in the shadow of climactic events. In peacetime competition for scarce funds, tankers and supply ships score badly against higher-profile combatants. The war in the Pacific provides an excellent example of major fleets with contrasting attitudes.

To go to war in either Europe or the Far East, the US Navy required to operate thousands of miles from its home bases. From quite early in the twentieth century the Americans developed what came to be known as the Rainbow plans, in which was evolved a war strategy against all likely powers. Plan Orange, the best known, catered for hostilities against Japan. It assumed that the Philippines were indefensible and would be overrun. To recover them and to move against Japan herself meant the steady advance of a battle fleet through the hostile territory of the mandated island groups, up to 7,000 miles from the US western seaboard. One fortunate result of the studies was the building-up of Pearl Harbor, on Hawaii, into a full fleet base, although it was still incomplete in 1941. A similar plan for the forward island of Guam ran foul of the Washington Treaties, which forbade the fortification of western Pacific islands.

Experience of operating in European waters during World War I had shown the US Navy the

value of a block of shipping, termed the Fleet Train, dedicated to the supply and maintenance of forward-based squadrons. Little was actually done between the wars, however, and a new organisation needed to be created when the fleet began its massive buildup following the outbreak of war in Europe in 1939.

The British Pacific fleet

When, in December 1941, a Pacific war became a reality, Pearl Harbor was established as the hub of an immense network, backed directly from resources within the United States. Only Australia and New Zealand had the space and resources to accommodate and feed the hundreds of thousands of military personnel readying for huge amphibious operations. Further forward, supply dumps and fuel stocks were set up at such exotically-named spots as Espiritu Santo, Bora Bora and Pago Pago, maintained by a steady stream of commercial tonnage. Here were loaded the fast fleet oilers and logistics ships that actually accompanied the fighting fleet. As the Japanese were forced back problems of supply grew; distances became ever greater and new garrisons proliferated, along with their now-dependent populations. A major shortcoming of Japanese naval policy was that of giving its considerable submarine fleet the rigid priority of attacking naval targets. Had the Japanese used them, other than for one brief period, to work against the long and vulnerable American supply routes the effect would have been serious.

To assist in front-line recovery and repair of battle-damaged ships came fleet tugs, salvage and specialist repair vessels, destroyer and submarine tenders, hydrographic survey ships and net tenders, a fragmented, floating fleet base that moved slowly forward with the tide of war.

British experience was different. The Royal Navy's transition from sail to steam had brought about the creation of a comprehensive network of coaling stations and fleet support bases. Warships could thus be directly sustained on foreign stations, often being refitted locally and even rotating crews without return to the United Kingdom. With such guaranteed access to facilities and an Atlantic, as opposed to Pacific, based tradition, British ships tended to be short-legged compared with their American peers.

Pre-war studies had shown, as they had the

Right: A submarine tender (or 'depôt ship') can provide forward support facilities for a whole submarine flotilla, although the USS *Beaver* is here seen in 1918 in calmer Californian waters.

Left: Refuelling at sea, or RAS, was the key to extended operations in the vast arena of the Pacific war. Here, the fleet oiler *Cahaba* tops up the battleship *Iowa* and a carrier simultaneously.

Right: Specialist cargo ships (AK) complemented the oilers by providing all types of provision. Here, the carrier *Essex* is resupplied by the *Mercury* (AK.42) off Okinawa in April 1945.

Americans, that a Mobile Fleet Base Organisation would be required if the assumption was made that permanent bases would be lost in war. Only in 1939, far too late, was a start made on such a scheme and the loss of Singapore and Hong Kong only served to underscore the cost of political apathy.

When, with the war in Europe effectively won, the Royal Navy was able to put together a credible Pacific Fleet with which to assist its ally it, too, required mobile support facilities. Already controlling 560 merchantmen, aggregating some 2.5 million grt, the Admiralty demanded a further 134 ships, soon increased to 154. To ensure that sufficient tonnage remained to supply the United Kingdom's basic requirement of 24 million tons of imports annually, the Prime Minister himself had to intervene to rule that the size of the British Pacific Fleet should be limited to the ability to support it, and not vice versa.

Modification and mobilisation of suitable shipping was painfully slow and the Americans, with their fine, purpose-built logistics fleet, marvelled at the eclectic mass of shipping, wearing many ensigns, that supported the British. Only with much mutual tolerance and direct assistance was the Royal Navy able to operate effectively alongside its ally.

Left: **Kurita's sudden appearance off Samar was a near-disaster for the Americans. Here, the escort carrier *Gambier Bay* desperately manoeuvres to avoid salvoes of heavy-calibre Japanese shells.**

THROUGHOUT THE WAR in the Pacific, the Imperial Japanese Navy sought a 'decisive battle', a Trafalgar-style annihilation that would establish absolute sea supremacy. In the Philippines, during October 1944, they had their opportunity.

On 20 October, the Americans staged the latest in their series of massive amphibious operations, putting the Sixth Army ashore on the central Philippines island of Leyte. Offshore lay the array of support shipping upon which the operation depended, and this the Japanese proposed to destroy. Their objective was to attack the Leyte anchorage with powerful surface forces which would arrive simultaneously from both north and south. These would have to thread their way through the maze of islands to issue on time from the San Bernardino Strait to the north and the Surigao Strait to the south.

By this stage of the war, seapower was measured by strength in aircraft carriers, and the Americans had forced a series of attritional battles in which the Japanese had lost the greater part of their trained aircrew. They thus had carriers but few aircraft, and depended upon land-based air cover. This, however, had also been greatly diminished by a series of sweeps mounted from the decks of Admiral Mitscher's 16 Third Fleet carriers.

Key
BATTLE
5 LEYTE GULF

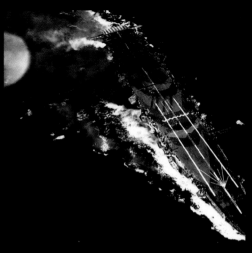

Critically short of bunker fuel, the bulk of the Japanese fleet was now based around Singapore, close to available sources. For the purpose of the operation, four separate formations were involved. From Singapore would come Vice Admiral Kurita's powerful squadron, tasked with forcing the San Bernadino Strait and from the same base, Vice Admiral Nishimura would sail for the Surigao Strait. En route, he would be reinforced by a smaller group under Vice Admiral Ozawa. His role was important, his command including four of the navy's virtually aircraft-less carriers. These were meant to be located by the Americans, providing an irresistible lure to entice Admiral Halsey's powerful Third Fleet, which was tasked with covering the landing. In its absence, the Japanese would have a free hand. What resulted was a series of related actions, fought over several days and known, collectively, as the Battle of Leyte Gulf.

Aware that their landings in the Phillipines would provoke a violent response, the Americans had made their dispositions in good time. On 23 October, therefore, as Kurita skirted the western Philippines, he encountered American submarines, which sank two heavy cruisers (including Kurita's flagship) and disabled a third. Carrying on, Kurita spent the following day fighting his way across the island-girt Sibuyan Sea in the face of successive carrier-based air strikes. These finally accounted for the loss of the super-battleship Musashi and, disheartened by her loss, Kurita temporarily reversed course. This critical manoeuvre was reported to Halsey who, believing the threat from Kurita to be passed, promptly took off northward with the whole Third Fleet to tackle Ozawa, whose presence had just been detected. Unknown to the American admiral, however, Kurita reversed course a second time and, by midnight on the 24th, his still powerful force had threaded the now-unwatched San Bernardino Strait.

To the south, meanwhile, Nishimura and Shima, whose forces remained separate, steamed toward the Surigao Strait, watched but not immediately attacked. Even as Kurita was making his way through the San Bernardino these two formations were fighting their way through a bottleneck of an approach, carefully sown by the Americans with a series of nocturnal ambushes by torpedo boats and destroyers. Already badly mauled, Nishimura arrived at the top end of the strait, only to run into a waiting gunline of six veteran battleships. These were actually part of Admiral Kinkaid's Seventh Fleet and had the role of bombardment and gun support. Instead, they crossed the Japanese 'T' in classic style, virtually annihilating the southern force, which lost both its battleships.

As Halsey's overwhelming strength closed to obliterate Ozawa, Kurita approached his objective from the north. Off the east coast of Samar, however, he ran into another Seventh Fleet group in the shape of Rear Admiral Sprague's 16 little escort carriers. These, equipped for shore support, suddenly found themselves fighting for their very existence. Transmitting a series of emergency calls, Sprague threw at Kurita everything that was to hand. His desperate defence convinced the already fatigued Japanese admiral that he had encountered the full force of Mitscher's fleet carriers. Following a period of indecisive manoeuvring, he retired, less three heavy cruisers. The obvious emergency persuaded Halsey to detach half his force, but it was too late to intervene, allowing Kurita to withdraw with little further loss.

On much the same scale as Jutland, the collective encounters cost the Japanese about 300,000 tons of warships against the Americans' 35,000 tons and, after October 1944, the Imperial Japanese Navy no longer constituted a significant threat.

Above left: Kamikaze suicide aircraft made their first appearance at Leyte Gulf. Elsewhere in the Philippines, the heavy cruiser *Louisville* is here about to be struck by one.

Above: Virtually devoid of aircraft, Ozawa's carriers were used successfully as live bait to lure Halsey off-station. The light carrier *Zuiho* belches dark funnel smoke. The paler smoke is from anti-aircraft fire.

Below: Bombed and blazing, the Princeton CVL is closed by the light cruiser *Birmingham*. When the carrier suddenly blew up there was fearful loss of life among those on the cruiser's upper deck.

Standards to Box Boats

From keel-laying to launch in just ten days. This Liberty ship goes down the ways watched by the President himself and the shipping magnate Henry J. Kaiser.

STANDARD WAR-BUILT SHIPS

SUBMARINE WARFARE during World War I caused such enormous losses in merchant shipping that British shipbuilding yards had to work at full capacity to provide replacements. To facilitate construction a range of standard designs, lettered 'A' to 'D' types, was introduced, enabling everything from engines to steel sections to be series-produced. It was, however, early in 1917 before the programme was started, and produced only 106 ships, totalling some 665,000 deadweight tons (dwt) before the armistice. Each ship averaged about 300 days under construction. The American programme of 'Hog Islanders' produced a further 122 ships, but this was between August 1918 and January 1921, therefore too late to be of use to stem the emergency.

Rapid wartime expansion and boom conditions translated quickly into over-capacity and depression in peace. The British industry, with its huge base and worldwide interests, survived, albeit in a much-reduced state. The Americans, not great ship operators, saw their industry in danger of total collapse. To protect what it saw as a national asset, Congress passed the Merchant Marine Act in 1936, thus creating the US Maritime Commission. This was empowered to fund the construction of 50 ships per year for 10 years, enabling hard-pressed operators to rejuvenate their fleets at reasonable outlay. Four baseline standards were to be produced, three dry cargo and one tanker.

The 'Libertys' to the 'Victorys'

The first contracts were let in 1938 but, when the European war erupted in 1939, the Commission foresaw the need of an emergency programme. Between August 1940 and July 1941 a further 200 contracts were awarded.

America's move was remarkably prescient for, once again, the British merchant fleet became the target of a ruthless and skilled enemy. In October 1940, a British technical mission rapidly toured American and Canadian facilities, seeking the provision of 86 standard ships. They brought their design with them, an uncomplicated tweendecker capable of lifting 10,000 dwt and powered by a triple-expansion engine taking steam from old-fashioned Scotch boilers. Building already at the North Sands yard of Joseph L. Thompson, was the first, named *Empire Liberty*.

Within weeks, 60 contracts were placed in the United States and 26 in Canada. This level of British investment allowed the Americans to create the

first of many specialist ship facilities to suit their new, all-welded construction techniques. For this, they completely redrew the British ship plans. The Canadians pursued the more-traditional methods of construction, i.e. all-riveted. This cleared British yards to concentrate on the massive and endless task of repairing war-damaged ships.

The Americans (initially very unhappy at building such 'low-tech' ships) built a series of 'North Sands' hulls, known as the 'Oceans', but passed he programme on to the Canadians, who continued to build them as 'Forts' and 'Parks'. The redrawn American type was christened the 'Liberty', officially an EC2 (or an Emergency Cargo Ship of a length between 400 and 450 ft). Very austere, the first, named appropriately *Patrick Henry*, was launched in September 1941, some 10 weeks before the cataclysm of Pearl Harbor propelled the United States, too, into war. Few knew that the ship was the forerunner of 2,700 such, many completed in strange guises ranging from hospital ships to animal transports. Most went on to give between 20 and 25 years of service.

Increasingly prefabricated, the 'Libertys', which initially took 250 days to build, were eventually completed in a few weeks. The record was for a hull to be launched less than five days after being laid down. With America now in the war, construction targets moved from 9 million grt in 1942 to an unbelievable 15 million for 1943.

During 1943, with an eye to postwar operation, an up-rated derivative, the VC2 'Victory' type, went into production in parallel with the 'Liberty'. With a 15-knot speed, against 11, and a slightly higher deadweight capacity, they were a little larger.

Driven by steam turbines, the 'Victorys' also had a raised forecastle for improved seakeeping, and more comprehensive cargo gear. Over 500 were built.

Tanker construction commenced with a dozen 18-knot, turbine-driven T3s (i.e. of between 500 and 550 feet, 152–168m, in length). All were acquired by the US Navy, four of them being converted to auxiliary aircraft carriers. The main programme, for some 525 hulls, comprised the smaller T2 type. As these were required to make 13½ knots, beyond the capacity of a reciprocating engine, and the gear-cutting industry was too stretched to provide gearing for steam turbine drive, the ships took an unusual turbo-electric installation.

Beside ship repair, British yards still produced over one million dwt annually of newbuilding. This comprised mainly short runs of a wide range of types, including 'B', 'C' and 'D' type freighters, 'Shell' and 'Norwegian' type tankers, colliers and coastal tankers. A significant group comprised the 12 (later extended) 15-knot, 12,000 dwt Standard Fast Cargo Liner. Lack of space precludes the mention of many more of these ships which won the war simply by being built at a higher rate than the enemy could sink them.

THE REVOLUTION IN CARGO HANDLING

Main picture and below: Old style handling of timber involved the labour-intensive handling of many small bundles. In contrast the commodity is shipped today in specialist large-hatch ships and in pre-packed bundles that can be handled similarly to containers.

TO THE OLD-TIME SHIP DESIGNER any type of opening in a hull was both a source of weakness and a potential flood path. As a result, tiny hatches meant that cargo had to be manhandled into the wings of the hold by a veritable army of dockers. The process was slow, but labour was cheap and time spent alongside the dock was commensurate with that taken on passage at sea. Progress with iron and steel shipbuilding improved matters somewhat, with ship design developing from an art to a science.

Old-style hatches were, indeed, a source of weakness. Portable hatch beams were overlaid with stout wooden hatch boards, and covered with a tarpaulin secured with battens and wedges. Even fitted correctly, this laborious arrangement could be carried away in heavy conditions.

During the 'thirties, therefore, the Tyneside firm of MacGregor patented a hatch cover comprising a number of steel pontoon sections. When closed, these were sealed hydraulically onto the hatch coaming. Released, they could roll along the coaming and, turned upright, be stowed compactly like a set of books. One man and a winch could do the job in 20 minutes. With the onset of rain, the hatch could be covered equally quickly to protect sensitive cargo. Only after World War II did the rolling steel hatch cover enter general service, in various configurations including side rolling. Its great strength enabled hatches to be greatly increased in size, allowing most cargo to be spotted directly from above.

The demands of amphibious warfare during World War II introduced the principle of roll-on, roll-off, with wheeled and tracked vehicles having access to, from and within a landing ship by means of movable powered ramps. Dock landing ships introduced the float-on and float-off of smaller craft, themselves preloaded.

By the late 'fifties the increasing expense of ships, crews and infrastructure brought demands for improvements – shorter times on passage and alongside, and fewer ports of call. Some Scandinavian owners, such as Johnson, had long championed the shipboard crane as quicker and less labour-intensive than the usual combination of simple and inexpensive 3-ton derricks (or cargo booms). The general acceptance of cranes was paralleled with the increasing use of fork-lift trucks, lowered into the tweendecks to shift loads. For their uninterrupted operation, tweendeck hatches had to be made flush-fitting, with coamings eliminated and replaced for strength by deep steel members below.

Roll-on/Roll-off and containers

Regular seasonal movement of perishables, such as Fred. Olsen's tomato trade with the Canaries, justified considerable investment in specialist pallet-handling ships. Each standard-sized pallet could be loaded at its point of origin and transported complete to its point of delivery. As, at no stage, did the produce require to be handled directly, while it remained in environmentally-controlled conditions, both wastage and insurance claims fell dramatically. Pallet carriers could also load and discharge quickly. Investments, ever more expensive, were now weighed carefully against perceived benefits and pay-back time. A primary aim was to reduce the need to handle cargo.

Good examples here are sawn timber and rolls of newspaper. Softwood, used in immense quantities by the construction industry, stems mainly from Canada and the upper Baltic. Of low density, this product will fill the ship and be loaded as a high deck cargo, with the ship still not down to her marks. Until the 'sixties, dockers armed with spikes would fit each sawn length separately to form a solid mass. Topsides, it was confined by timber stanchions erected along the sides of the ship. With the coming of large hatches and fork lifts timber began to be handled in pre-packed bundles of standard volume, again not broken down except by the end-user.

Roll-on roll-off permitted newsprint, notoriously wet-sensitive, to be covered and secured to trailers for its complete journey, with only the tractor units changing. All types of heavy goods could, of course, be carried but direct derivatives of these ships were the familiar car/passenger cross channel ferry and the pure car carrier (PCC), the latter an unlovely box-shaped vessel with up to 13 internal decks crammed with several thousand export cars.

Truly global in their activities, the oil and chemical industries required ever-larger indivisible loads to be shipped. Traditional heavy-lift derricks, capable of perhaps 100-ton loads, were largely superseded in the 'fifties by the complex and costly German Stülcken derrick with up to three times the capacity. The layout of the ship itself, however, still

imposed limitations, speeding the acceptance of commercial ships derived from naval LSDs. Able to flood down, such ships can float on barge-mounted cargoes of immense size, for instance complete container cranes and ever smaller ships.

Described below, the container brought the largest revolution to date. It was the ultimate 'through' package, being stuffed and secured at source, sealed under customs licence and stripped only at its destination. It meant an enormous investment in ships, boxes, shore terminals, computer systems and land-based transport. It also meant the scrapping of thousands of traditional break-bulkers and the loss of livelihood to tens of thousands of seamen. Whether it is truly 'ultimate', only time will tell.

Left: Motor vehicles, as a cargo, are high value, high volume and low deadweight, demanding specialist multi-decked ships. UECC is a Franco-Norwegian consortium running a pool of smaller vessels between UK and European continental ports.

THE DECLINE OF TRADITIONAL MARITIME FLAGS

Below right: Until the late 1950s the UK operated the world's largest active fleet. Thirty years later, the Red Ensign was in 13th place, with just two per cent of the world's tonnage. Other traditional mercantile powers, such as France and the Netherlands, have fared even worse.

TO THE SHIPPING LAYMAN, a phenomenon of the last half-century has been the apparent withdrawal from the industry of traditionally-powerful maritime nations. Ninety years ago, in 1908, the world fleet of seagoing steam ships numbered nearly 15,000, aggregating about 32.2 million gross registered tons (grt). Of these, over 6,300 ships, totalling about 52 per cent by tonnage, were British. Following, in order, were Germany (11.3 per cent), the United States of America (5.8), France and Norway (3.9 each). By 1991, the world total had mushroomed 13-fold to about 430 million grt, of which 22 per cent wore the Liberian flag, 17 per cent the Panamanian, and 16 per cent the Cypriot, Bahamian or Bermudan. Where, at the beginning of the century, six ships out of ten would have sported such as London, Liverpool or Hamburg on their counters, much the same proportion would now bear Monrovia, Limassol or Nassau.

The answer, as ever, lays in economics. Shipping is an industry that, necessarily, transcends national boundaries. Some flags, including the British, are very involved in 'cross-trading', or operations between states other than their own. In doing so, they come into direct competition with discriminatory measures, adopted by many emergent states to favour their own industries, but also with a range of flags whose shipowners pay little or no tax. However efficient a company, it cannot compete on such terms.

Flags of convenience – and necessity

The cost of operating a ship falls under three broad headings – fuel, capital costs and running expenses. The proportion consumed by each depends upon the type of ship. For a quarter-million ton tanker, fuel will account for a quarter of overall cost but, for a long-haul container ship, which must maintain schedules, it may be as high as 40 per cent. For a coaster, which spends proportionately longer alongside, it will be only half this. In order to be replaced, ships must pay for themselves within a working lifetime, so between 30 and 50 per cent of expenditure is capital cost. The remainder, running

costs, is greatly influenced by crew, administration and port charges. For their size the larger examples have small crews and their respective 25 and 30 per cent costs reflect the high administration and cargo handling charges associated with the container business. A coaster, with a large crew in relation to her size, and making frequent port calls, will see nearly half its costs associated with running charges. In the short term, costs may be cut by slow steaming, for a knot or two less will dramatically reduce fuel bills. Ships may be retained a year to two longer before replacement. Crew costs, however, with wages inflated for the owners by social security and payroll taxes, are on-going. Good working practices and automation may reduce crews in the first instance but a cheaper crew is a great attraction.

By international law, ships have to be registered and wear a flag appropriate to their port of registration. Owners are not, in general, obliged to join their own national registry. As costs vary greatly between one 'flag' and another there may be considerable advantage in operating through a nominal company established elsewhere. Registers that accept shipping foreign to them are called Open Registers and their flags commonly termed Flags of Convenience (FOC). There are also quasi-FOCs, such as the British Bermudan and Isle of Man, and

the French Kerguelen, where a traditional 'closed' register will still apply some of the requirements of the parent flag.

Flag changes are nothing new. Early in World War II, for instance, many American ships shifted to Panamanian in order to circumvent neutrality laws and continue trading to the United Kingdom.

Flags of developed nations impose taxation, set and maintain standards and stipulate the required number of qualified nationals to be recruited for officers and crew. In contrast, the lower end of the FOC spectrum is virtually requirement-free. A handy-sized bulker may pay an annual registration and survey fee of only a few thousand dollars, but the contributions of many such ships make a large difference to the economy of a small state. In return, they allow owners a very free hand.

Good FOCs are as strict as any in the business, the worst often hit the news in being arrested by Admiralty marshals or detained by port authorities for infringement of mandatory codes. Crews here have no enforceable rights, while companies spawn second or third-generation offshoots whose provenance is convoluted to the point where ownership cannot be established. Attempts by such FOCs to improve standards have often been met simply by mass defections to other flags.

Although traditional flags dislike open and quasi-open registers which, they maintain, distort free competition, nearly half the world's shipping is linked to them. Reputable organisations join them to survive and, indeed, they are often referred to as 'Flags of Necessity'.

Above left: Effective strikes in 1960 and 1966 by members of the Nation Union of Seamen improved the lot of many but cost the companies so dearly that they looked at other options. Here, Union-Castle and P & O ships lay idle at Southampton in 1966.

Above : Today's seamen need to master wider ranges of skills and training is both more formal and more expensive. Here a class is learning the technique of launching a large inflatable raft, introduced in the late 1950s

THE REVOLUTION IN SHIPBUILDING

FOLLOWING THE INDUSTRIAL Revolution, the British not only owned the bulk of the world's metal shipping but also built it. Ships were remarkably similar, varying mainly in size and in the detail that suited them to their owner's particular trade. The many yards along the Tyne and the Tees, the Clyde and the Mersey were thinned-out by the great 1930s' depression but the survivors continued to build traditional types in a traditional fashion. There was little reason for innovation. A ship was first framed-up, her form, a series of harmonious curves, already visible. Hull and deck plating, much of it furnaced and rolled to complex curvature, was then riveted to the frames, an exhausting, noisy and dirty process.

The desperate need for shipping during World War II changed all this. Ship designers sought speed and ease of construction. Every process and feature was queried and, if not eliminated, simplified. Hulls, formerly graced by continuous sheerlines and camber, now comprised a series of flat planes. Complex curvature in bow and stern plating was replaced almost entirely with simply-curved plates, using knuckles if necessary. Continuous tank-testing ensured that simplicity of construction was not bought at too high a cost in hydrodynamic efficiency.

Unlike 'one-offs' for an individual owner, standard ships were just like one more series-built commodity. Welding revolutionised construction. Not demanding the same degree of physical stamina as riveting it could be, and was, undertaken by large numbers of women. Hull and superstructure were reduced to simple modules, built anywhere and brought to the shipyard only for final assembly. As downhand welding was quicker and more reliable, means were developed for the safe inversion and alignment of ever-larger agglomerations of modules.

The half-million tonners

Austere war-built standard ships formed the bulk of most post-war fleets, with general shortage of resources preventing their rapid replacement by owner-specified, bespoke tonnage. By the time that replacement programmes did get under way, austerity was past and ships were of a higher grade, faster, more versatile, and of ever-increasing size. Many older yards lacked the space, resources or, simply, the will to respond to the new demands and, once the demand for 'low-tech' tonnage disappeared they went out of business, one by one.

Opposite: Large ships are now built almost exclusively in graving docks. The French-built cruise liner *Sovereign of the Seas* demonstrates the extreme forms and high technology that demands covered construction.

Left: Ships built in modules can be dismantled in modules. An aluminium high-speed ferry has here had a section of shell plating removed to fleet-in a 16-cylinder diesel propulsion unit.

Below: Harland and Wolff at Belfast specialises in the construction of large bulk carriers. Here, a complete and already fitted-out superstructure module is being positioned by a Goliath crane.

The 1960s saw the dynamics of 'economies of size', as tankers and bulk carriers increased in size at a phenomenal rate. Quarter-million tonners became commonplace, with a fair number of others exceeding 350,000 dwt and a handful exceeding a half-million. Hulls of this magnitude could not be launched conventionally, requiring to be assembled in docks and floated out. Million-ton docks and the Goliath cranes that served them represented a huge investment. They needed to be created on greenfield sites, and these were selected in countries where labour was cheap. Japan prospered mightily, having not only the labour pool but also the ingenuity to harness computer technology to the processes of both design and engineering production.

The parallel midbodies of large bulk carriers incorporate, for instance, literally acres of identical, stiffened rectangular shell plates. Production lines for these were completely automated. For smaller plate components, wastage was cut dramatically through the ability of computer-aided draughting (CAD) to 'nest' complex shapes onto a single plate. With the individual shapes and their registration programmed to digital tape, they were cut and bevelled automatically by numerically-controlled (NC) flame cutters. Edge profile and finish were produced as specified, and ready for welding.

To guarantee quality control and to avoid delays due to weather, building processes are commonly under cover, with the construction hall forming a 'T' with the building dock, which extends into the hall. Inside, prefabricated modules are assembled into major blocks, already well advanced in fitting-out. The after end, incorporating machinery and accommodation, takes longest to complete

and is the first to be lowered into the dock.

At the correct point in a tightly-defined schedule, this module is then moved bodily along the support ways to make room for the next module ahead. Once this is aligned and connected, the combination is moved for the next block to be added, and so on. The ship, in effect, is being extruded from the construction hall, her bow section being added last. The key to such focused activity is minutely-detailed planning. Because of the effort involved, economics demand that a yard produces a portfolio of standard designs, capable of a degree of 'personalising' for individual owners. In time, the new technologies filtered down to even the smallest yard.

Cost considerations remain paramount. Cheaper Japanese yards wrested business from the more expensive Europeans. In turn, however, Korea has taken Japan's place, while China, Malaysia and Indonesia are set fair to continue the process. Europe's diminishing share comprises mainly the 'high-tech' end of the market, such as liquified gas carriers and large cruise ships.

OIL AND GAS TANKERS

Right: Rapid industrialisation and population growth saw hugely increased demand for lubricating oils. Bulk shipment was introduced in the 1860s but many merchantmen, such as the *Chigwell* of 1880, accepted cargoes of 'case oil'.

OIL SEEPING NATURALLY from the ground has been used for fuel and lighting for centuries. In such as Burma and China it has likewise long been transported in riverine and coastal craft. However, the major stimulus for the exploitation of oil, not least for its lubricating qualities, came from the rapidly-industrialising areas of Europe and the United States.

Following the 1859 discovery of United States oil, it was being shipped to Great Britain within three years. Ships either retained their general cargo configuration, shipping oil in stackable rectangular cans ('case-oil') or had oil tanks retro-fitted, conformally with their hull. To minimise the dangers of free surfaces, tanks were kept small or fitted with expansion trunks to reduce the area of the ullage space.

Oil of Russian origin was cheaper but was produced around the land-locked Caspian Sea. A fleet of craft compatible with the local inland waterways was, as a consequence, built by two of the Swedish Nobel brothers. Their *Zoroaster* of 1878 had her conformal tanks removed, increasing capacity by using the ship's shell plating as tanks. She also burned oil for propulsive purposes. Three follow-ons developed the concept further, having engines sited more safely right aft and adding longitudinal to transverse bulkheads to reduce individual tank sizes.

The *Gluckauf*, built at Wallsend to German account in 1886, is usually regarded as the ancestor of the modern tanker. She was of 2,700 dwt and

took the Nobels' ideas further by isolating the limits of the cargo tanks by means of cofferdams, and arranging piping, pumping and valve layout in a coherent and accessible manner.

There followed a proliferation of tanker-building and the formation of companies which would become synonymous with the industry, including the ancestors of Esso and Shell, two of the seven great 'oil majors'. Up to about 1910 there were many sailing tankers, both bulk and case-oil carriers, but these were limited to some 4,000 dwt apiece. Once designers learned how to cater for the large stresses imposed by engines-aft machinery on an unloaded hull, ship size increased. Even before World War I Eagle Oil had ten ships of 16,000 dwt in service or on order.

Suez – its influence on shipping

A combination of war losses and a post-war boom found the oil majors with insufficient tonnage, a shortfall solved largely by Scandinavian independent owners working to profitable charters. They quickly became a feature of the inter-war tanker scene.

Until World War II, most oil was refined at the point of origin, so that the majority of tankers were transporting refined products such as aviation spirit

Left: By the late 1970s oil demand was increasing so rapidly that million-ton tankers were confidently forecast. Middle-eastern crises changed all that, and only a handful of ships exceeded 500,000 deadweight tons.

or diesel oil. By the 1950s, however, oil-importing economies, such as those of Western Europe and Japan, were requiring an ever-greater range of oil-derived products, while the areas of production were also experiencing increasing political instability. New refineries were thus constructed, close to the new industrial zones. Tankers now fell into two groups, the long-haul crude-oil carriers running from the main centres of production in the Middle East, West Africa and Central America, and the smaller 'products carriers' that distributed refined products to the consumers.

The ever-increasing range of products made carriers complex and expensive, with intricate cargo handling arrangements designed to prevent cross-contamination of the many 'parcels' that might be carried.

AS larger crude carriers could shift cargo more cheaply, sizes increased quickly. The standard 18,000-tonner of 1945 had become 30,000 dwt by the early 1950s and, a decade later, the 70,000-tonner, which was the maximum that the Suez Canal could accommodate in a loaded condition. The first 100,000 dwt ships were already at sea, however, and sizes again soon doubled to the maximum that could transit the Canal in ballast, returning via the Cape fully loaded, a round trip of some 18,000 miles. The 200,000-tonner known as a VLCC (Very Large Crude Carrier), had deep draught and slow manoeuvrability, and had profound effects on waterways and the migration of ports downstream to deeper water.

With war closing the Suez Canal in 1967 extra voyage time caused a tanker shortage. New buildings, no longer constrained, increased further in size. The 300,000 dwt ULCC (Ultra-large) made its appearance but, although the million-tonner was confidently predicted, the cost of modifying port

infrastructures confined the growth to a small handful of 550,000 dwt ships.

Since World War II, natural and petroleum gas have become a significant energy source. Shipped in highly specialised ships, the product is liquefied by a combination of pressurisation and refrigeration. Liquefied natural/petroleum gas (LNG/LPG) carriers move the product from the Caribbean, Indonesia/Malaysia and North Africa in heavily insulated cylindrical or spherical tanks. Long haul ships may have a capacity of some 125,000 cubic metres and smaller distributors, 15,000.

Below: Liquified natural (LNG) and petroleum (LPG) gas is now shipped in vast quantities by sea, one major route being Australia-Japan. In the great spherical tanks of the Moss system, the gas is carried in a pressurised and refrigerated state.

SUPPORTING THE OFFSHORE OIL INDUSTRY

THE FIRST EXPLOITATION OF OIL beyond the tideline was made using equipment mounted on pontoons, which could be towed into position and then ballasted down to provide a stable working platform. Deeper water sites had to await the jack-up rig. This, usually triangular, pontoon has a tubular or lattice leg at each corner which can be 'spudded' into the seabed. Thus supported, the pontoon deck can then raise itself up the legs to a level safely above the surface. When drilling has been completed, the procedure is reversed and it is towed away for the next task.

The Gulf of Mexico, where most developments occurred, has a benign climate outside the hurricane season, and an eclectic range of local craft earned their living tending the rigs. Specialist items, however, such as long bundles of drilling pipe, special cements and high density muds, led to the introduction of a supply vessel suited to the task. The marine equivalent of a pick-up truck, this has a short, high forecastle encompassing basic accommodation and supporting a wheelhouse. The after two-thirds has a low-freeboard deck, completely clear and bounded along the sides by high protective bulwarks, fitted with stout lashing rails.

As laying alongside a rig is not possible in open sea conditions, the supply vessel's mode of operation was to drop an anchor and back down to the rig, using her twin screws to maintain line. Constant engine orders are required to keep the after deck within plumbing range of the rig's crane and, before the days of heave compensation, shifting heavy or bulky loads could be an exciting occupation in a heavy swell.

When, in 1966, gas and oil were struck in the North Sea, the industry effectively shifted forward a gear, for depths quickly became considerable and conditions were anything but benign. Fortunately the semi-submersible platform had made its appearance. It features a (usually) rectangular working deck, supported on the longer sides by huge hollow legs, based on permanently-submerged buoyant pontoons. For transit, the lower members are pumped out to increase freeboard and to reduce the wetted area. In operation, the platform is simply ballasted down to bring the working deck to the required height above the surface. As waves pass through the structure, it has very little motion in a seaway.

Production platforms

Semi-submersibles are usually self-propelled but, for operations, must be located by heavy anchors, two at each corner. The rig's crane will transfer an anchor (attached by its cable to the rig) to the supply ship, which runs out a considerable distance before releasing it. An anchor's holding power depends upon the weight of a scope of heavy cable acting as a spring, preventing snatch loads being transferred to the anchor. Positioned, the platform will have eight such anchors, deployed at 45-degree intervals.

It will be apparent that the basic supply vessel has had to become a versatile anchor-handler and tug in addition. While retaining its layout, the Offshore Supply Vessel (OSV) has grown considerably, from the original 310 gross tons with 1,200 bhp to 1,600-tonners with 13,000 bhp. It has acquired a large winch, used both for towing and anchor handling, and a full-width stern roller. An island wheelhouse gives all-round visibility, while slow-speed manoeuvring, effected by joystick control from a central console, is greatly enhanced by transverse thrusters. To meet the ever-present risk of fire aboard platforms, the OSV carries powerful monitors and is built with a designated rescue zone and the necessary facilities for survivors.

Viable oil wells, once proven, are capped and await the production platform. First to arrive is the immense tubular lattice structure of the jacket. Shipped out on its side, it is skidded off its flat barge,

Below: Oil is the lifeblood of industry. Flowing continuously from offshore to refinery, it is distributed in many refined forms to the consumer. In the depths of winter an inland waterway ice-breaking tug clears the way for a tanker barge.

Left: Offshore production and storage units are anchored permanently over a field's production centre. Shuttle tankers may load directly from them with crude for the refinery.

Below: The huge tubular jacket has here been positioned and sunk over a seabed template. Taking advantage of calm conditions, a giant floating crane is lowering the platform which crowns it

floated into the vertical, positioned over the pipe template and gently flooded to settle on the seabed, where it is secured by piling. Atop the jacket, prefabricated modular components of up to 300 tonnes apiece are positioned by some of the world's largest floating cranes.

There is a great air of urgency, as operations are expensive and 'weather windows' unpredictable. A small township of interconnected accommodation and production platforms may be created for large fields, the agglomeration processing the output of a number of wells. Oil may be piped or shipped to shore-side refineries.

The considerable quantities of necessary pipe, in 40 ft (12.2 m) lengths, are shipped aboard special pipe carriers and transferred to a specialist barge where it is welded into a continuous length and laid over a long jib (or 'stringer') as the barge is slowly winched forward on a pair of anchor cables.

If shipped ashore, specially-fitted shuttle tankers locate themselves over a Single Point Mooring (SPM). This, effectively a submerged buoy, is attached to a turret-mounted loading assembly which allows the tanker to 'weathervane', or lay to weather, during the loading process.

Many other craft are involved along the way, from the Seismic Survey Ships towing arrays of air guns, to rock dumpers which cover and support the pipelines from scour and anchors, and maintenance ships with divers and, increasingly, remotely-operated vehicles (ROV).

HEAVY LIFT SHIPS

Right: Lauritzen's Dan Lifter is ballasted to sit on the bottom in shallow water to allow large loads to be floated into position. Here, she brings back the bomb-damaged LSL *Sir Tristram* from the Falklands.

Below: Blue Star Line is one company that still profitably operates cargo liners. One or two of the fleet are equipped for exceptional loads. The *Timaru Star*'s Stülcken derrick can plumb both No.2 and No.3 hold.

AS RECENTLY AS WORLD WAR I it was necessary for an item such as a railway locomotive to be broken down into several component parts in order to be transported by sea. Because European colonial powers exported a considerable quantity of rolling stock to their dominions this was a considerable time-wasting activity. In European ports, large floating cranes were perfectly capable of handling such loads complete but similar facilities were unusual abroad, and the individual weights were beyond the capacity of a ship's cargo gear. Reassembly of such items as major electrical plant required skills unobtainable in colonial territories.

Soon after World War I a Norwegian shipowner, Christen Smith, secured a contract to ship 200 steam locomotives from the Tyne to Angola. With adequate cranage available at either end, he had his ships strengthened to take the vehicles complete. It occurred to him that, as so much time had been saved by this simple procedure, there would be greater savings using a ship that could handle and stow heavy loads herself.

Thus was founded the Belships fleet. High-class cargo liners, such as those of the Clan, Strick and Hansa lines, which traded to less well-equipped colonial ports, commonly carried a single 30 or 50-tonne derrick, but Smith's fleet were true specialists. To provide wide, unobstructed deck space for bulky items, machinery was sited aft (unusual in dry cargo ships of the time). A small island bridge structure divided the long No. 1 hatch from equally long Nos 2 and 3 abaft it. Each hold was served by a single 100-tonne derrick, together with a full outfit of more conventional 5-tonners. Hatch covers were

load-bearing, seated on exceptionally deep coamings for stiffness. Side decks were obstruction-free and their strengthening obviated the need for pillars in the hold below.

Because loads were often bulky as well as heavy, derricks required a long outreach. This translated into more powerful scantlings and a greater moment imposed on the ship, which thus listed heavily during cargo handling. Large ballast capacity was thus incorporated, both to counteract such lists and to restore stability range when the ship carried heavy deck loads. Belship's basic design was so successful that, during World War II, British yards built 14 7,800 grt ships to a very similar layout, and ten handy-sized derivatives of 3,540 grt.

Amphibious warfare

Following the war, the oil business, in particular, required to shift ever-larger indivisible items of cargo, and considerable attention was devoted to the problem. Derricks were heeled to one side of a mast, restricting operations to that side of a ship but able to serve two hatches. Pads on retractable arms could be lowered hydraulically onto a quay to confer stability on moving heavy loads, although the resultant point loading could often be beyond the capacity of the quay apron to support it.

The 'ultimate' heavy-lift derrick was introduced in the 1950s by the Hamburg firm of Sülckenwerft. Rated at up to 330 tonnes, these huge units were heeled between a pair of massive tapered posts, whose rotatable caps allowed the derrick to work two hatches. Improvements in electronic control permitted two such derricks to work together, virtually doubling lift capacity. This trend was later continued with sided cranes.

With the 1960s came the onset of containerisation and the general demise of the classic cargo liner. Heavy lift was similarly affected, borrowing new techniques based on those introduced during World War II.

Amphibious warfare had demanded the handling and transport of huge numbers of heavy armoured vehicles. This resulted in the LST, which combined unobstructed deck space with interconnecting lifts and ramps. In turn, this led to the specialist roll-on/roll-off (RoRo) ship, with its ability to take aboard huge, trailer-mounted loads.

The wartime requirement to move pre-loaded assault craft on ocean passages brought about the Landing Platform (Dock), or LPD, able to flood down to load and discharge smaller craft displacing several hundred tonnes. Now known as Float-on-Float-off, or FloFlo, the principle is used widely.

The versatile concept of the Dock Ship, a Dutch development, combines both principles. Her capacious well, closed by a stem gate, can accept huge floating loads. Alternatively, pontoon sections can be added to create both a tween deck and a weather deck, allowing RoRo cargo to be carried on three levels. Further, the narrow side decks flanking the well support tracks for a pair of 500-tonne capacity gantry cranes. Projecting horns take the tracks beyond the transom.

A final concept is the pontoon barge which can be sunk in shallow water. A very large load, such as an immobilised ship, is then floated over it and positioned before the pontoon is pumped out, gently lifting her from the water to be carried away. This method was used to bring Brunel's *Great Britain* home from the Falklands.

It was then a short step to develop the technique into an open-decked version of an LPD, well capable of lifting and transporting a ship the size of a guided-missile destroyer.

Below: Mammoet Shipping's *Happy Buccaneer* operates like a naval LSD, flooding down to accept barge-mounted heavy cargoes over a lowerable sterngate.

ROLL-ON/ROLL-OFF

Below: The blue-banded funnel of Wilhelmsen once graced cargo liners. Quarter ramps on its RoRos connect their cavernous interiors direct with the quayside. Their loadbearing capacity will accept most wheeled cargo.

SOME COMMODITIES ARE NOT suitable for shipment by container. A good example is heavy specialised vehicles for earth-moving or road construction. Another is the wide range of so-called 'forest products', e.g. sheets of hardboard or chipboard, which stow to compact, dense-masses, and heavy rolls of newsprint, which are notoriously damp sensitive. Both are best loaded onto trailers or pallets. Then, of course, there are the hundreds of thousands of cars that are continuously shipped around the world to suit international tastes. These are the types of trade in which the roll-on/roll-off ship earns its keep.

As explained earlier, RoRo concepts such as unobstructed inboard spaces, ramps and elevators originated with the LSTs of World War II. Enhanced by the inventive genius of firms such as MacGregor International, these quickly moved on to take their part in the 1960s' shipping revolution.

RoRos vary in size and capability from the small, largely open construction, single-decked ferries that link offshore islands with the mainland to the 50,000-ton giants that operate, for instance, between north-west Europe/Scandinavia and eastern United States/Canada ranges. Between these extremes are a wide variety of ships, all with a box-like family resemblance.

This appearance is due to the type being volume, rather than weight, critical. To cite a comparison. A 150,000 grt ULCC, designed for

high-density cargo, will have a deadweight of about 300,000 tons, but low-density RoRo shipments mean that a large 58,000 grt carrier will be of only some 45,000 dwt. This nicely illustrates that a gross ton is a unit of the ship's reckonable enclosed space while a deadweight ton relates to the actual weight of cargo that she can carry.

As long-haul RoRos operate in direct competition with more economic pure container ships over sections of their voyage itineraries they, too, require to be 'container friendly'. This means that they can stow boxes on the weather deck, which is sometimes fitted with permanent guides for the purpose, and in the forward holds. This arrangement, together with their fine lines and comparatively high speed, means that bow doors cannot be fitted. To permit a 'drive-on/drive-off' facility, without too much on-board manoeuvring, careful internal design is therefore required. Contributing to this is the massive stern ramp, angled across the transom, which folds upwards against a prominent gantry structure when the ship is at sea. Internal ramped access to the lower vehicle spaces severely restrict's the headroom available for the machinery spaces.

The RoRo's generally lofty appearance, coupled with some widely-publicised sinkings, have given the popular misconception that the concept is fundamentally unsound. Certainly, it can be unforgiving if poorly operated and may respond unpredictably to collision damage but, on both counts, considerably less so than the average aircraft. In a RoRo, the lowest continuous vehicle deck is the freeboard deck. This is sited a specific distance above the load waterline and spaces below it are sub-divided by watertight bulkheads. Any two spaces may be flooded without the ship sinking. Properly designed and run they can absorb great punishment, as evinced by the case of the *Atlantic Conveyor*. Hit by a pair of large anti-ship missiles, she blazed uncontrollably for days but finally sank only through this causing structural failure.

RoRo dangers and car carriers

What a RoRo cannot tolerate is free water on the freeboard deck. This vast open area, vital to an economic stowage factor, offers a free surface. Water will, inevitably, move to one side, with a consequent shift of its centre of gravity (CG). This will cause the ship to slump moving the CG even further and usually accentuating the cause of the flooding, and

Left: A modern ark, the Pure Car Carrier (PCC) can stow a veritable town-full of cars. Shoebox topsides, grafted onto a fine-lined hull, contain a multitude of interconnected decks.

Below: Following several notable capsizes, caused by the free-surface effect of water on the main deck, many RoRos were fitted with external bulging to extend their stability range.

initiating a rapid capsize. Doubling the walls of the garage space to reduce the effects of collision badly affects the revenue-earning space. Adding sponsons along the sides, to increase the stability range, increases form resistance and the cost of fuel.

One of the more bizarre sights met with at sea is the Pure Car Carrier, or PCC. Lofty topsides have to merge with fine underwater sections for speeds of up to 20 knots, resulting in exaggerated flare at either end and pronounced discontinuities in the form of knuckles. The small crew is housed topside in a superstructure that is barely noticeable. The current largest can stow over 6,000 cars on up to 14, low headroom decks. Fitted with prominent quarter and 'midships ramps, and a multitude of internal ramps, they are designed to move their cargoes with zero damage, but to load and discharge in minimum time. Exhaust fumes are a major resulting problem and an external feature of most PCCs is the array of ventilators along the upper deck edges. An unusual feature of this trade is the high proportion of PCCs owned or run by the car manufacturers themselves in order to retain full control over shipments.

THE RISE OF THE SUPER-FERRY

Above: Beauty of sorts. The lines of the classic ocean liner contrast with those of the super-ferry, its modern counterpart. Super-structures are greatly enclosed for a maximum of outside cabin space.

THE EXPLOSIVE DEVELOPMENT in air travel following World War II resulted in the rapid demise of the classic ocean liner. Worldwide travel became affordable to the many for the first time, as economies picked up. Rising standards of living were closely reflected by individual car ownership. Already familiar with jetting to the sun, everyman wished also to use his car to 'do it himself' on foreign soil closer to home. From the United Kingdom, however, his choices were limited, as ferries to the near continent were still run by the lineal descendant of the railway companies that had first begat them. They were geared to moving foot passengers across an unavoidable barrier that separated one train and the next. Facilities, both at terminals and aboard ship, ranged from basic to plain dire.

It did not have to be like this. On the Baltic there existed a growing network of routes, many of them international and of quite substantial length. Scandinavian standards were (and remain) high, and

operators adapted quickly to the growing demand by car-accompanied passengers. Experience produced the drive-through concept, with bow and stern doors permitting a first-on, first-off approach, with no on-board manoeuvring. Passengers represented a captive audience with time on their hands. Wooed with good-class restaurants and, on international routes, the delights of tax-free shopping, they could be persuaded to spend freely. Operators were thus encouraged to improve facilities even further.

As Baltic standards improved, with introduction of newer and larger tonnage, first generation ships were displaced. Thoresen's three Viking ferries appeared on the mid-Channel services from Southampton like a breath of fresh air, their six-hour daylight passage being long enough to demonstrate that improved standards would be rewarded elsewhere.

On the shorter Channel routes from Dover the British firm of Townsend established itself with its strong 'Free Enterprise' image. With transit times

Left: Short-haul ferries require maximum through-put for profitability. Port infrastructure thus has to be tailored for rapid loading and discharge, as seen here at Dover.

too brief for the encouragement of leisurely onboard activities, ships were designed more to maximise revenue-earning space and to minimise turnround times. No overnight cabin space was needed, reducing volume demand and staff requirements. Restaurants were replaced by simple, quick-service cafeterias. Although freight-only services already existed, a considerable flow of commercial vehicles, attracted by the short delay in crossing, was also drawn, accentuating the trend to the maximisation of garage space.

Mini cruisers and on-board facilities

Changes in travel habits are illustrated by the fact that British Rail's early-1950s' ferries accommodated ten passengers for each car carried, indicating a still-large train-travelling public. Ten years later, Townsend's first ship showed a change of ratio to 5.5 to one. More recent ships have reduced this further to only 3.5 to one. These ships are worked intensively, making up to five return trips per day. As loading and discharge thus occupies a considerable proportion of their time, much investment goes into complex internal ramping to smooth vehicle flow. Such expenditure has to be matched with shore facilities including linkspans.

Even short-haul ships such as these have grown inexorably (to a current 26,000 grt) but are specialised to the point where they are not easy to switch to alternative routes. Their size is largely a commercial response to the unfair challenge posed by the Channel Tunnel, with its vast hidden subsidies.

It is on the longer, overnight routes, again particularly on the Baltic, that the ferry has continued its remarkable development to 'super' status. Passages are skilfully marketed as 'mini-cruises', supported by a host of facilities added to enhance the staple pleasures of foreign travel and 'duty-frees'. What has occurred is a re-emergence of the luxury liner concept, with the difference that passengers now view their trip more as an end in itself than simply a means of taking passage as part of a longer travel sequence.

Upper Baltic ships are approaching 60,000 grt (exceeded by only very few of the classic ocean liners of the past) and have reverted to a 5.5 to one passenger to car ratio. Such huge ships adopt features like six-deck-high 'atria' onto which inboard cabins look out. Laid out as promenades, they are served by gilded elevators and lined with exclusive

shopping facilities. This opulent, leisurely ambience is enhanced by health clubs, beauty parlours and pools, casinos, bistros and restaurants of the best class. Ticket costs are pitched at levels that make a prospective trip attractive, for it is on board his ship that the ferry operator makes his profit.

This style of luxury ferry is currently very much a European concept but, with the United Kingdom already connected by the two-day passage to northern Spain, longer passages are certainly future possibilities. Further development in North Africa could, for instance, generate sufficient demand for Mediterranean routes to be established. Despite its generally more benign climate, the Mediterranean has attractions served currently by short-haul ferries and cruise liners.

Below: Speed in crossing currently takes precedence over comfort. High-speed hull forms may not always be the answer to routes where wind and sea predominate from specific directions.

CRUISE SHIPS

BEFORE THE 1950s, when air travel began to challenge and deplete the world's fleet of passenger liners, sea travel was commonplace, but was looked upon as a means to an end. To take a voyage for its own sake was unusual. Cruises, for a dedicated few enthusiasts however, were available from companies giving employment to low-season tonnage or similarly eking out an extra season or two from superseded units slated for disposal.

During the 1960s and 1970s, established companies found passenger operations increasingly uneconomic, and either sought to find new employment for their ships or off-loaded superfluous good-quality tonnage onto the sales market. Familiar names – Union Castle, Royal Mail, Canadian Pacific, French Line, Holland-Amerika and so many more – either disappeared or looked to be in immediate danger of doing so. Several entrepreneurial companies thus acquired their first ships for a proverbial song and began to heavily promote cruising for the mass market. Their timing was well calculated for incomes were rising and charter air rates were tumbling.

Cruising in luxury from one exotic location to another was targeted first at the lucrative American market, whose Florida ports were, in any case, conveniently close to the Caribbean or to Bermuda. Ships remained on station, locally maintained, their crews rotated, in order to maximise the number of cruises per ship per season. For an increasingly-interested European market the 'fly-cruise' combination was ideal, the necessary return trip to Florida occupying little precious vacation time.

Ex-passenger liners, switched to cruising, usually lacked the luxury features increasingly expected by this new class of tourist. Where suitable, ships were thus given extensive – and expensive – rebuilds, paid for by remodelling accommodation to increase the number of berths.

Throughout the 1980s cruising prospered, if fitfully. Mediterranean and Indonesian itineraries vied with the Caribbean. For the discerning there was Alaska or even the fringes of the polar seas. Conversions were no longer adequate, elderly liners, even with elaborate makeovers, still contriving to look elderly, while becoming increasingly difficult to comply with toughening safety standards. Built for ocean passages, with fine lines, deep draught and machinery designed for high continuous output, they did not conform to cruise-liner parameters.

As these first generation ships gravitated through ever cheaper operators before being scrapped, purpose-designed ships, ever larger, ever more bizarre in styling, emerged. For now, in the 1990s, cruising has come of age, and scores of thousands of berths are being marketed.

Today's cruise ship resembles a huge motor yacht, her form a sharp and modernistic forward end wedded to a wide-transomed, boxy, parallel mid-body. Outside cabins command a premium, so accommodation decks are piled ever higher. With earlier promenade deckspace usurped by cabins, air is sought on the acres of topside sundeck, liberally provided with pools and bars. Lifeboats, which would have interfered with the view, have been banished downward to a recess in the hull proper from where, at least, it is a shorter drop to the water.

Belying her topsides appearance, a cruise ship's submerged hull form is advanced and efficient. Shallow draught is necessary to maximise the number of accessible cruise destinations. Twin screws are, therefore, provided to reduce their diameter and to improve manoeuvrability. Cruising involves frequent docking and undocking, so up to six side thrusters may be provided, along with efficient flapped rudders to make the ship, in most conditions, independent of expensive tugs.

Even larger ships are planned, the long-heralded 250,000-ton *Phoenix World City* being dwarfed by the 2,880 ft (877.8 m), difficult to believe and horribly-named, *World of ResidenSea*. This behemoth will feature 286 apartments for continuous, condominium-type ownership. To be completed in 2001, the vessel will remain at sea to assist inhabitants to avoid tax liabilities!

Right: For many 'beauty and the beast'. Cruise ships may mean the sudden descent of thousands of tourists on ancient locations ill-equipped to cope with their requirements.

Below: Large numbers of passengers require much space: most prefer outside accommodation. The result is a high-sided hull with a long, parallel midbody and no traditional promenade decks.

Opposite: Passenger enjoyment and corporate identity enjoy high priority during the cruise ship's design process. The resulting appearance is far removed from that of the classic passenger vessel and is something of an acquired taste.

Floating hotels

Flexible diesel-electric propulsion is usually specified. Shafts are short and directly-driven by 200-ton electric motors rated at possibly 20 megawatts (27,000 ehp) apiece. Power derives from multiple diesel-generator units, which may be sited remotely. They can handle hotel and propulsion loads together or, if the demand is low, be shut down individually for economy or maintenance.

Most types of shipbuilding have been subsumed by Far East yards but cruise ships, being orderd at a phenomenal rate, have remained a European speciality. Size and luxury are pre-eminent, the traveller being overwhelmed by vast, nine-deck atria, banks of gilded elevators, fountains and arcades of fine shops, theatres seating 1,400 and double-level gymnasia.

At the time of writing (1998) some 40 cruise ships, aggregating nearly three million grt, are on order. There has been an explosion in size. The 80,000 tons or so of the two Cunard 'Queens' were a record for some 60 years but, of the above total, five exceed 100,000 tons apiece and three no less than 149,000 tons, each accommodating 3,100 passengers.

INLAND WATERWAY SHIPPING

Above: Barge life may appear idyllic, but competition is fierce. This laden craft is on the River Main, part of the important Rhein-Main-Danube route connecting the North Sea to the Black Sea.

ANYBODY WHO HAS TRAVELLED the Rhine and heard the day-round thump of marine diesels will be aware of the prodigious quantity of commercial traffic that the river carries. They may not appreciate, however, that it is only the trunk of a veritable tree of navigable rivers that include the Meuse, Moselle and Neckar and, via the Main, there is access to the Danube and, thence, the Black Sea.

Man's adventure with ships began on inland waterways and the world's great natural drainage systems – suitably improved where required – still provide ready access for specialist craft, deep into the continental masses. Several major examples, the Nile, Congo and Zambezi, the Yangtze and the Mekong, Amazon and Ganges, have never

spawned the wide variety of specialist commercial traffic typical of the European and American networks. The enormous Russian system harnesses a combination of river, lake and canal to link the Caspian and Black Seas with the Baltic and White Seas, and in North America, the Mississippi-Missouri and the St Lawrence/Great Lakes, all serve advanced economies.

Since medieval times, the Rhine and its tributaries have attracted industry reliant on watercraft to bring raw materials and to distribute finished goods. It has been Rotterdam's good fortune (echoing that of New Orleans) to stand at the junction of ocean going shipping and inland waterway craft, acting as centre and trans-shipment point for bulk and manufactured cargoes.

The traditional workhorse of the European scene is the familiar, engines-aft barge, built in several size ranges with dimensions configured to the locks on the waterways for which they are designed. Loaded, the barges have little freeboard and proceed with sidedecks awash. Often home to both skipper and family the barge frequently carries the family car atop the hatches. Fore and aft lines also support flapping washing and, often, a toddler given free range on a short harness.

River navigation varies with the season. Spring brings melt water from the mountains, high water levels and swirling currents. By late summer water levels are low, shoals abound and navigable channels narrow. While deep water enables a barge to load a full cargo, clearance under the many bridges ('air draught') is greatly reduced. Shallow water increases air draught but reduces the quantity of cargo that can be loaded, the craft riding proportionately higher.

Containers to Gainsborough

Since the late 1970s, a new style of ship, the low air-draught coaster, has proliferated. Able to work coastwise around Europe and to penetrate the major waterways, these 'paragraph' ships are designed to take full advantage of all classification rules. On a rateable net tonnage of about 1,000 nrt a typical example can load 3,000 tons dwt. The wheelhouse is sited atop a hydraulically-powered telescopic pillar and together with the masts, can be lowered to decrease air draught. It can also be raised to heights suitable to give visibility over a deck load of containers. Like all modern ships, these are 'container friendly', with parallel cargo sections and clear, unobstructed holds. Heavy steel hatch covers can be operated rapidly, while being strong enough to accept deck loads. Without waste of time and money in trans-shipment, a low air-draught coaster could load at, say, Strasbourg, and discharge at a minor port such as Gainsborough in the heart of Lincolnshire. Found also on the very extensive Russian waterways network, such sea/river ships are rapidly displacing more conventional coasters.

European operators have also adopted the American practice of 'push-towing'. Dumb barges and empty motor barges were commonly towed by powerful tugs on conventional short scopes but more common today are 'barge trains'. Rectangu-lar barges, lashed into blocks two wide and up to three long, are pushed as a rigid mass by multi-engined rectangular tugs. They are far from the quarter-mile long trains met with on American waterways, but can still shift several thousand tons in waterways that are more constricted and more densely populated.

Somewhat fallen from grace are the LASH and BACO systems, introduced in the 1970s to link Europe with American and African waterways respectively. Both extended the container concept, using specialist ships to transport stacks of box-shaped barges, or 'lighters'. These were moved by tugs around waterways and to and from the anchorages used by their carriers.

Road and rail have long robbed waterways of their significance in passenger traffic. The stately, wood-built sternwheelers of the Mississippi-Missouri, with their airy promenade decks and studied, gracious living, were very much part of the Southern scene. Their appearance and their characteristic sounds – melodious steam siren, Calliope steam organ, and the measured thump of their great steam engine – have been relegated to tourist entertainment. Similar, but more functional Nile vessels are more likely to be moving sightseers in air-conditioned comfort to Abu Simbel than perspiring peasants to the local souk. We are the poorer for their passing.

Above: 'Push-towing' of connected barge trains has been widely adopted on major European waterways. As with hard-towing of motor vehicles, the system allows more positive control.

Below: Pretty and practical. The beamy, pontoon-style hull of the traditional Mississippi sternwheeler successfully combines shallow draught with high-stacked accommodation.

TUGS AND TOWAGE

Main picture: A 1930s
vintage Swedish
motorship being
manoeuvred by three
tugs. The towing
industry has declined
because modern ships
of this size would
have side thrusters,
controllable pitch
propellers and
advanced rudders
to manoeuvre
themselves.

TUGS HAVE THE DISTINCTION of being one of the first types of craft to which steam power was applied. Indeed, it was steam power that brought about the tug. Sailing ships could be delayed for days by contrary winds from sailing or berthing, a situation unprofitable for shipowners but potentially disastrous for the Admiralty. Thus, by the mid-1820s, of several hundred steam paddle craft operating in European waters, most were passenger-carrying packets but many were tugs. These worked in ports, especially fishing ports, and estuaries, and in towing barges on canals.

For long, inefficient machinery caused small craft such as tugs to be 'short legged'. Cruising tended to be limited to patrolling the chops of the Channel in quiet weather to solicit the masters of incoming sailing ships. Rival tugs would compete fiercely to sell their services. In those days of poor communications, however, many a fine sailing ship, dismasted by storm, had to be abandoned as a derelict. Any tug getting a line aboard could have attempted a lucrative salvage operation under the universally-recognised Lloyd's Open Form agreement, with its famous 'No cure, No pay' terms.

At the close of the century, steam merchantmen were already of considerable size and value but, with machinery still fragile and landfalls in thick weather still dependent upon dead reckoning, casualties were frequent. The Dutch tug operator L. Smit identified a role for a new and larger type of tug which could both aid casualties at sea and undertake protracted tows. His venture thrived, especially as, by World War I, radio was being generally introduced, enabling casualty and rescue tug to communicate.

By the 1920s, Smits found it worthwhile to begin posting salvage tugs at specific stations abroad, usually at nodal points of busy shipping lanes. Dutch pre-eminence in this field was reinforced by the addition of the rival tug firm of Bureau Wijsmuller and the salvage specialists Van den Tak.

During World War II tugs, often accompanying convoys, worked incessantly to bring home casualties and their priceless cargoes. The eight large 'Bustler' class tugs of the Royal Navy owed much of their design to Dutch practice.

Larger tugs of this period were typically diesel-powered for 3,000 bhp. Individual rating was by 'static bollard pull', i.e. the tensile force that a tug could exert in a line when developing maximum power. Traditionally, one ton of bollard pull required 100 bhp, so the above tugs were rated at about 30 tons. Postwar improvements, particularly the enclosure of the propeller within a patent duct to improve flow into it, has improved the ratio somewhat.

Decline and development of tugs

From the 1950s, ships began to increase rapidly in size, tugs necessarily doing likewise. Higher standards of navigation and enforced regulation of traffic, however, began a long decline in casualty rates. Despite the occasional high-profile wreck, business for expensive salvage tugs declined remorselessly. Previously powerful fleets of Dutch, German and British tugs were drastically thinned, and foreign-stationed salvage tugs are now history.

left: Purpose-built salvage tugs have declined as marine accidents have greatly reduced. Multi-purpose offshore support ships, such as the *Pacific Blade*, are, however, well equipped to double in the role.

Where a modern 2,800 bhp sea-going tug would be some 200 ft (61m) in length, a good, multi-purpose harbour and coastal tug would typically be of 1,800 bhp and 105 ft (32 m). These and smaller units are under a wider range of design influences. For instance, unlike American tugs, which site their towpoint well aft, European craft always tend to a point close to amidships. If a towline under high tension is allowed to achieve an angle too wide on the beam, the tug can be dragged bodily sideways, i.e. 'girded', and is in immediate danger of capsize. Conventional, propeller-driven craft obviously cannot develop a transverse thrust to get out of this situation, hence the rise in popularity of 'water tractors'. These are propelled by Voith Schneider cycloidal units (whose vertically-mounted blades revolve in a horizontal circle, the incident angle of each blade being continuously adjusted to direct thrust in a desired direction), or azimuth thrusters, typified by the Japanese Z-peller, and the German Schottel, whose complete nozzle-mounted propeller may be angled in any direction. Such installations obviate the need for a conventional rudder while giving a tug exceptional manoeuvrability.

Another major influence on tug design has been the blurring of distinction between it and that of the Offshore Supply Vessel (OSV). Larger OSVs undertake towing and anchor-handling as part of their remit, being powerfully equipped as a result. They customarily carry water and foam monitors, portable pumps and other gear, once the preserve of the salvage tug and what heavy gear is not carried can be flown out in hours by helicopter. The classic salvage tug has therefore been effectively superseded.

Smaller harbour tugs have lost much trade through the growing trend of modern merchantmen to be equipped with transverse thrusters, permitting them to berth and unberth without assistance.

CONTAINER SHIPS

GOODS WHICH, IN TRANSIT from supplier to consumer, need to be trans-shipped between sea, rail and road transport, benefit by being packaged so as to minimise handling. Such a range of transport is termed 'intermodal' and some organisations are large enough to embrace all three. Thus the four British inter-war railway companies used heavy, 4-ton wooden boxes to shift single shipments between the United Kingdom, Eire and the Continent.

To be universally acceptable, containers needed to be larger, however, and experiments began in the late 1940s using the ubiquitous ex-Service LSTs of the Atlantic Steam Navigation Company. By 1964, trading as Containerways, the company was running a regular container service on trailers.

The distant Canadian company of White Pass & Yukon Railway was truly intermodal, hauling freight by sea from Vancouver to Skagway, thence by rail to White Horse and by road to further, more remote, destinations. It early adopted containers to speed up cargo transfer from one mode to another, its great innovation being to stack the boxes aboard ship in guides. Thus, the company's diminutive *Clifford J. Rogers* of 1955 could claim to be the world's first cellular container ship.

Trailered containers made poor use of ship capacity and the Pan Atlantic Shipping Company also experimented with cellular stacking and, along with Waterman Steamship, was purchased by Malcolm McLean in 1955. McLean was another intermodal operator and had opened up a regular Houston–New York coastal service, using converted standard C2 cargo ships.

The principle gained momentum with Matson opening a service in 1958 from the West Coast to Hawaii, soon extended to the Far East. They, too,

Below: As container ships grow ever larger their terminals need to enlarge to accommodate them. Channels must be deepened and, as this picture emphasises, cranes need to have sufficient headroom and outreach.

experimented with deck-loaded stacks before embarking on the full conversion of C2s and C3s. Such war-built workhorses, together with larger C4s and T2 tankers (often lengthened, or 'jumboised'), proved suitable both for the surgery involved and their subsequent service.

McLean's Sea-Land company's operations were centred on Elizabeth, New Jersey, where it constructed the world's first international, purpose-built container terminal. Most major American lines quickly followed suit, but European companies were more cautious, baulking at the huge investment involved. When, in the mid 1960s, they moved, it was in the form of consortia in order to pool assets. This brought together previously bitter business rivals, such as Hamburg-Amerika and Norddeutscher Lloyd which linked to create HAPAG Lloyd, now a major player.

For operations to be truly intermodal worldwide, a standard range of containers was required. While some large organisations may yet run their own sizes in parallel, the standard box was of a nominal 20 × 8 × 8 ft, as defined by the International Standards Organisation (ISO). The other standard, a 40-footer, has twice the capacity, but the 20-foot equivalent unit (or TEU) is that by which container ship capacities are reckoned.

Boxes and 'brass plate' companies

Boxes are both strong and accurately made as they may be stacked up to 13 deep and weigh up to a loaded 24 tonnes apiece. Corner pillars, which must take the compressive stresses involved, have be aligned to just 10 mm on length and 5 mm on width for a 40 ft container. Within the strict limits of the corner pillars, containers may vary greatly, with hard or soft tops, insulated walls, open flats and tank types being most common.

A number of major ports had, by the early 1970s, become nodes of a worldwide network of container trunk routes. Large, long-haul ships called at a minimum number of these, depending upon smaller, 'feeder' ships to distribute containers to and from their terminals on shorter hauls. Very soon, every short-sea trader required to be configured to be 'container friendly'.

For maximum flexibility, most long-haul ships were 'Panamax'-designed, with major dimensions compatible with the Panama Canal locks. Second-generation ships, which emphasised speed, were fine-lined, with space for 2,600–3,000 TEU. An oil crisis later, third-generation ships were slower and more capacious, being beam – rather than length – limited. A 20 ft container can accommodate 21.7 tonnes of cargo but usually contains much less. With an average 15 tonnes per unit, a 39,000 dwt ship can load 2,600 TEU, but would require a lower density of 13 tonnes per unit to take aboard her full capacity of 3,000 TEU.

New trends are to 'post-Panamax' ships which, no longer limited by dimension, have leapt to some 6,600 TEU, as typified by A.P. Møller's S class ships. Already, however, German shipyards are pushing an 8,000 TEU design, which could exceed 100,000 dwt. Only a few major ports could accept such vessels at the moment, both in terms of draught limitations and terminal cranes, whose height and outreach have to be increased to suit.

The spread of containerisation effectively spelt the end of the traditional cargo liner. Fleets of superb ships, such as those of the British Blue Funnel and Ellerman Lines, the Dutch Rotterdam Lloyd and Nederland Lines and the Norwegian Wilhelmsen Line, to name a very few, disappeared as their owners became largely 'brass plate' companies as part-owners of 'box-boats'.

Above: Currently the world's largest, the 'S'-class ships of A.P. Møller can stow over 6,000 TEU. This picture, of the Southampton terminal, gives an idea of the scale and problems of the container industry.

Below: As the large, inter-continental container ship discharges in the background, a small feeder ship loads in Gladstone Dock, Liverpool.

Into the Nuclear Age

ON 27 AUGUST 1943, the British sloop *Egret* became the first warship to be sunk by guided missile. The weapon was an Hs 293 which, with the larger FX1400, was designed by the Germans to be launched from high-flying aircraft. They were essentially glide bombs, the aimer in the aircraft operating their control surfaces via a radio link. Although they achieved a commendable rate of success, notably in the sinking of the Italian battleship *Roma*, their command link proved easy to jam, while the weapons themselves were quickly copied by the Americans.

The threat of such missiles and the Japanese Kamikaze posed new problems for warship defences. An interim measure was a range of radar-laid, heavier-calibre guns, pending the development of surface-to-air missiles. The first generation of these, typified by the Americans Terrier and Talos, proved to be too bulky to have the necessary agility in flight. Together with their massive guidance and handling systems they also proved too expensive for retro-fitting into war-built cruiser hulls in order to effect their modernisation.

Early systems could control only one missile at a time but modern solid-state, multi-frequency radars can 'share' their attention over many channels. Complex trainable launchers and associated

Main picture: Vertical launch of missiles obviates the requirement of a complex and vulnerable launcher and handling system. It also enables salvo firing and the loading of a mix of weapons.

Insert: The demise of the once-mighty Soviet fleet is a phenomenon of our time. Its Slava-class cruisers were dominated by the eight inclined launchers for SS-N-12 anti-ship missiles, capable of carrying a 1,000 kg conventional or nuclear warhead over 300 miles.

GUIDED MISSILES AT SEA

handling systems have been superseded by milk-crate-like vertical launch assemblies where canister-loaded missiles are simply slotted into a cellular frame.

Also borrowed from the Germans by the Americans was the crude but effective V-1. As the ramp-launched Loon, it was tested on submarines and aircraft carriers. Its 900 kg (1,985 lb) payload and 150-mile (240 km) range was developed by 1953 into a nuclear warhead and 500 miles (800 km) range at trans-sonic speed. The new weapon was called Regulus.

This was the era of the Cold War and it was desirable to be able to strike deeply into an opponent's territory other than with vulnerable manned aircraft. Where Regulus was a cruise missile, its successor, Regulus II, later renamed Polaris, was vertically-launched on a ballistic trajectory. Matched to the newly-developed nuclear submarine, Polaris and its Poseidon and Trident successors, have evolved to be able to threaten any point on the World's landmasses. Paralleled by equivalent French and Soviet systems, these missiles mount a continuous deterrent to major attack on their respective states.

Surface-to-surface missiles

Fearing the threat posed by the West's amphibious forces and carrier groups, of which it possessed neither, the Warsaw Pact states of the Cold War built fleets of land-based bombers, carrying heavy, stand-off air-to-surface missiles, and a range of ship-killing surface-to-surface missiles. Of the latter, the cruiser-launched SS-N-3 could cover 300 miles (500 km) at a speed of Mach 1.5. Although it required an associated aircraft to give mid-course correction, it was capable of engaging an aircraft carrier from beyond the effective range of its aircraft.

The smaller SS-N-2A, a sub-sonic missile known as Styx was carried by minor warships and a host of cheaply-produced small craft, of which many were transferred to client states. On 21 October 1967 the West was galvanised when the Israeli destroyer *Eilat*, patrolling off Alexandria, was sunk without warning by two SS-N-2As launched by Egyptian boats that had not even left harbour.

Having concentrated on surface-to-air missiles to the virtual exclusion of surface-to-surface weapons, the West's navies had quickly to make up lost time. France's MM38 Exocet, followed by the American Harpoon, proved excellent and, by virtue of regular updates, remain in service after more than two decades.

For defence against incoming anti-ship missiles, either 'hard' or 'soft' kill measures can be used. The former seek to destroy the weapon either through a hail of small-calibre projectiles (e.g. from Phalanx or Goalkeeper guns), or by agile anti-missile missiles such as the Sea Wolf. Soft kills are achieved by confusing the missile with a combination of electronic countermeasures, clouds of reflective chaff and infrared flares.

For some considerable time, anti-submarine escorts carried standoff weapons such as Asroc or Ikara, ballistic and cruise vehicles respectively, which carried a lightweight torpedo to the vicinity of a submerged target before releasing it. Such systems have been largely superseded by the manned helicopter which uses sonobuoys and dunking sonar to track a prospective target prior to torpedo release. Helicopters can also deploy anti-ship missiles, such as Sea Skua and Penguin, which can devastate smaller targets.

Pin-point targeting of objectives hundreds of miles inland is possible with cruise missiles such as the Tomahawk. This is able to follow a highly evasive track, with its radar comparing the terrain below with a pre-programmed, onboard digitised contour map, prepared from data obtained by satellite measurement.

Future generations of missiles will fly at hypersonic speed and use miniaturisation to improve accuracy and resistance to countermeasures.

Left: Modern compact missile systems give even minor warhips considerable fire-power. The craft, herself, however, is extremely vulnerable to attack by shipborne helicopter.

Below: The gutted hulk of HMS *Sheffield* in the Falklands War is a reminder that even minor powers may purchase the latest in high-technology weaponry. Although in no danger of sinking, the ship was in a combat zone and could not be saved.

MODERN ESCORTS

Right: Blank faces on the foreward and after superstructures of the American 'Ticonderoga'-class cruisers accommodate the four multi-element, phased-array antennas of their three-dimensional Aegis radars.

Below: Blohm und Voss, Hamburg, designs, builds and licences its range of MEKO escorts. The basic hull of each is configured to accept an optional fit of weapons and sensors, as fitted in this Turkish example.

WHILE IT REPRESENTS AN important category of warship, the term 'escort' is not precise. An escort for a carrier attack group will probably require different characteristics to one accompanying an amphibious force. Mass-produced escorts for convoys require to be uncomplicated and cheap. As high-value formations may also be covered by nuclear submarines, we need also to confine ourselves to what might be termed 'surface escorts'.

A first important point is that, in a real shooting war, there are never enough escorts. As future wars will be short, there will be no time to build them, so any peacetime decision on quantity versus quality will be critical. With this in mind, the German MEKO concept makes considerable sense. The acronym means Mehrzweckskombination, or Multi-purpose, and relates to a set of standard hulls with ready-connected apertures into which may be slotted a choice from a menu of weapon and sensor systems. Hulls may be ordered as 'fitted for, but not with', being configured for specific missions by the later interchanging of stockpiled system modules.

In earlier times, a boiler malfunction might keep a warship in dockyard hands for weeks; today, a gas turbine change may be effected in hours. Assuming a ship life of, say, 25 years, and the current rate of electronic progress, a conventionally-designed ship would be unavailable for a total of several years, undergoing several siginificant updates in addition to the time-honoured major mid-life refit. MEKO can greatly reduce such wasted time and, with a higher utilisation factor, fewer ships may be required.

'Escorting' involves a wide range of activities, possibly demanding a mix of anti-air (A/A), anti-submarine (A/S) and anti-ship capability. Escorts should also be able to look after themselves to avoid becoming a liability in requiring to be escorted themselves. As modern systems are volume – rather than weight critical, such versatility needs space which, of course, predicates a large hull. Designing down to an accountant-dictated, specific hull size does not work, as evinced by the British types 22 and 42, both of which had to be successively 'stretched'. Early, economy-driven units proved incapable of economic updating and had to be discarded. Steel for hulls is relatively cheap, larger hulls make better seaboats, hydrodynamically they are more easily driven and they offer more scope for subsequent updating. Adequately-sized ships are thus more economic in both the short and the long term.

Smaller, less capable but stealthy

'Top drawer' escorts are, therefore, likely to be large and, even in the best-endowed fleet, comparatively few in number. A prime example, the 27 American 'Ticonderogas', began life as second-generation destroyers, descended from the 28-strong 'Spruance' class. They were re-classified cruisers to reflect their enhanced status in being built around the SPY-1A or 1B Aegis radar system. Slow-rotating antennas have been replaced by four-quadrant phased arrays, which comprise thousands of electronic elements that may be switched in any combination and at any rate to shape and/or direct beams for the purpose of search, target tracking or missile guidance. Cooperative Engagement Capability (CEC) allows data to be shared between ships to, say, facilitate layered defence or the control of one ship's armament by another.

One or two complex and vulnerable missile launchers and loading systems have been super-

seded by Vertical Launch Systems, (VLS) which provide simple milk-crate type storage and launch facilities for, currently, up to 61 missiles. Canister-loaded, these may comprise any combination of say, 1,000-mile (1,600 km) range Tomahawk land attack cruise missiles, 70-mile (112 km) range Harpoon anti-ship missiles, 40-mile (64 km) range Standard A/A missiles or 9-mile (14 km) range ASROC A/S missiles. Aegis' capacity is such that the weapons may be salvo-fired and controlled in order to swamp an opponent's defence.

The size of a 'Ticonderoga', indeed of any credible escort, allows it to accommodate two helicopters. These capable aircraft 'are, after possibly a nuclear submarine, the most effective A/S system.

They can deploy their own 'dunking' sonar and a pattern of sonobuoys, analyse their output and share the data with other aircraft and ships. They can carry a brace of A/S torpedoes as well as target the ship's weapons and can carry one or two light air-to-surface missiles, capable of knocking-out light combatants. On-board electronic countermeasures (ECM) can protect both themselves and the ship. Finally, they may be fitted with a laser-based system for detecting shallow-laid mines. Such versatility requires that two aircraft are carried to guarantee the serviceability of one.

Smaller budgets dictate smaller and less capable ships, but today's frigates and corvettes, the latter exemplified by the 1,075-ton 'Eilat' type, can still deploy a respectable mix of guns, tube- and VLS-launched missiles and a helicopter, while incorporating advanced 'stealth' features which make it difficult for incoming missiles to target them.

Above: The long forecastle of the British Type 42 frigate *Edinburgh* results from the stretching of the design. The stiffened sheer strake was to cure cracking, and the forward bulwark wetness, in South Atlantic conditions.

SUPER CARRIERS

TODAY'S CAPITAL SHIP IS, indisputably, the giant aircraft carrier. Deploying enormous striking power wherever there is salt water to float them, they can exert enormous influence on a situation without the political complications of becoming actively involved. Only the United States can afford such vessels although several other fleets operate smaller types.

The trend to growth had its origins in the Pacific War, where the advantages of large air wings were quickly established. This, and the need for a protected flight deck, saw the *Midway* (CV-41) class displace 45,000 tons against the 27,500 tons of the preceding 'Essex' type.

The successful outcome of the great Pacific carrier battles gave the admirals considerable influence in postwar planning. Their arguments for greater aircraft bomb loads and greater strike radius resulted in an aircraft with a designed take-off weight of nearly 45 tons. The situation was complicated by the advent of nuclear weapons, the strategy for the use of which was yet to be defined. Inter-service rivalries, however, saw the air force making a powerful bid to be the means of strategic weapon delivery, and the navy could not allow this.

A new carrier, to operate this proposed aircraft (designated the ADR-42) had its design governed by its weight and size, a need to transit the Panama Canal lock system, and a requirement for both protection and a 33-knot speed. Provisionally named *United States* (CVA-58) she was dimensioned around 18 ADR-42s and 80 fighter aircraft. With a design displacement of 79,000 tons, an overall length of 1,088 ft (331.6 m) and a beam at the waterline of only 125 ft (38.1 m) this necessitated the flightdeck to be sponsored out to a width of 190 ft (57.9 m). Interestingly, the ship would have had no island.

The proposal, for commencement in 1949, represented a huge extrapolation of then-current experience and, with the development of a far smaller nuclear strike bomber, the AJ-1 Savage, it appeared less than viable. Skilful lobbying by the air force succeeded in getting the project cancelled even before construction began.

Carriers in the nuclear age

In June 1950, however, the outbreak of the Korean War re-emphasised the indispensibility of aircraft carriers for out-of-area operations. The CVA-58 project was promptly re-instated, this time around yet another strike bomber, the A3D Skywarrior, a 27-tonner which went into production in place of the Savage. Its size and weight governed catapult length and power, size of elevators and internal hangar height. New developments, benefiting the design, were the British inventions of the steam catapult and the angled flight deck, the one enabling heavier aircraft to be launched safely and the other allowing a deck-park to be maintained alongside simultaneous flying-off and landing operations.

Successfully compressed to within a 60,000-ton design displacement, the carrier, named *Forrestal* (CVA-59), owed much to the aborted *United States* project, and was the first true super carrier. Completed in 1955, she was followed by five near sisters at approximately one year intervals. On an overall length of 1,039 ft (316.7 m) they carried about 90 aircraft, including 32 Skywarriors. Only about half the aircraft could be stowed below.

The CVA-59 design was highly successful and has been the basis of continual evolution. Next in line was the *Enterprise* (CVAN-65), the first to be given nuclear propulsion. She operated the A-5 Vigilante, which was marginally smaller than the A3D, and was the last of the manned naval strategic bombers, which were displaced by submarines deploying the new Polaris inter-continental missile.

Left: USS *George Washington* (CVN-73) entered service in 1991. As defence dollars become scarcer there will be revived the periodic argument of how many carriers, and of what size, give best value.

Despite regular reviews to justify its continued building rather than smaller and questionably cheaper designs, the super carrier has continued to evolve. Their own enormous cost is inflated by that for necessary·capable escorts and replenishment ships, not to mention the cost of the 80+ air wing. With the scrapping of smaller, specialist 'decks', the big carriers have had the attack component of their air wings diluted with anti-submarine aircraft, helicopters and specialist aircraft for early warning, electronic warfare and communications.

Although two further oil-fired units were built during the long evaluation of the *Enterprise*, the following ship, *Nimitz* (CVN-68) was the first of seven nuclear-powered sisters, being commissioned at intervals which guarantee that twelve big carriers will always be available. With the *Nimitz* series, the design has been stretched to 1,088 ft (331.6 m) overall, the size of the aborted CVA-58, but, unlike that proposal they are 134 ft (40.8 m) in waterline beam and 251 ft (76.5 m) in width over the flight deck.

Well maintained, and given a periodic updating under the service life extension programme (SLEP), these ships should have a useful life of 50 years. To follow this quiet remarkable run, the US Navy is examining radical new ideas in its CVX programme. This new generation may revert to conventional propulsion if a replacement for the steam catapult, possibly electromagnetically powered, can be perfected.

MODERN SUBMARINES

Right: Ballistic missile submarines are, in practice, rarely seen on the surface. Now restricted to Ohio-class units, such as the *Alabama* here, submerged patrols are mounted out of Georgia and Washington state.

Below: Nuclear-propelled fleet submarines, such as this British *Trafalgar*, are capable of being modified to fire cruise missiles. This gives them land bombardment capacity, with nuclear warheads if necessary.

ALTHOUGH ANY NAVY WORTHY of the name includes a submarine element such craft were, until recently, built by only a few nations. In an era of few contracts, however, hard bargaining has seen 'technology transfer' to others, such as Australia, Argentina and Turkey.

Usually referred-to as 'boats', rather than as 'ships', submarines fall into three major groups. These are the strategic missile carriers (SSBN), nuclear propelled attack boats (SSN) and 'conventional' diesel-electric craft (SSK).

With the dismantling of the apparatus of the Cold War, SSBNs have been greatly reduced in number by international agreement, but are still operated by the United States, Russia, the United Kingdom, France and China. Their task is to patrol undetected, their cargo of inter-continental ballistic missiles ready to be programmed to strike at spe-

cific points deep within the territory of a potential opponent. They are meant to be a deterrent, to be unleashed only when their own, or allied, state has been similarly attacked.

Such missiles are huge, the Trident D-5, for instance, weighing over 57 tons at launch. Its near 14-metre (46 ft) length, standing in 20 to 24 vertical silos, determines the SSBNs depth of hull and, thus, its diameter and length. Because their missiles are of such a size, both American Trident boats and Russian 'Typhoon' class SS-N-20 carriers have hull diameters in the 11 to 12.5-metre (36–41ft) range, permitting several internal deck levels. Their length, at about 171m (561ft), is almost exactly that of Winchester Cathedral, which is why they conceal themselves in deep oceans.

Attack submarines, the SSNs, are often appropriately termed 'hunter killers'. Where surface

An SSN spends much time loitering, listening on passive sonars which may be either hull-mounted or in the form of a towed array. She will advertise her presence in using an active sonar only to achieve an accurate range and bearing to target. From her weapon tubes she may lay mines, fire lightweight or heavy torpedoes (depending upon the target), launch encapsulated versions of anti-ship missiles such as Exocet and Harpoon, or target remote land sites with encapsulated Tomahawk cruise missiles.

One of the most formidable warships at sea today, an SSN can run down virtually any surface ship and attack a wide range of targets from distances that make counter attack difficult.

As the elite group of navies that operate nuclear submarines obviously intends to retain its advantages and expertise, the majority of the world's boats are still diesel-electric SSKs. Generally smaller than SSNs, they are significantly cheaper both to acquire and to maintain.

Potentially far quieter than its nuclear cousin, the 'conventional' can lay quietly on the bottom or move stealthily in shallow waters. The great limitation remains however, for the need to periodically recharge the batteries. For this atmospheric air is required to run the diesel engines. Consequently, much research is currently being directed at increasing the period between necessary 'snorting' routines. Practical solutions include fuel cells, air-independent diesels and Stirling engines. All, however, still require stored energy or oxygen, and cannot entirely eliminate periodic contact with the surface.

Current SSKs are formidable craft in their own right and are extremely difficult to detect. Nonetheless, the 'nuclear club' is largely abandoning them in favour of all-nuclear submarine fleets. The exceptions, Russia and China, are both considerable exporters of such boats.

Future submarines may lose their fin, as optics and other sensors are removed from retractable masts and are re-sited 'off-board'. Their data will be conveyed down to the boat by fibre-optic strands in a tow cable and reconstituted on displays and readouts anywhere on board. Fin-less, a boat would be faster and quieter, and not prone to making large changes in attitude when turning quickly. Without masts, her internal layout could be much improved.

A further development might well see a submarine deploying one or more unmanned underwater vehicles (UUV) for the purposes of extending her sensor range, as weapon delivery systems or to act as decoys.

Left: The 31 American ballistic missile submarines of the Benjamin Franklin and Lafayette classes spanned development from the 2,500-mile A-2 Polaris to the 4,350-mile C-4 Trident. Here, the intemediate USS *Rayburn* (SSBN 635) shows all her 16 C-3 Poseidon launch tubes with top caps raised.

Below: To the world's relief, the break up of the Soviet Union resulted in a huge reduction in the number of nuclear warheads lurking in the deep oceans. Unfortunately, other states are seeking to join the 'nuclear club'.

warships can exercise 'graded response', reacting as required to incidents ranging from infringement of fishing rights to an all-out nuclear exchange, an SSN lacks such flexibility. Like generations of preceding boats, they are effective only if shooting to kill.

Nuclear energy, developing power for an indefinite period without the need of atmospheric air, revolutionised submarine design. Married to a hydrodynamically clean hull, such plant can produce submerged speeds well in excess of 30 knots and, in some reported cases, even 40 knots. Paradoxically, the SSN rarely proceeds at such speeds because of the noise created. In the undersea theatre, to be undetected is to win.

Nuclear v diesel electric

Long submerged patrols by SSNs, which rarely have need to surface, are ameliorated for their crews by the boats' surplus electrical power, which provides a fresh and properly-conditioned internal atmosphere, with unlimited fresh water and heat.

Tomorrow's Ships

FOR REASONS OF PROVIDING steadier gun platforms, or to ease the sensitivities of Victorian digestive systems, nineteenth century ship design threw up some quirky solutions. Examples included the circular Russian 'Popoffkas', packets with saloons suspended on gimballed supports, and long cargo carriers, built in sections and hinged to allow differential movement in the vertical plane. Ship science was still in its infancy and such ideas failed because they were effective over only a small band of sea conditions and, sometimes, positively detrimental in others.

Two principles, however, those of the planing hull and the hydrofoil, which were introduced in the 1890s, have gone on to evolve through a century of refinement. Propelling a conventional hull through water encounters resistance, mainly from wave making and friction between water and hull. Both the above principles reduce resistance by raising the hull in the water. The planing hull uses flat bottom sections to develop a lift component with increasing speed, greatly reducing submerged volume. In the case of the hydrofoil, fully submerged or surface-piercing wing-type foils can develop lift forces sufficient to raise the hull completely clear of the water. With both, high speeds, typically 50 knots, are possible but hydrodynamic laws limit them to a modest size and lightweight construction.

Pure planing craft can be very fast in relatively calm conditions but begin to slam hard in rising sea states, necessitating speed reduction to avoid structural damage. A better solution is to design the craft with round-bilge, displacement form forward and flat planing sections aft. A great improvement in 'seakindliness' is thus purchased at the cost of some speed reduction.

While battle fleets have little application in peacetime for small, high speed warships, the principle is well represented in such as rigid inflatable boats (RIB) and clandestine insertion craft for special forces. By far the most examples are seen in recreational dayboats.

Once the hull is foil-borne, a hydrofoil is little affected by sea state but, to maintain high speed in

Main picture: Incat's high speed ferries use SWATH technology. The hulls have a small waterplane area and wave-piercing entry to exploit its power.

Below: Hydrofoil technology, such as that employed on this passenger-carrying Boeing Jetfoil, is very mature. The control system ensures a comfortable ride, but is complex.

RAPIDE

ADVANCED HULL FORMS

poor conditions, they require submerged control surfaces governed by a control system taking data from numerous sensors. A successful hydrofoil design requires a thorough knowledge of the dynamics of both the craft and the sea.

While a hydrofoil may provide a steady gun platform, its limited size and light construction sees it poorly represented in all navies except the Russian. It is, however, much used for high speed passenger ferries.

Catamaran craft date from antiquity and, although offering generous deck space, do not typically incorporate advanced hull design. An exception is the high speed ferry which combines the advantages of wide-beam passenger accommodation with 'wave-piercing' hulls. The forward run of these is designed so as to cut through waves without either lifting to them or being driven down by them. As fine compromise is involved it is not surprising that a design may fail spectacularly under the wrong conditions.

Speed, space and survivability

A recent derivative of the catamaran is the Small Waterplane Area/Twin Hull, or SWATH. Its origins lay in a 1942 Anglo-Canadian proposal for an aircraft carrier and it relies for its buoyancy on two deeply-submerged, torpedo-shaped hulls. These support narrow vertical struts which rise to a height sufficient to support a transverse deck, constructed like a stiff eggbox. A conventional hull, acted upon by a typically random sea, exposes and submerges a proportion of the hull's volume in a continuously variable and asymetric manner. The hull counters this disturbance either by moving downwards under gravitational force or upward under the upthrust of buoyancy. Continuous fore-and-aft and transverse asymetry will result in motions and accelerations in all major axes.

In a SWATH, however, quite large perturbations in sea level will act on only a small volume of the side struts which, as a result, experience far smaller disturbing forces and, consequently, less motion. This has important design implications for craft which need, say, to operate helicopters in very poor conditions, or to maintain patrols in sea states high enough to quickly exhaust a crew.

SWATHs have their machinery safely buried in the lower hulls, while hits on their struts are not likely to prove seriously damaging. Because of their large wetted area they are not particularly fast and, as passenger ferries, they have the disadvantage of a deep draught for their size.

Currently exciting wide interest is a trimaran hull for warships. A fine-lined main hull is here stabilised by two, equally slim, outrigger hulls, the whole bridged by a spacious upper deck. The concept promises a combination of space, speed, stealth and survivability, the 'S' ingredients so vital to successful warship design which, like all naval architecture, is a balance of carefully-weighted compromise.

Above left: A trimaran form is being seriously evaluated as that for a future combatant. It promises a useful combination of large deck area, survivability and, with machinery in the outriggers, low exhaust signature.

Above: Her retractable foils clearly visible beneath the surface, the US naval hydrofoil *Pegasus*, makes 50 knots. Displaying little water while foil-borne, such craft create minimal wash.

MANOEUVRING AND PROPULSION

Above: A wave-piercing high speed ferry executing a tight turn. There is very little wave making, the wash being due primarily to the waterjet propulsion. Note the small list angle

THE MORE SPECIALISED a ship, the more specific her requirements, not least for manoeuvring and propulsion. Large ferries on tight schedules need to access constricted terminals; a seabed operations vessel (SOV) must maintain her exact position regardless of wind and current; a conventional submarine, although reliant on battery power, requires to remain submerged for long periods, and so on. Providing solutions to such problems is the task of the industry's many specialist firms.

The cruise ship, which sometimes requires to access and leave tight locations without recourse to expensive tug assistance, and the SOV, which must occupy an exact location in the face of weather and without the benefit of visible fixed reference points, have much the same problem but with slightly differing priorities. Each, in a nutshell, requires responsive directional thrust.

Conventional, shaft-mounted propellers can develop thrust only directly ahead or astern. At low speeds, conventional rudders have little effect. The transverse, tunnel-mounted thruster, sometimes provided both forward and aft, is able to move a ship bodily on or off the quay, or pivot it. To maintain a given position against disturbing forces such as wind and tide, however, requires azimuth thrusters, in which the complete active assembly can be rotated about the vertical axis to direct the thrust as required. Several such thrust sources must operate together to give balanced equilibrium. Thrusters such as these may protrude permanently below the ship or, less vulnerably, fold down or be lowered from a vertical trunk.

Lacking visible reference points at sea, such a ship will lay several transponders on the seabed, surrounding the point of interest. On a continuous basis, she then acoustically ranges onto each in turn, any variation in initial distance being translated into a vectored 'error signal' transmitted to the thruster group, which responds with thrust in

the correct magnitude and direction to restore her position, reducing the error signal to zero. A chosen position may be maintained indefinitely with fingertip control.

Azimuth thrusters, sited right aft, can also replace both conventional propeller and rudder, greatly simplifying the after end. Early units comprised directional propellers driven by vertical shafting from a power unit in the hull above. In recent years it has become customary to drive the propellers with an integrally-mounted electric motor sited in the unit. These so-called 'podded' drives are typified by the Finnish Azipod and German Siemens-Schottel ranges, which cover powers from five to 30 megawatts (6,700 to 40,200 hp). Recent references for the Azipod include paired units for cruise ships exceeding 70,000 grt. If arranged with the propeller ahead of the pod, the former is more efficient through working in a virtually undisturbed water stream.

Left: Cable layers have particular requirements for accurately following prescribed tracks. The two tunnel thrusters assist greatly but are effective only at slow foward ship speed.

Propulsion systems – old and new

There is currently great public interest in fast ferry travel. For these craft conventional propellers are efficient up to only about 25 knots, beyond which they are liable to experience thrust breakdown due to their limited diameter and high revolutions. Above 30 knots, therefore, the waterjet, which does not experience such problems, is superior. As no part of a waterjet assembly extends below the hull, it is also well-suited to service in very shallow water, while it is capable of rapid change of thrust direction, including reversal, through deflection of the jet efflux.

There is a huge potential market for 'conventional' diesel-electric submarines (SSK), which are far less expensive to operate than nuclear boats (SSN). Their drawback, of course, is their frequent need to access atmospheric air in order to recharge their batteries, while the SSN can remain submerged indefinitely. Practical Air Independent Propulsion (AIP) systems are now available, however, enabling SSKs to stay down for three to five times longer.

The British firm of Cosworth has pioneered closed-cycle diesel (CCD) engines, whose exhaust gas is "scrubbed" clean of products of combustion (water and carbon dioxide (CO_2)) and then re-enriched with oxygen and trace gases before being passed back into the engine.

The Swedes are developing the Stirling engine, whose principle was first propounded in 1816. In this machine, diesel fuel is burned near-silently in an oxygen-rich atmosphere within a pressure vessel. The resulting high pressure gas drives a balanced reciprocating engine from which it exhausts at a pressure still high enough to be discharged from the submerged boat without the aid of noisy pumps.

Fuel cells are favoured by the Germans. First developed in 1839, these reverse the basic principle of water electrolysis by combining oxygen and hydrogen to produce electricity, with heat and water as by-products. The water is discharged by pumping but the heat needs to be dissipated.

Other than in the case of CCD, AIP systems are currently able to provide power sufficient only for auxiliary propulsion, their endurance governed by a boat's capacity for oxygen and fuel sources.

Below: HMS *Sandown* is a single role mine-hunter. She is propelled by Voith-Schneider cycloidal propulsors, which act somewhat akin to a helicopter's rotor blades to produce near-maximum thrust in any direction, giving unparalleled manoeuvrability.

LITTORAL WARFARE

Below: Hovercraft in the assault role are able to use many beaches inaccessible to conventional landing craft. Lower blade tip velocities and ducts have much reduced noise.

Below right: In service since 1984, the American LCAC hovercraft is configured to fit four to an assault ship's docking well. It can carry 60 tons at a loaded speed of 40 knots.

FOR NEARLY A HALF-CENTURY following World War II, East and West pursued a Cold War policy of threatening each other with saturation nuclear attack. The greater majority of their warheads were deployed by monstrous submarines (SSBN) carrying inter-continental ballistic missiles (ICBM). Fleets of both sides were concerned largely with the safeguarding of their own SSBNs and the tracking/destruction of those of the enemy, if possible before they could launch their lethal cargoes.

During the Cold War era both sides had to address a perceived threat that could be defined clearly in terms of both characteristics and scale. With the declared end of this protracted stand-off, however, military staffs faced a dilemma. Treasuries, noting a greatly-reduced threat, demanded a 'peace dividend' of run-down Services and slashed defence budgets, while the Services themselves no longer had a major threat which could be used as a focus for justifying forces of significant strength.

The Falklands War of 1982 and the Gulf War of 1991 gave pointers to the direction in which military thought was moving i.e. limited action against rene-gade states that bucked world social conventions to an unacceptable degree. As it is possible to purchase nuclear or biological expertise, together with the means of long-range delivery, such states can pose a very real threat. Although it is not an easy task to evolve a credible rationale for a major Western state being mortally threatened by a Middle Eastern despot armed with anthrax-laden ballistic missiles, new force structures are based on it, the domino effect of alliances making it theoretically possible.

Both the Falklands and the Gulf involved limited war in pursuit of political objectives; those objectives realised, hostilities ceased. Both involved maritime power projection, effectively an extension of amphibious warfare doctrine evolved during World War II and requiring the naval and mercantile assets to safely transport military forces perhaps thousands of miles to a theatre of operations. Such a force sends a series of signals to assist in a political settlement of differences. Its despatch demonstrates resolve on the part of the despatcher. Its comparatively protracted time in transit allows space for reflection and negotiation. Having arrived,

Left: As landing vehicles, hovercraft have the advantage of being able to cross shallows, mud flats, saltings or swamps to put their assault troops ashore.

the force may be held overtly in international waters, a cogent argument for a last-ditch political agreement. Only when negotiation fails is the force unleashed and hostilities commenced.

Within the force, inter-Service cooperation is essential. Only an army can conquer and hold territory. Only maritime forces can take it there, and for these to operate satisfactorily, local air superiority must be established. This demands capable aircraft working from capable decks. During transit, the force may have to defend itself against air, surface or submarine attack. To be maintained at its theatre of operations, it must enjoy secure lines of communication for the purposes of supply etc.

Responding to crisis

From the naval aspect, what has been termed the littoral region is of vital interest. This embraces both the inshore waters which need to be controlled in order to support operations ashore and the coastal strip of land that can be controlled from the sea. Interest has thus moved from the primarily 'blue water' operations of the Cold War era to a more confined and cluttered inshore theatre where technology will be stretched to instantly and unambiguously identify friend from foe.

Most of the traditional elements of a fleet will still be apparent. For an ocean passage, there is surface and nuclear submarine escort with carrier aircraft backup. To dominate inshore waters, efficient mine detection and mine clearance and, again, carrier-based air power is needed until bases ashore can be established. In the landing phase, there is a requirement for naval gunfire support, but this is currently poorly provided and is in no way replaced by the multiple rocket launcher systems borrowed from the army. To be independent of conventional ports, specialist ships are required – helicopter

assault ships for the seizure of key points, assault landing ships to put ashore the main attack waves, roll-on/roll-off vessels and heavy lift ships to follow up with transport, light armour, heavy equipment and supplies.

In the current absence of heavy naval guns, it would fall to expensive cruise missiles to provide deep fire support. The aborted American 'arsenal ship' proposal would have provided a low-freeboard platform bearing hundreds of mixed missiles in vertical launchers, capable of being targeted and fired by any ship of the force with Cooperative Engagement Capability (CEC).

An essential component for these new concepts is speed of response. Only the Americans have addressed this by the forward-basing of combat-loaded 'pre-positioning' ships and the acquisition of the full range of shipping mentioned above. Great Britain is not in this situation because the catastrophic run-down of her merchant marine has left her dependent upon the hire of expensive and non-guaranteed neutral sources.

Below: The *PAP 104* vehicle is used by minehunters to locate, identify recover or blow up 'mine-like objects'. Electrically propelled, it is controlled remotely via a trailing fibre-optic cable.

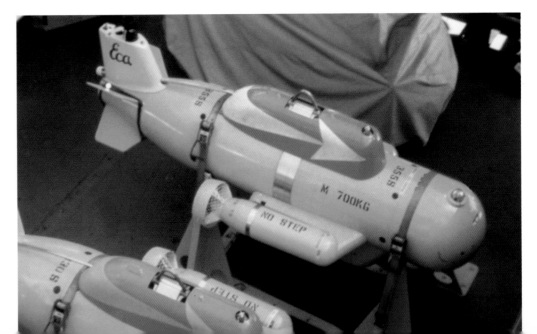

TOWARDS THE UNMANNED MERCHANTMEN

Right: Even at low speeds, very large ships cannot stop quickly, neither are their rudders very efficient. Simulators enable the would-be shiphandler to set up his own problem, and practice realistically without the risk of collision.

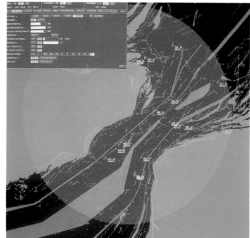

Above: Exceptionally busy waterways such as the Dover Strait, shown here, are made safer by defining 'separation zones' wherein the bulk of the traffic is obliged to head in the same direction.

EVEN WITH CURRENT technology, unmanned merchantmen are quite feasible. Certain types of vessel, particularly those carrying passengers will, of course, always require a crew, but long-haul carriers of bulk materials or containers may spend weeks at sea, proceeding at constant speed. Crews are expensive both to hire and to service. Their presence aboard, and the necessary resulting safety systems, considerably complicate the ship: conversely, their absence would lead to cheaper operation and reduced overheads on goods carried.

In an analogy to the 'huffler', who once earned a living joining Thames barges for an hour or two to assist their two-man crew to shoot low bridges, temporary crews would join and leave a ship at port limits to assist in berthing, cargo handling and preparing for sea. Between ports limits the ship would be on her own, the output from a hundred sensors and diagnostic points being relayed regularly by satellite to a 24-hour control centre. From here, in emergency, an operator could override the ship's systems for a direct 'hands-on' control.

Every on-board system, from main engines to radio transmitters, would be duplicated, their health checked constantly by self-diagnostic routines. Those concerned that a lack of crew would bring about a wave of strandings and pollution should remember that the great majority of marine accidents are brought about by human error.

Picture this ...

Let us follow a hypothetical case. Our bulker has completed loading at the terminal and is secured for sailing under the watchful eye of the company's representative. While alongside, the ship's systems have undergone a check by specialists and the ship itself examined for essential maintenance.

Propulsion is by diesel-powered azimuth thrusters, so rudders are not required. Once cast off, the ship tracks bodily sideways without the need for tugs to align herself with the port fairway. From here to the port limit a bottom-laid cable connects a series of transponders. Any axial misalignment with, or derivation from, the track represented by this cable is immediately detected and the thrusters angled to correct the error. Pilotage will be unnecessary.

Left: A separation zone at work. A large geared bulker, a container ship and a chemical tanker are in close proximity, yet pose no danger to each other. The problem is the distant passenger ferry, whose route dictates that she crosses both traffic zones.

Below: Radars are greatly enhanced by their ability to super-impose on the plot layered data such as shore lines and hydrographic information. Contacts can be plotted over a period of time to establish any risk of collision.

That our ship is unmanned is indicated during daylight hours by specific daymarks and, maybe, a distinctive paint scheme and, by night, by particular light groups. Even now, port approaches are dangerous places for pleasure craft, with large ships unable to undertake evasive action. Nonetheless, the berthing crew will remain aboard as a required safety measure until dropped off at port limits.

The ship here takes its departure from a transponder at a known point. Thence, the voyage will comprise a series of transits between pre-programmed waypoints. It is a simple task for the on-board computer to continuously compare positions along the line joining two waypoints with those given by a global positioning system (GPS). Any leeway due to wind or current will be detected and immediately corrected, as with any sophisticated autopilot.

In heavily congested areas, traffic separation schemes will ensure that ships in a given vicinity should generally be proceeding in the same direction. There will, however, always be 'rogue' vessels which cross the paths of ships, such as passenger ferries, and fishing craft moving erratically.

Our ship has several radars, optimised for overlapping range bands. They are equipped with a Closest Point of Approach (CPA) facility so that any other ship coming within a pre-determined distance will trigger the necessary precautionary action. Returns from all ships within radar range will be monitored for course and speed, the radar being able to extrapolate these to predict any likely infringement of the CPA. Like the computer of a chess game, programmed with the rules of the game and able to assess an opponent's move before making the necessary counterplay, our ship's computer is programmed with the Collision Regulations, controlling the ship according to the action of other ships. Infringement of the CPA will, in any case, have alerted the company's operational control centre, which can override with manual control should the situation warrant it.

The company centre will also have world weather forecasts available. If severe conditions lay ahead for our ship, threatening damage or delay, she will be re-programmed with a new set of waypoints to take her clear. This decision is simplified because the ship, among all other data, can transmit local barometric pressure, relative windspeed and wave height, and, via strain-gauged elements, the stresses being imposed on the hull.

Risk of fire in machinery spaces can be obviated by shutting them down and purging them with an inert atmosphere. In certain parts of the world, where piracy is a problem, there is no reason why the ship should not be manned temporarily by a specialist security force appointed by the operators.

Ships without crews, like unmanned trains or aircraft, are totally practicable and, with suitable system redundancy, totally safe. Public opinion, however, has yet to be educated to the fact that technology can be superior to human decision-making.

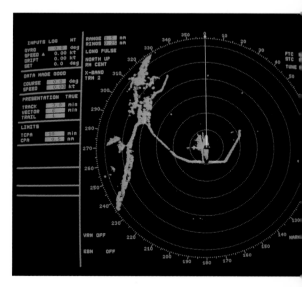

GLOSSARY

AMC – Armed Merchant Cruiser. Merchant ship, usually a passenger liner, armed for service as an auxiliary warship

Asdic – Shipborne equipment for sonic detection of submerged submarines

Avgas – Service abbreviation for aviation fuel

Beakhead – Triangular space at extreme forward end on a sailing warship

Breakbulk – Mixed cargo

Brig – A two-masted sailing ship, square-rigged on both mastst

Bring to – Loosely, to bring a ship to a halt

Broach – Dangerous situation of slewing so as to bring a heavy following sea on to the beam

Bulge – Flanking space added to hull to improve stability or to counter under-water attack

Camber – Slope of deck from centre line to deck edge

Cargo boom – See Derrick

Carronade – Short, light carriage gun firing a relatively heavy shot over a limited range

Chokepoint – Heavily-used waterway capable of being closed to traffic in time of war

Coaming – Raised sides of accommodation or cargo hatches

Cofferdam – Double bulkhead, typically to separate a dangerous cargo from an adjacent space

Conference – Several companies in the same trade, working within agreed rules rather than open competition

Corvette – World War II: small anti-submarine escort of simple design

Counter – Overhanging part of a ship's stern

Crank – Liable to excessive and unpredictable angles of heel

Deadwood – Solidly timbered, extremely narrow hull sections at foot of stem and sternposts

Deckhead – Overhead, or ceiling, of a compartment

Depth charge – Explosive anti-submarine weapon designed to be fired at pre-set depth

Derrick – Spar, pivoted at its foot and fitted for cargo handling

Director control – Salvo gunfire slaved to a single master station

DWT – Deadweight Tonnage. With deductions, the actual weight of cargo that a ship can carry

Dumb – Equipped with no means of propulsion

E-boat – German motor torpedo boat. More correctly, S-boat (Schnellboot)

Fixed ammunition – Cartridge and projectile combined as single element (see Quick Firer)

Free surface – Undivided surface area of slack, i.e. partially empty, tank

Frigate – World War II: Anti-submarine vessel with capability superior to that of a corvette

GRT – Gross Registered Tonnage. A measure of the capacity of a ship (One gross ton = 100 cubic feet)

Go about – To change tack, i.e. put wind on other side, in a sailing ship

Gyro control – To use a gyroscope as a stable reference

Hard chine – Line of discontinuity between two areas of hull plating, often between bottom and sides (cf Round Bilge)

Hog – Tendency of hull to droop at ends when supported amidships (cf Sag)

Holystone – Abrasive block for the scouring of wood-laid decks

Jeune á'cole – Nineteenth century French naval thought favouring, inter alia, torpedo craft over capital ships

Knuckle – Similar to Chine (qv) but usually higher on hull

Landfall – First sight of land following an open-sea passage

Length (bp) – Length between perpendiculars, i.e. on summer loadline, the length from forward side of stem to after side of rudderpost

Length (oa) – Length overall, i.e. extreme length of hull

Lift – In square rigger, support lines from mast to either end of yard

Mach number – Speed referenced to the velocity of sound at sea level

Metacentric height – Measure of stability. The vertical distance between ship's centre of gravity and her transverse metacentre

Moment – Product of a force and the distance through which it acts

Muzzle velocity – Speed at which projectile actually leaves gun

NRT – Net Registered Tonnage, i.e. gross tonnage (qv) less deductions for non-earning capacity

Nautical mile – Varies with latitude but usually assumed to be 6,080ft (1,852m). One nautical mile per hour equals one knot

Period – Time between successive wave crests passing a fixed point or time for peak-to-peak oscillation in such as roll or pitch

Quickfirer(QF) – Small, rapid-firing gun, usually using Fixed ammunition (qv)

Racer – Radial track, recessed into deck, to assist in training of guns

Rider – In wooden warships, short lengths of timber laid, often diagonally, between major members to increase rigidity

Round bilge – Radiused transition between side and bottom surfaces (cf Hard Chine)

Sag – Tendency of a hull to droop amidships when supported at either end (cf Hog)

Scantlings – Recommended dimensions, etc., of components used for a given size of vessel

Sheer – Rise of deck toward bow or stern

Shroud – Standing rigging giving transverse support to mast

Sloop – Loose term for many types of small sailing ship or warship

Snort – Anglicised form of Schnorkel, an air induction and exhaust trunk allowing submarines to run diesel engines while submerged

Sonar – See Asdic

Sponson – Gun platform projecting from side of ship, allowing a measure of axial fire

Staithe – Berth specially fitted for loading coal

Static head – Pressure, increasing with depth of water, e.g. as experienced by submerged submarine

Steeve – To pivot a bowsprit toward the vertical

Tabernacle – Rectangular trunk supporting heel of mast above deck level and incorporating pivot to allow mast to be lowered

Ten-year-rule – Rolling means of limiting defence spending by British Government between wars, based on assumption of no major war involvement for ensuing decade

Tonne – Metric ton, equally 1,000kg or approximately 2,200lb

Transponder – Electronic beacon which emits signal on being correctly addressed

Tumblehome – Inward slope of ship's sides. Reverse of flare

Tweendeck – Intermediate deck in ship's hold

Ullage – Vertical distance between surface of liquid cargo and top of tank

Van – Leading division in a line of battle

Waterplane – Horizontal section of hull at waterline at any instant

INDEX

Hamlyn would like to thank the following for their kind permission to reproduce the photographs and in particular Peter Kent of The Imperial War Museum London, Bob Todd of The National Maritime Museum London and Dave Manning of the US Naval Historical Foundation, Washington.

AKG, London 14 Top, 17 Bottom, 21 Bottom, 28 left (detail), 35 Bottom, 43, 70 (detail); Beken of Cowes 161 Top, 180 Bottom Left; Bibliothek fur Zeitgeschichte, Stuttgart 66, 125 Bottom, 126 Top Right, 127, 129 Top, 134-135, 140 right; Blohm und Voss, Hamburg 174 Bottom; Bridgeman Art Library, London/New York 29 Top, left Endpaper bottom left (detail), Left Endpaper centre (detail), 4 Bottom Left (detail), /Guardian Royal Exchange Insurance Collection, Richard Willis, The Engagement Between the Bonhomme Richard and the Serapis off Flamborough Head, 1779 49, /Guildhall Art Gallery, Corporation of London, William Clarkson Stanfield, The Victory Towed to Gibraltar 29 Bottom, /Kunsthistorisches Museum, Vienna, Nicholas Hilliard, Sir Francis Drake, 1581 33 right, /Musee des Beaux-Arts, Tourcoing, Paul Chabas, The Corner of the Table 112 Bottom, /National Maritime Museum, London, Anonymous, Sovereign of the Seas, prestige ship of Charles I 22 Bottom Right, 39 Bottom, /National Portrait Gallery, Smithsonian Institution, Portrait of John Paul Jones, c.1781, engraved by Carl Guttenberg 48, /Pepys Library, Magdalen College, Cambridge 21 Top, /Private collection, H Graf, SM Linienschiff Kaiser Friedrich III, 1990 (litho) 74, /Private Collection, Harley Crossley, Brittanic and Mauretania in Ocean Dock, Southampton, WWI, 1986 (oil on canvas) 111 Bottom, /Society of Apothecaries, London, Nicolas Hilliard, The Armada, 1588 (detail) 20 left, /Stapleton Collection, UK 92 Main Picture; Corbis UK Ltd Left Endpaper right, 2-3, 167 Bottom, Left Endpaper bottom centre (detail), Right Endpaper top right (detail); DERA 181 left; E.T. Archive 8 Main Picture, 10 Centre Left, 16, 31, 32 right, 40 Top, 46, 92 Bottom, 110 Bottom, /Imperial War Museum, Charles Pears, HMS Courageous in Dry Dock at Rosyth Winter, 1919, oil 76 left, /National Maritime Museum, Willem van de Velde the younger, Resolution in a Gale (detail) Right Endpaper bottom left; Mary Evans Picture Library 1, 4 Top, 8 Top Centre, 9, 11, 12 right, 32 left, 33 left, 35 Top, 37 Bottom, 40 Bottom, 43 Top, 44, 60, 64, 72 left, 73 Top, 80, 84 Top Left, 89 Top Right, 93, 97 Top, 99 Bottom, 102 Bottom, 108 Top Left, 110 Left, 111 Top; Fotoflite 147 Centre, 158, 159, 161 Bottom, 169 Top, 171 Top, 180 Main Picture, 187 Top; Hugh McKnight 166, 167 Top; Hulton Getty Picture Collection 37 Top, 42, 47, 65 Top Right, 65 Bottom, 67 Top, 71, 75 Bottom, 77 Top, 79 Centre Right, 84 Centre, 87 Bottom, 88-89, 89 Bottom, 94, 95 Centre, 96 Bottom Left, 96-97, 98, 99 Top, 102 Top, 112 Top, 113; Hull Maritime Museum 39 Top, 116–117 Bottom, John Ward, Whalers in the Arctic, c.1835 38; Image Bank/Eddie Hironaka Right Endpaper above left; Imperial War Museum, London 58, 59 Bottom, 68-69, 72-73, 75 Top, 76-77, 78-79, 79 Top Right, 83, 84-85, 85 Bottom, 87 Top, 88 Bottom, 90, 118 Main Picture, 119, 120-121, 123 Bottom, 124, 125 Top, 126 Bottom, 128 Top, 130 Right, 134 Bottom Left, 135 Bottom, 138, 139 Bottom, 140 left, 141; Jane's Information Group 175, 178 Bottom, 185 Bottom; National Maritime Museum, London 14 Bottom,

19, 22, 25, 34, 52, 53, 62, 63, 82, 86 (detail), 95 Top, 100, 101, 103 Top Right, 109 Bottom, 114 Left, 115 Top, 115 Bottom, 123 Centre Right, 154; Matra BAe Dynamics 172 Main Picture, 173 Top; Museum of Fine Arts, Boston/Henry Lillie Pierce Fund, Joseph Mallord William Turner (1775-1851), Slave Ship, 1840, oil on canvas 59 Top; Military Archive and Research Services 178 Top; The Military Picture Library/Peter Russell 183 Bottom, /Tony Simpson 184 left, /Yves Debay 185 Top; Museum in Docklands, PLA Collection 104-105, 106, 114-115, 148 left, 150; National Museums and Galleries of Northern Ireland, photograph reproduced with the kind permission of the Trustees and by kind permission of the Furness Withy Group, Kenneth Denton Shoesmith, Motor Class Vessel 108 Bottom; Octopus Publishing Group Ltd./David Loftus Right Endpaper centre left; Courtesy of NR Omell Gallery, London/Thomas Whitcombe, Shipping off Deal, oil on canvas 30; P&O 109 Top, Left Endpaper centre left (detail), Right Endpaper top left (detail), Right Endpaper bottom right (detail), Left Endpaper top (detail), 4 Bottom Right (detail), Charles Pears, Ranchi, 1925 5 Bottom Left, /European Ferries 163 Bottom, /Princess Cruises 164, 165, /Stena Line 151 Right, 163 Top; Courtesy Peabody Essex Museum, Salem, Mass. Charles Robert Patterson, Montezuma, American ship, photo Jeffrey Dykes 41; Popperfoto 5 Bottom Right, 132; Reeve Photography/Primagraphics 186; Rex Features 152, 170; Royal Armouries, Leeds 18 Right, 24; Royal Naval Museum, Portsmouth 122-123, 133 Top; Royal Exchange Art Gallery/Charles Pears, The Lawhill off Falmouth, c.1937 6-7; Science Photo Library/David Parker 187 Bottom; Science & Society Picture Library Cover, 10 Top Right, 15, 17 Top, 23 Bottom, 26, 27, 36, 45, 50, 51, 54, 55, 61, 68 Bottom, 103 Centre, 103 Bottom; Southampton City Council 18 left; Southern Daily Echo, Southampton 151 left; Seaco Picture Library 153 Top, 182, 183 Top; Shell International Photo Library 155, 156, 157; Silja Line, Sweden 162; Topham Picturepoint 107, 116, 117 Top Right, 147 Top, 148-149, 149 Bottom, 168-169, 171 Bottom; TRH Pictures/Avco Lycoming 184 right, /Harland and Wolff 153 Bottom, /Press Association 173 Bottom, /US Navy 179 left, 181 right; US Naval Historical Foundation, Washington 56, 57, 65 Top Left, 67 Bottom, 81, 91, 118 Bottom, 128-129, 130 left, 131, 133 Centre, 133 Bottom, 135 Centre, 136, 137, 139 Top, 142, 143, 144, 145, 146, 172 Bottom Left, 174 Top, 176-177, 179 right; Vasa Museum, Stockholm 23 Top; Werner Forman Archive/Viking Ship Museum, Bygdoy 12 left, 13 right; Wilh.Wilhelmsen, Norway 160.